The Poetry of Ṭáhirih

The Poetry of Ṭáhirih

by

John S. Hatcher and Amrollah Hemmat

GR

George Ronald
Oxford

George Ronald, *Publisher*
46 High Street, Kidlington, Oxford OX5 2DN

A catalogue record for this book is available from the British Library

ISBN 0-85398-460-3

Permission to quote from *Memorials of the Faithful* by 'Abdu'l-Bahá, translated and annotated by Marzieh Gail, published in Wilmette, Illinois in 1971, has been granted by the National Spiritual Assembly of the Bahá'ís of the United States and by the publishers, the United States Bahá'í Publishing Trust.

Cover designed by Alexander Leith
Typeset by Stonehaven Press, Knoxville, Tennessee

Contents

The numbers below each chapter refer to the numbers given to the poems so that they might be easily identified with the Persian rendering at the back of the book.

Acknowledgements

We would like to express our gratitude to the many individuals who have assisted us in our work on this project. In particular we would like to thank the Research Department of the Bahá'í World Centre for advising us about published sources for some of the poems, the Persian Affairs Desk of the National Spiritual Assembly of the Bahá'ís of the United States and in particular Mr Bijan Bayzaee for providing a copy of valuable work by his father, the late esteemed scholar. We would also like to thank Mr Bayzaee for other printed material as well as his most excellent assistance in the final production of poems in the original language.

Among others who assisted us were Mr Shukru'llah Ashchi and Mrs Shahrzád Ashchi, who provided us with a copy of a rare manuscript, an anthology of Bahá'í poems; Mr Hormatullah Mahdi and Mrs Rizvan Mahdi for providing copies of several important writings of the Báb and for assisting us in obtaining reference sources and producing the poems in the original; Dr Frank Lewis for sharing his translations and notes on some poems; Mr Kavian Milani for providing us with rare poems; and Mr Aziz Hakimian for reviewing some of our interpretations.

Finally, we would like to express our appreciation to Mr Parviz Dadresan for providing us with printed material and initial advice on the interpretation of some poems; Mr Mohammad Ebrahim Joneidi, Mrs Parvin Joneidi and Mr Ehsanollah Hemmat for carefully reviewing the poems in the original language and advising us on alternative interpretations. In particular, we are indebted to Mrs Joneidi's grammatical analysis of Arabic terms and explication of alternative meanings to some of the more troublesome couplets.

Preface

While the first two chapters together with the introduction and notes for each individual poem should give the reader a solid background for discovering some of the possible meanings of the poems in this volume, the reader would do well to understand several important facts about this project.

First of all, there is at this time no authenticated collection of the entire canon of Ṭáhirih's poetry in Persian and no collection in English. As we have indicated throughout, some of the poems in this volume are disputed as being hers, and there are many poems that have not yet been published in the original or in translation that we intend to publish in a future volume. Likewise, there are poems which we have included that contain variant readings among extant collections and we have pointed out these differences when we felt it necessary to do so.

The order in which we have put the poems is entirely the result of our interpretation of thematic structure for this collection and should not be taken as any authoritative division among Ṭáhirih's work as regards genre, subject or chronology. In addition to providing titles of our own devising for the poems, we have included a number for each poem which indicates the number we have assigned the original poems as they appear in this volume in the same order as our translations.

The difficulty of Ṭáhirih's work – besides the inherent difficulty of any sophisticated poetry – is twofold, as we discuss in Chapter Two. One problem is the need to become accustomed to the extremely elliptical nature of her allusions, as well as to the essential ambiguity that is an inevitable part of poetry in general, but particularly of poetry which is heavily allusive and symbolic. In short, one must be willing to spend time and energy to 'recover the allusion' (as T. S. Eliot put it) and not attempt to impose some restrictive or definitive interpretation on these verses.

Another difficulty lies in the reader's need to understand the major historical events that form the background to this period in Bábí-Bahá'í history, particularly those events immediately prior to the Declaration of the Báb in 1844 up through the establishment of the Bábí community by Bahá'u'lláh in Ba<u>gh</u>dád (until Bahá'u'lláh was further exiled in 1863).

The need to understand something of this background can be stated simply: the Heroic Age of the Bahá'í Faith begins with the Declaration of the Báb on 23 May 1844; and Ṭáhirih was not only an integral part of these dramatic events, she was at the heart of this history until her execution/martyrdom in 1850:

> May 23, 1844, signalizes the commencement of the most turbulent period of the Heroic Age of the Bahá'í Era, an age which marks the opening of the most glorious epoch in the greatest cycle which the spiritual history of mankind has yet witnessed. No more than a span of nine short years marks the duration of this most spectacular, this most tragic, this most eventful period of the first Bahá'í century.[1]

For the purpose of becoming acquainted with this historical context that forms the cultural backdrop against which many of these poems take their meaning, we recommend that the reader consult works such as Shoghi Effendi, *God Passes By*; *The Dawn-Breakers*, translated and edited by Shoghi Effendi; Balyuzi, *The Báb*; and Martha Root, *Ṭáhirih the Pure*. Likewise, the reader would find extremely helpful *A Basic Bahá'í Dictionary* by Wendi Momen and *A Basic Bahá'í Chronology* by Glenn Cameron with Wendi Momen. It goes without saying that the reader would also do well to have access to *Selections from the Writings of the Báb* and the works of Bahá'u'lláh which constitute the heart of Bahá'í scripture.

Finally, what we have accomplished here is a beginning. It is not intended to be definitive, complete or flawless. We have tried to blend solid scholarship with a poetic feel for Ṭáhirih's work to make the ideas, character and art of this outstanding figure available to English-speaking audiences. At the very least, we hope this work conveys some sense of the degree to which Ṭáhirih's art reflects the character, insights and steadfastness of these heroes without whom the Bahá'í Faith would not have succeeded.

Dedicated to the women
of this and every age and dispensation
without whose brilliance and heroism
the Cause of God would not exist today

Chapter One

A Glimpse at the Life of Ṭáhirih

> A woman chaste and holy, a sign and token of surpassing beauty, a burning brand of the love of God, a lamp of His bestowal, was Jináb-i-Ṭáhirih.
>
> *'Abdu'l-Bahá*[2]

There have been books and plays written about the life of Ṭáhirih. Her reputation as a poetess of surpassing talent and as a heroine and martyr of the Bábí Faith goes quite beyond the annals of the Bábí and Bahá'í religions. But it is not our purpose here to go into great detail about her remarkable life. Rather we wish to make a few observations about Ṭáhirih that we have derived directly from the experience of translating and studying her art, followed by statements of 'Abdu'l-Bahá and of Shoghi Effendi about the impact of Ṭáhirih on the early history of the Bahá'í Faith.

Anyone familiar with even the bare essentials of Ṭáhirih's life is probably somewhat aware of her personality and courage. She was outspoken, defiant, undaunted by tradition or the station of cleric or king. From childhood she could converse with anyone on equal footing and surpassed the reputed scholars of her day in both her specific learning and in her rhetorical prowess. Through independent study she discovered the writings of Shaykh Aḥmad-i-Aḥsá'í and Siyyid Káẓim-i-Rashtí and through a dream vision she recognized the Báb as soon as she read some of His writing, even though she never met Him in person.

From that point on, her life was never the same again. She devoted herself entirely to service to the Báb as Qá'im and to the Cause He revealed such that she was the only woman among the first of His 18 disciples (the 18 Letters of the Living). But even before this fulfilment of her search for the Promised One she could not countenance pretentiousness in any form and brazenly defied any attempts to suppress her thirst for knowledge, in spite of her father's high position and antipathy towards these new teachings. She blatantly rejected any attempts to placate her, even so far as rejecting marriage to the king, Náṣiri'd-Dín Sháh.

When there was no alternative to being faithful to her calling, she was forced to abandon her home, husband and three children, and she never looked back. From this point on she was well aware that the only sure fate awaiting her in time would be her own martyrdom, something about which she had absolutely no fear or concern. Indeed, in her verse and in her actions, she reveals an inner longing to attain the presence of or nearness to God beyond the constraints of earthly existence.

In every situation she invariably revealed herself to be a woman of unsurpassed wit, wisdom, intellect, action and courage. And yet what she reveals in the poems in this volume is something beyond the almost allegorical nature of her life's story. She shows herself in these verses to possess a rather amazing intellect – an almost other-worldly knowledge about some of the most esoteric and abstruse matters of theology, cosmology and ontology.

The reader is free to decide whether these qualities of mind and spirit derive from her early interest in learning or more directly from some higher spiritual station she possessed, some source of inspiration or revelation from the spiritual plane of existence. Most probably her talents as a poet, her prowess as a thinker and her courage in the face of fierce persecution and eventual execution were a combination of both personal will and divine assistance. Yet, one undeniable fact we derive from reading her poetry is that she had foreknowledge of a number of events in Bahá'í history long before they occurred. She predicts, indeed she foresees, her own martyrdom. She is fully aware that Bahá'u'lláh is Mustag͟háth͟ ('He Who is Invoked'), the promised Prophet foretold by the Báb as 'Him Whom God shall make manifest'. She foresees that Bahá'u'lláh will restore the shambles that remained of the Bábí Faith after the execution of the Báb and herself and she even alludes to the respite (a ten-year period) that would occur before Bahá'u'lláh would reveal Himself in 1863. In fact, in one Tablet Bahá'u'lláh states that among His most ardent followers was:

> . . . the Point of Ecstasy Jináb-i-Ṭá, upon her be the glory of God the Most Glorious. For a long time she was with this Servant and would not have bartered a moment of her visit with this servant for the kingdom of this world or the next. Indeed, she did not wish to be separated from me for even a moment, but what happened was destined to occur. And so many were the verses and poems she uttered regarding this wondrous Faith. And among them that mention the Abhá Countenance was an ode, one verse of which reads:
>
> If Bahá were to cast away the veil from His face,
> A hundred thousand like Azal would appear.[3]

Her allusions to the nature of creation and cosmology in the last section of poems (several to Bihjat) show that she is aware that there are other planets where human life abides[4] and where there is the same sort of spiritual evolution that is occurring on this planet.[5] She frequently explains the essential verities governing the Prophetic Cycle that concludes with Muḥammad and culminates in the appearance of the Báb and Bahá'u'lláh. What is more, she indicates in her poetry that the long-awaited Day of Resurrection prophesied in the scriptures of past religions and throughout the Qur'án has occurred with the advent of the Báb and, further, that she is the 'Trumpet' of that momentous event, an appellation that should give us pause as to exactly how lofty her station may have been.

Though it is not possible for us to determine her station, it is clear from her life's story that she had an other-worldly knowledge and it is likewise apparent in her actions at Badas͟ht and in her teaching and guidance of the community that she was no ordinary disciple but, along with Quddús, Mullá Ḥusayn and Vaḥíd, was one of the foremost leaders of the Bábí Faith.

In her poetry she frequently alludes to the essentially spiritual nature of creation as time and time again she states that all created things are infused with divine attributes. She articulates in no uncertain terms the concept that all human beings have free will, a power that is a gift of God and a gift that imposes a judgement on each human being to fulfil what she alludes to in one poem as the 'wish of Adam': that all people fulfil two requisites for spiritual development, the first of these being recognition of the Prophet through the beauty of His attributes and the second being an expression of this knowledge in action.

Because she possesses this ambiguous and mysterious spiritual station, she speaks in her poetry with many voices and points of view. Sometimes she speaks with the voice of authority. At other times she speaks as a believer among believers. Sometimes she seems to function as an intermediary between the believers (like Bihjat) and the Prophet. As readers approach these pieces, then, they must keep an open mind as to which voice is speaking and in what circumstances. For while we have attempted to make some logical groupings of these verses, we leave it to the reader to pierce the poetic veils of these poems which, as much as possible, we have left as we found them.

'Abdu'l-Bahá's Tribute to Ṭáhirih[6]

A woman chaste and holy, a sign and token of surpassing beauty, a burning brand of the love of God, a lamp of His bestowal, was Jináb-i-Ṭáhirih.[7] She was called Umm-Salmá; she was the daughter of Ḥájí Mullá Ṣáliḥ, a mujtahid of Qazvín, and her paternal uncle was Mullá Taqí, the Imám-Jumʻih or leader of prayers in the cathedral mosque of that city. They married her to Mullá Muḥammad, the son of Mullá Taqí, and she gave birth to three children, two sons and a daughter; all three were bereft of the grace that encompassed their mother, and all failed to recognize the truth of the Cause.

When she was still a child her father selected a teacher for her and she studied various branches of knowledge and the arts, achieving remarkable ability in literary pursuits. Such was the degree of her scholarship and attainments that her father would often express his regret, saying, 'Would that she had been a boy, for he would have shed illumination upon my household, and would have succeeded me!'[8]

One day she was a guest in the home of Mullá Javád, a cousin on her mother's side, and there in her cousin's library she came upon some of the writings of S͟haykh Aḥmad-i-Aḥsá'í.[9] Delighted with what he had to say, Ṭáhirih asked to borrow the writings and take them home. Mullá Javád violently objected, telling her: 'Your father is an enemy of the Twin Luminous Lights, S͟haykh Aḥmad and Siyyid Káẓim. If he should even dream that any words of those two great beings, any fragrance from the garden of those realities, had come your way, he would make an attempt against my life, and you too would become the target of his wrath.' Ṭáhirih answered: 'For a long time now, I have thirsted after this; I have yearned for these explanations, these inner truths. Give me whatever you have of these books. Never mind if it angers my father.' Accordingly, Mullá Javád sent over the writings of the S͟haykh and the Siyyid.

One night, Ṭáhirih sought out her father in his library, and began to speak of S͟haykh Aḥmad's teachings. The very moment he learned that his daughter knew of the S͟haykhí doctrines, Mullá Ṣáliḥ's denunciations rang out, and he cried: 'Javád has made you a lost soul!' Ṭáhirih answered, 'The late S͟haykh was a true scholar of God, and I have learned an infinity of spiritual truths from reading his books. Furthermore, he bases whatever he says on the traditions of the Holy Imáms. You call yourself a mystic knower and a man of God, you consider your respected uncle to be a scholar as well, and most pious – yet in neither of you do I find a trace of those qualities!'

For some time, she carried on heated discussions with her father, debating such questions as the Resurrection and the Day of Judgement, the Night Ascent of Muḥammad to Heaven, the Promise and the Threat, and the Advent of the Promised One.[10] Lacking arguments, her father would resort to curses and abuse. Then one night, in support of her contention, Ṭáhirih quoted a holy tradition from the Imám Jaʻfar-i-Ṣádiq;[11] and since it confirmed what she was saying, her father burst out laughing, mocking the tradition. Ṭáhirih said, 'Oh my father, these are the words of the Holy Imám. How can you mock and deny them?'

From that time on, she ceased to debate and contend with her father. Meanwhile she entered into secret correspondence with Siyyid Káẓim, regarding the solution of complex theological problems, and thus it came about that the Siyyid conferred on her the name 'Solace of the Eyes' (Qurratu'l-'Ayn); as for the title Ṭáhirih ('The Pure One'), it was first associated with her in Badas͟ht, and was subsequently approved by the Báb, and recorded in Tablets.

Ṭáhirih had caught fire. She set out for Karbilá, hoping to meet Siyyid Káẓim, but she arrived too late: ten days before she reached that city, he passed away. Not long before his death the Siyyid had shared with his disciples the good news that the promised Advent was at hand. 'Go forth,' he repeatedly told them, 'and seek out your Lord.' Thus the most distinguished of his followers gathered for retirement and prayer, for fasts and vigils, in the Masjid-i-Kúfih, while some awaited the Advent in Karbilá. Among these was Ṭáhirih, fasting by day, practising religious disciplines, and spending the night in vigils, and chanting prayers. One night when it was getting along toward dawn she laid her head on her pillow, lost all awareness of this earthly life, and dreamed a dream; in her vision a youth, a Siyyid, wearing a black cloak and a green turban, appeared to her in the heavens; he was standing in the air, reciting verses and praying with his hands upraised. At once, she memorized one of those verses, and wrote it down in her notebook when she awoke. After the Báb had declared His mission, and His first book, 'The Best of Stories',[12] was circulated, Ṭáhirih was reading a section of the text one day, and she came upon that same verse, which she had noted down from the dream. Instantly offering thanks, she fell to her knees and bowed her forehead to the ground, convinced that the Báb's message was truth.

This good news reached her in Karbilá and she at once began to teach. She translated and expounded 'The Best of Stories', also writing in Persian and Arabic, composing odes and lyrics, and humbly practising her devotions, performing even those that were optional and supernumerary. When the evil 'ulamá in Karbilá got wind of all this, and learned that a woman was summoning the people to a new religion and had already influenced a considerable number, they went to the Governor and lodged a complaint. Their charges, to be brief, led to violent attacks on Ṭáhirih, and sufferings, which she accepted and for which she offered praise and thanks. When the authorities came hunting for her they first assaulted S͟hams-i-Ḍuḥá mistaking her for Ṭáhirih. As soon, however, as they heard that Ṭáhirih had been arrested they let S͟hams go – for Ṭáhirih had sent a message to the Governor saying, 'I am at your disposal. Do not harm any other.'

The Governor set guards over her house and shut her away, writing Bag͟hdád for instructions as to how he should proceed. For three months, she lived in a state of siege, completely isolated, with the guards surrounding her house. Since the local authorities had still received no reply from Bag͟hdád, Ṭáhirih referred her case to the Governor, saying: 'No word has come from either Baghdád or Constantinople. Accordingly, we will ourselves proceed to Baghdád and await the answer there.' The Governor gave her leave to go, and she set out, accompanied by Shams-i-Ḍuḥá and the Nightingale of Paradise (the sister of Mullá Ḥusayn) and her mother. In Baghdád she stayed first in the house of Shaykh Muḥammad, the distinguished father of Áqá Muḥammad-Muṣṭafá. But so great was the press of people around her that she transferred her residence to another quarter, engaged night and day in spreading the Faith, and freely associated with the inhabitants of Baghdád. She thus became celebrated throughout the city and there was a great uproar.

Ṭáhirih also maintained a correspondence with the 'ulamá of Káẓimayn; she presented them with unanswerable proofs, and when one or another appeared before her she offered him convincing arguments. Finally she sent a message to the Shí'íh divines, saying to them: 'If you are not satisfied with these conclusive proofs, I challenge you to a trial by ordeal.'[13] Then there was a great outcry from the divines, and the Governor was obliged to send Ṭáhirih and her women companions to the house of Ibn-i-Álúsí, who was muftí of Baghdád. Here she remained about three months, waiting for word and directions from Constantinople. Ibn-i-Álúsí would engage her in learned dialogues, questions would be asked and answers given, and he would not deny what she had to say.

On a certain day the muftí related one of his dreams, and asked her to tell him what it meant. He said: 'In my dream I saw the Shí'ih 'ulamás arriving at the holy tomb of Imám Ḥusayn, the Prince of Martyrs. They took away the barrier that encloses the tomb, and they broke open the resplendent grave, so that the immaculate body lay revealed to their gaze. They sought to take up the holy form, but I cast myself down on the corpse and I warded them off.' Ṭáhirih answered: 'This is the meaning of your dream: you are about to deliver me from the hands of the Shí'ih divines.' 'I too had interpreted it thus,' said Ibn-i-Álúsí.

Since he had discovered that she was well versed in learned questions and in sacred commentaries and Texts, the two often carried on debates; she would speak on such themes as the Day of Resurrection, the Balance, and the Ṣiráṭ,[14] and he would not turn away.

Then came a night when the father of Ibn-i-Álúsí called at the house of his son. He had a meeting with Ṭáhirih and abruptly, without asking a single question, began to curse, mock and revile her. Embarrassed at his father's behaviour, Ibn-i-Álúsí apologized. Then he said: 'The answer has come from Constantinople. The King has commanded that you be set free, but only on condition that you leave his realms. Go then, tomorrow, make your preparations for the journey, and hasten away from this land.'

Accordingly Ṭáhirih, with her women companions, left the muftí's house, saw to arranging for their travel gear, and went out of

Baghdád. When they left the city, a number of Arab believers, carrying arms, walked along beside their convoy. Among the escort were Shaykh Sulṭán, Shaykh Muḥammad and his distinguished son Muḥammad-Muṣṭafá , and Shaykh Ṣáliḥ, and these were mounted. It was Shaykh Muḥammad who defrayed the expenses of the journey.

When they reached Kirmánsháh the women alighted at one house, the men at another, and the inhabitants arrived in a continuous stream to seek information as to the new Faith. Here as elsewhere the 'ulamá were soon in a state of frenzy and they commanded that the newcomers be expelled. As a result the kad-khudá or chief officer of that quarter, with a band of people, laid siege to the house where Ṭáhirih was, and sacked it. Then they placed Ṭáhirih and her companions in an uncovered howdah and carried them from the town to an open field, where they put the captives out. The drivers then took their animals and returned to the city. The victims were left on the bare ground, with no food, no shelter, and no means of travelling on.

Ṭáhirih at once wrote a letter to the prince of that territory, in which she told him: 'O thou just Governor! We were guests in your city. Is this the way you treat your guests?' When her letter was brought to the Governor of Kirmánsháh he said: 'I knew nothing of this injustice. This mischief was kindled by the divines.' He immediately commanded the kad-khudá to return all the travellers' belongings. That official duly surrendered the stolen goods, the drivers with their animals came back out of the city, the travellers took their places and resumed the journey.

They arrived in Hamadán and here their stay was a happy one. The most illustrious ladies of that city, even the princesses, would come to visit, seeking the benefits of Ṭáhirih's teaching. In Hamadán she dismissed a part of her escort and sent them back to Baghdád, while she brought some of them, including Shams-i-Ḍuḥá and Shaykh Ṣáliḥ, along with her to Qazvín.

As they travelled, some riders advanced to meet them, kinsmen of Ṭáhirih's from Qazvín, and they wished to lead her away alone, unescorted by the others, to her father's house. Ṭáhirih refused, saying: 'These are in my company.' In this way they entered Qazvín. Ṭáhirih proceeded to her father's house, while the Arabs who had formed her escort alighted at a caravanserai. Ṭáhirih soon left her father and went to live with her brother, and there the great ladies of the city would come to visit her; all this until the murder of Mullá Taqí,[15] when every Bábí in Qazvín was taken prisoner. Some were sent to Ṭihrán and then returned to Qazvín and martyred.

Mullá Taqí's murder came about in this way: One day, when that beṣotted tyrant had mounted his pulpit, he began to mock and revile the great Shaykh Aḥmad-i-Aḥsá'í. Shamelessly, grossly, screaming obscenities, he cried out: 'That Shaykh is the one who has kindled this fire of evil, and subjected the whole world to this ordeal!' There was an inquirer in the audience, a native of Shíráz. He found the taunts, jeers and indecencies to be more than he could bear. Under cover of darkness he betook himself to the mosque, plunged a spearhead between the lips of Mullá Taqí and fled. The next morning they arrested the defenceless believers and thereupon subjected them to agonizing torture, though all were innocent and knew nothing of what had come to pass. There was never any question of investigating the case; the believers repeatedly declared their innocence but no one paid them any heed. When a few days had passed the killer gave himself up; he confessed to the authorities, informing them that he had committed the murder because Mullá Taqí had vilified Shaykh Aḥmad. 'I deliver myself into your hands,' he told them, 'so that you will set these innocent people free.' They arrested him as well, put him in the stocks, chained him, and sent him in chains, along with the others, to Ṭihrán.

Once there he observed that despite his confession, the others were not released. By night, he made his escape from the prison and went to the house of Riḍá Khán – that rare and precious man, that star-sacrifice among the lovers of God – the son of Muḥammad Khán, Master of the Horse to Muḥammad Sháh. He stayed there for a time, after which he and Riḍá Khán secretly rode away to the Fort of Shaykh Ṭabarsí in Mázindarán.[16] Muḥammad Khán sent riders after them to track them down, but try as they might, no one could find them. Those two horsemen got to the Fort of Ṭabarsí, where both of them won a martyr's death. As for the other friends who were in the prison at Ṭihrán, some of these were returned to Qazvín and they too suffered martyrdom.

One day the administrator of finance, Mírzá Shafí', called in the murderer and addressed him, saying: 'Jináb, do you belong to a dervish order, or do you follow the Law? If you are a follower of the Law, why did you deal that learned mujtahid a cruel, a fatal blow in the mouth? If you are a dervish and follow the Path, one of the rules of the Path is to harm no man. How, then, could you slaughter that zealous divine?' 'Sir,' he replied, 'besides the Law, and besides the Path, we also have the Truth. It was in serving the Truth that I paid him for his deed.'[17]

These things would take place before the reality of this Cause was revealed and all was made plain. For in those days no one knew that the Manifestation of the Báb would culminate in the Manifestation of the Blessed Beauty and that the law of retaliation would be done away with, and the foundation principle of the Law of God would be this, that 'It is better for you to be killed than to kill'; that discord and contention would cease, and the rule of war and butchery would fall away. In those days, that sort of thing would happen. But praised be God, with the advent of the Blessed Beauty such a splendour of harmony and peace shone forth, such a spirit of meekness and long suffering, that when in Yazd men, women and children were made the targets of enemy fire or were put to the sword, when the leaders and the evil 'ulamás and their followers joined together and unitedly assaulted those defenceless victims and spilled out their blood – hacking at and rending apart the bodies of chaste women, with their daggers slashing the throats of children they had orphaned, then setting the torn and mangled limbs on fire – not one of the friends of God lifted a hand against them. Indeed, among those martyrs, those real companions of the ones who died, long gone, at Karbilá – was a man who, when he saw the drawn sword flashing over him, thrust sugar candy into his murderer's mouth and cried, 'With a sweet taste on your lips, put me to death – for you bring me martyrdom, my dearest wish!'

Let us return to our theme. After the murder of her impious uncle, Mullá Taqí, in Qazvín, Ṭáhirih fell into dire straits. She was a prisoner and heavy of heart, grieving over the painful events that had come to pass. She was watched on every side, by attendants, guards, the farrás͟hes, and her foes. While she languished thus, Bahá'u'lláh dispatched Hádíy-i-Qazvíní, husband of the celebrated K͟hátún-Ján, from the capital, and they managed, by a stratagem, to free her from that embroilment and got her to Ṭihrán in the night. She alighted at the mansion of Bahá'u'lláh and was lodged in an upper apartment.

When word of this spread throughout Ṭihrán, the Government hunted for her high and low; nevertheless, the friends kept arriving to see her, in a steady stream, and Ṭáhirih, seated behind a curtain, would converse with them. One day the great Siyyid Yaḥyá, surnamed Vaḥíd, was present there. As he sat without, Ṭáhirih listened to him from behind the veil. I was then a child, and was sitting on her lap. With eloquence and fervour, Vaḥíd was discoursing on the signs and verses that bore witness to the advent of the new Manifestation. She suddenly interrupted him and, raising her voice, vehemently declared: 'O Yaḥyá! Let deeds, not words, testify to thy faith, if thou art a man of true learning. Cease idly repeating the traditions of the past, for the day of service, of steadfast action, is come. Now is the time to show forth the true signs of God, to rend asunder the veils of idle fancy, to promote the Word of God, and to sacrifice ourselves in His path. Let deeds, not words, be our adorning!'

The Blessed Beauty made elaborate arrangements for Ṭáhirih's journey to Badas͟ht and sent her off with an equipage and retinue. His own party left for that region some days afterward.

In Badas͟ht, there was a great open field. Through its centre a stream flowed, and to its right, left, and rear there were three gardens, the envy of Paradise. One of those gardens was assigned to Quddús,[18] but this was kept a secret. Another was set apart for Ṭáhirih, and in a third was raised the pavilion of Bahá'u'lláh. On the field amidst the three gardens, the believers pitched their tents. Evenings, Bahá'u'lláh, Quddús and Ṭáhirih would come together. In those days the fact that the Báb was the Qá'im had not yet been proclaimed; it was the Blessed Beauty, with Quddús, Who arranged for the proclamation of a universal Advent and the abrogation and repudiation of the ancient laws.

Then one day, and there was a wisdom in it, Bahá'u'lláh fell ill; that is, the indisposition was to serve a vital purpose. On a sudden, in the sight of all, Quddús came out of his garden, and entered the pavilion of Bahá'u'lláh. But Ṭáhirih sent him a message, to say that their Host being ill, Quddús should visit her garden instead. His answer was: 'This garden is preferable. Come, then, to this one.' Ṭáhirih, with her face unveiled, stepped from her garden, advancing to the pavilion of Bahá'u'lláh; and as she came, she shouted aloud these words: 'The Trumpet is sounding! The great Trump is blown! The universal Advent is now proclaimed!'[19] The believers gathered in that tent were panic struck, and each one asked himself, 'How can the Law be abrogated? How is it that this woman stands here without her veil?'

'Read the Súrih of the Inevitable,'[20] said Bahá'u'lláh; and the reader began: 'When the Day that must come shall have come suddenly . . . Day that shall abase! Day that shall exalt! . . .' and thus was the new Dispensation announced and the great Resurrection made manifest. At the start, those who were present fled away, and some forsook their Faith, while some fell a prey to suspicion and doubt, and a number, after wavering, returned to the presence of Bahá'u'lláh. The Conference of Badasht broke up, but the universal Advent had been proclaimed.

Afterward, Quddús hastened away to the Fort of Ṭabarsí[21] and the Blessed Beauty, with provisions and equipment, journeyed to Níyálá, having the intention of going on from there by night, making His way through the enemy encampment and entering the Fort. But Mírzá Taqí, the Governor of Ámul, got word of this, and with seven hundred riflemen arrived in Níyálá. Surrounding the village by night, he sent Bahá'u'lláh with eleven riders back to Ámul, and those calamities and tribulations, told of before, came to pass.

As for Ṭáhirih, after the breakup at Badasht she was captured, and the oppressors sent her back under guard to Ṭihrán. There she was imprisoned in the house of Maḥmúd Khán, the Kalántar. But she was aflame, enamoured, restless, and could not be still. The ladies of Ṭihrán, on one pretext or another, crowded to see and listen to her. It happened that there was a celebration at the Mayor's house for the marriage of his son; a nuptial banquet was prepared, and the house adorned. The flower of Ṭihrán's ladies were invited, the princesses, the wives of vazírs and other great. A splendid wedding it was, with instrumental music and vocal melodies – by day and night the lute, the bells and songs. Then Ṭáhirih began to speak; and so bewitched were the great ladies that they forsook the cithern and the drum and all the pleasures of the wedding feast, to crowd about Ṭáhirih and listen to the sweet words of her mouth.

Thus she remained, a helpless captive. Then came the attempt on the life of the Sháh;[22] a farmán was issued; she was sentenced to death. Saying she was summoned to the Prime Minister's, they arrived to lead her away from the Kalántar's house. She bathed her face and hands, arrayed herself in a costly dress, and scented with attar of roses she came out of the house.

They brought her into a garden, where the headsmen waited; but these wavered and then refused to end her life. A slave was found, far gone in drunkenness; besotted, vicious, black of heart. And he strangled Ṭáhirih. He forced a scarf between her lips and rammed it down her throat. Then they lifted up her unsullied body and flung it in a well, there in the garden, and over it threw down earth and stones. But Ṭáhirih rejoiced; she had heard with a light heart the tidings of her martyrdom; she set her eyes on the supernal Kingdom and offered up her life.

Salutations be unto her, and praise. Holy be her dust, as the tiers of light come down on it from Heaven.

Shoghi Effendi's Tribute to Ṭáhirih[23]

. . . a woman, the only one of her sex, who, unlike her fellow-disciples, never attained the presence of the Báb, was invested with the rank of apostleship in the new Dispensation. A poetess, less than thirty years of age, of distinguished birth, of bewitching charm, of captivating eloquence, indomitable in spirit, unorthodox in her views, audacious in her acts, immortalized as Ṭáhirih (the Pure One) by the 'Tongue of Glory', and surnamed Qurratu'l-'Ayn (Solace of the Eyes) by Siyyid Káẓim, her teacher, she had, in consequence of the appearance of the Báb to her in a dream, received the first intimation of a Cause which was destined to exalt her to the fairest heights of fame, and on which she, through her bold heroism, was to shed such imperishable lustre.

While Bahá'u'lláh was being so odiously and cruelly subjected to the trials and tribulations inseparable from those tumultuous days, another luminary of the Faith, the valiant Ṭáhirih, was swiftly succumbing to their devastating power. Her meteoric career, inaugurated in Karbilá, culminating in Badas͟ht, was now about to attain its final consummation in a martyrdom that may well rank as one of the most affecting episodes in the most turbulent period of Bahá'í history.

A scion of the highly reputed family of Ḥájí Mullá Ṣáliḥ-i-Baraqání, whose members occupied an enviable position in the Persian ecclesiastical hierarchy; the namesake of the illustrious Fáṭimih; designated as Zarrín-Táj (Crown of Gold) and Zakíyyih (Virtuous) by her family and kindred; born in the same year as Bahá'u'lláh; regarded from childhood, by her fellow-townsmen, as a prodigy, alike in her intelligence and beauty; highly esteemed even by some of the most haughty and learned 'ulamás of her country, prior to her conversion, for the brilliancy and novelty of the views she propounded; acclaimed as Qurrat i-'Ayní (solace of my eyes) by her admiring teacher, Siyyid Káẓim; entitled Ṭáhirih (the Pure One) by the 'Tongue of Power and Glory'; and the only woman enrolled by the Báb as one of the Letters of the Living; she had, through a dream . . . established her first contact with a Faith which she continued to propagate to her last breath, and in its hour of greatest peril, with all the ardour of her unsubduable spirit. Undeterred by the vehement protests of her father; contemptuous of the anathemas of her uncle; unmoved by the earnest solicitations of her husband and her brothers; undaunted by the measures which, first in Karbilá and subsequently in Baghdád, and later in Qazvín, the civil and ecclesiastical authorities had taken to curtail her activities, with eager energy she urged the Bábí Cause. Through her eloquent pleadings, her fearless denunciations, her dissertations, poems and translations, her commentaries and correspondence, she persisted in firing the imagination and in enlisting the allegiance of Arabs and Persians alike to the new Revelation, in condemning the perversity of her generation, and in advocating a revolutionary transformation in the habits and manners of her people.

She it was who while in Karbilá – the foremost stronghold of Shí'ah Islám – had been moved to address lengthy epistles to each of the 'ulamás residing in that city, who relegated women to a rank little higher than animals and denied them even the possession of a soul – epistles in which she ably vindicated her high purpose and exposed their malignant designs. She it was who, in open defiance of the customs of the fanatical inhabitants of that same city, boldly disregarded the anniversary of the martyrdom of the Imám Ḥusayn, commemorated with elaborate ceremony in the early days of Muḥarram, and celebrated instead the anniversary of the birthday of the Báb, which fell on the first day of that month. It was through her prodigious eloquence and the astounding force of her argument that she confounded the representative delegation of Shí'ah, of Sunní, of Christian and Jewish notables of Baghdád, who had endeavoured to dissuade her from her avowed purpose of spreading the tidings of the new Message. She it was who, with consummate skill, defended her faith and vindicated her conduct in the home and in the presence of that eminent jurist, Shaykh Maḥmúd-i-Álúsí, the Muftí of Baghdád, and who later held her historic interviews with the princes, the 'ulamás and the government officials residing in Kirmánsháh, in the course of which the Báb's commentary on the Súrih of Kawthar was publicly read and translated, and which culminated in the conversion of the Amír (the governor) and his family. It was this remarkably gifted woman who undertook the translation of the Báb's lengthy commentary on the Súrih of Joseph (the Qayyúmu'l-Asmá') for the benefit of her Persian co-religionists, and exerted her utmost to spread the knowledge and elucidate the contents of that mighty Book. It was her fearlessness, her skill, her organizing ability and her unquenchable enthusiasm which consolidated her newly won victories in no less inimical a centre than Qazvín, which prided itself on the fact that no fewer than a hundred of the highest ecclesiastical leaders of Islám dwelt within its gates. It was she who, in the house of Bahá'u'lláh in Ṭihrán, in the course of her memorable interview with the celebrated Vaḥíd, suddenly interrupted his learned discourse on the signs of the new Manifestation, and vehemently urged him, as she held 'Abdu'l-Bahá, then a child, on her lap, to arise and demonstrate through deeds of heroism and self-sacrifice the depth and sincerity of his faith. It was to her doors, during the height of her fame and popularity in Ṭihrán, that the flower of feminine society in the capital flocked to hear her brilliant discourses on the matchless tenets of her Faith. It was the magic of her words which won the wedding guests away from the festivities, on the occasion of the marriage of the son of Maḥmúd Khán-i-Kalantar – in whose house she was confined – and gathered them about her, eager to drink in her every word. It was her passionate and unqualified affirmation of the claims and distinguishing features of the new Revelation, in a series of seven conferences with the deputies of the Grand Vizir commissioned to interrogate her, which she held while confined in that same house, which finally precipitated the sentence of her death. It was from her pen that odes had flowed attesting, in unmistakable language, not only her faith in the Revelation of the Báb, but also her recognition of the exalted and as yet undisclosed mission of Bahá'u'lláh. And last but not least it was owing to her initiative, while participating in the Conference of Badasht, that the most challenging implications of a revolutionary and as yet but dimly grasped Dispensation were laid bare before her fellow-disciples and the new Order permanently divorced from the laws and institutions of Islám. Such marvellous achievements were now to be crowned by, and attain their final consummation in, her martyrdom in the midst of the storm that was raging throughout the capital.

One night, aware that the hour of her death was at hand, she put on the attire of a bride, and anointed herself with perfume, and, sending for the wife of the Kalantar, she communicated to her the secret of her impending martyrdom, and confided to her her last wishes. Then, closeting herself in her chambers, she awaited, in prayer and meditation, the hour which was to witness her reunion with her Beloved. She was pacing the floor of her room, chanting a litany expressive of both grief and triumph, when the farráshes of 'Azíz Khán-i-Sardár arrived, in the dead of night, to conduct her to the Ílkhání garden, which lay beyond the city gates, and which was to be the site of her martyrdom. When she arrived the Sardár was in the midst of a drunken debauch with his lieutenants, and was roaring with laughter; he ordered offhand that she be strangled at once and thrown into a pit. With that same silken kerchief which she had intuitively reserved for that purpose, and delivered in her last moments to the son of Kalantar who accompanied her, the death of this immortal heroine was accomplished. Her body was lowered into a well, which was then filled with earth and stones, in the manner she herself had desired.

Thus ended the life of this great Bábí heroine, the first woman suffrage martyr, who, at her death, turning to the one in whose custody she had been placed, had boldly declared: 'You can kill me as soon as you like, but you cannot stop the emancipation of women.' Her career was as dazzling as it was brief, as tragic as it was eventful. Unlike her fellow-disciples, whose exploits remained, for the most part unknown, and unsung by their contemporaries in foreign lands, the fame of this immortal woman was noised abroad, and travelling with remarkable swiftness as far as the capitals of Western Europe, aroused the enthusiastic admiration and evoked the ardent praise of men and women of divers nationalities, callings and cultures. Little wonder that 'Abdu'l-Bahá should have joined her name to those of Sarah, of Ásíyih, of the Virgin Mary and of Fáṭimih, who, in the course of successive Dispensations, have towered, by reason of their intrinsic merits and unique position, above the rank and file of their sex. 'In eloquence', 'Abdu'l-Bahá Himself has written, 'she was the calamity of the age, and in ratiocination the trouble of the world.' He, moreover, has described her as 'a brand afire with the love of God' and 'a lamp aglow with the bounty of God'.

Indeed the wondrous story of her life propagated itself as far and as fast as that of the Báb Himself, the direct Source of her inspiration. 'Prodige de science, mais aussi prodige de beauté' is the tribute paid her by a noted commentator on the life of the Báb and His disciples. 'The Persian Joan of Arc, the leader of emancipation for women of the Orient . . . who bore resemblance both to the mediaeval Heloise and the neo-platonic Hypatia', thus was she acclaimed by a noted playwright whom Sarah Bernhardt had specifically requested to write a dramatized version of her life. 'The heroism of the lovely but ill-fated poetess of Qazvín, Zarrín-Táj (Crown of Gold) . . .' testifies Lord Curzon of Kedleston, 'is one of the most affecting episodes in modern history.' 'The appearance of such a woman as Qurratu'l-'Ayn,' wrote the well-known British Orientalist, Prof. E. G. Browne, 'is, in any country and any age, a rare phenomenon, but in such a country as Persia it is a prodigy – nay, almost a miracle . . . Had the Bábí religion no other claim to greatness, this were sufficient . . . that it produced a heroine like Qurratu'l-'Ayn.' 'The harvest sown in Islamic lands by Qurratu'l-'Ayn,' significantly affirms the renowned English divine, Dr. T. K. Cheyne, in one of his books, 'is now beginning to appear . . . this noble woman . . . has the credit of opening the catalogue of social reforms in Persia . . .' 'Assuredly one of the most striking and interesting manifestations of this religion' is the reference to her by the noted French diplomat and brilliant writer, Comte de Gobineau. 'In Qazvín,' he adds, 'she was held, with every justification, to be a prodigy.' 'Many people,' he, moreover has written, 'who knew her and heard her at different periods of her life have invariably told me . . . that when she spoke one felt stirred to the depths of one's soul, was filled with admiration, and was moved to tears.' 'No memory,' writes Sir Valentine Chirol, 'is more deeply venerated or kindles greater enthusiasm than hers, and the influence which she wielded in her lifetime still inures to her sex.' 'O Ṭáhirih!' exclaims in his book on the Bábís the great author and poet of Turkey, Sulaymán Náẓim Bey, 'you are worth a thousand Náṣiri'd-Dín Sháhs!' 'The greatest ideal of womanhood has been Ṭáhirih' is the tribute paid her by the mother of one of the Presidents of Austria, Mrs. Marianna Hainisch, '. . . I shall try to do for the women of Austria what Ṭáhirih gave her life to do for the women of Persia.'

Many and divers are her ardent admirers who, throughout the five continents, are eager to know more about her. Many are those whose conduct has been ennobled by her inspiring example, who have committed to memory her matchless odes, or set to music her poems, before whose eyes glows the vision of her indomitable spirit, in whose hearts is enshrined a love and admiration that time can never dim, and in whose souls burns the determination to tread as dauntlessly, and with that same fidelity, the path she chose for herself, and from which she never swerved from the moment of her conversion to the hour of her death.

Chapter Two

Translating the Poetry of Ṭáhirih

> But poetry acts in another and diviner manner. It awakens and enlarges the mind itself by rendering it the receptacle of a thousand unapprehended combinations of thought. Poetry lifts the veil from the hidden beauty of the world . . .
>
> *Shelley*, 'A Defence of Poetry'

The Problem with Poetry

Poet Robert Hayden was fond of saying that poetry is the art of saying the impossible, by which he meant, we may presume, that the poet attempts to discover methods by which ineffable realities (emotions, ideas, sensations, beliefs) could be translated into some sort of verbal formula by which they could be understood. Also implicit in this statement is whether the same information might be conveyed in another, more direct method, or is there something valuable accomplished by the indirection with which poetry communicates to us the artist's vision – the process of gaining access to meaning is integral to the meaning itself.

Another thing Hayden was fond of noting is that often the most popular poetry – if poetry has any sort of popularity these days – is usually mediocre poetry because it can be easily understood. For while poetry, like all language, is a form of communication, if it merely reminds us of what we already know, then it probably does not stretch us beyond our present state of understanding, the very goal that worthwhile art demands of us.

Not that being reminded of what we know is unpleasant or without value, but great poetry, poetry with lasting merit, takes us from our present state of awareness to some place else, some place we may not have ever been before, some level of understanding we did not formerly have. But it is usually not an easy trip because the vehicle with which poetry transports us from here to there is figurative language – metaphors, symbols, allusions and other difficult rhetorical devices that force us to meditate, to ponder, to use that part of our minds that is not often exercised.

And what part is that? These are the myriad analogical skills whereby we must discover the puzzling similarities among the diverse realities around us. We are urged to possess the cleverness to discern how language employs poetic devices to reach out beyond itself, to point us to some larger idea.

Of course, language itself does this. All language is inherently poetic because it is by nature symbolic. When we say the word 'tree', we have in mind not a word but an object (or a whole group of objects) which this sound in the English language has come to symbolize or represent. Even then we have our own personal perception and response. If we live in a tropical climate, we may immediately think of a palm. If we live in a northern clime, we may envision an evergreen.

In other words, language is already a form of art even before it becomes used artistically. Even when we are trying to employ this unique human capacity to express ideas in words in the most direct and literal form, we inevitably founder and fail and fall short of exactitude. But the poet, the good poet, is attempting something beyond description. The good poet, Auden was fond of noting, uses an algebraic process whereby that which is unstated, that which is implied (the unknown, the 'x') must be discovered by the diligent reader who must figure out inferentially what the poet has implied symbolically.

For this reason, students of poetry quickly realize that the poets who endure through the ages, those who are over the course of time considered to be the 'good' poets or the 'great' poets, most often happen to be the poets who are not always easy to understand. And why is that? Because poets of quality are not satisfied with the usual way of expressing thoughts and feelings. They rarely presume that they have discovered some new verity about human existence so much as they can provide a new perspective on eternal verities, a window on reality that will somehow make that reality more intimate, more immediate, more accessible, more relevant to our daily existence.

So it was that John Donne in his famous but difficult poem 'A Valediction Forbidding Mourning' compares himself and his beloved to the 'stiff twin legs of a compass' and expects us, his audience, to solve the puzzle (the algebraic equation, if you will) of how these essentially different realities relate to one another. Furthermore, Donne must have believed that this exercise he forced us into would give us a better understanding of this love relationship than we might have got had he employed some more direct, some more 'arithmetic' method of adding one adjective to another: e.g. 'We *love* each other! We *really* love each other! I mean *really, REALLY* love each other!!!'

The good poet, the demanding poet, thus writes for a small audience, people who think it worth their time to go through the intense and sometimes agonizing process of trying to figure out what the artful use of language is trying to tell us. And why does the poet seem intentionally to be so indirect, to make these puzzles that obscure his meaning? Why is he or she willing to sacrifice the plaudits of the masses for the usually posthumous appreciation of a small coterie of critics?

On some level the poet, the artist in general, thinks the means by which the idea is communicated is as important as the idea itself – or, perhaps more accurately, that the medium and the message are inseparable. In other words, possibly the poet could have found some less poetic way of getting the idea or feeling across. But poetry, indeed all art, assumes that there is something valuable in the art itself, the beauty of the language, the beauty of the image, the attempt to give sensually perceptible form to the unseen world of what Plato called the realm of 'ideas'. It is an idea that might be stated as simply as the inscription the persona in Keats' 'Ode on a Grecian Urn' reads at the end of this classic poem about the relationship between the artist and the idea: 'Beauty is Truth, truth Beauty – That is all ye know on earth and all ye need to know.'

And yet the beauty, the art of poetry, is not always obvious, any more than the beauty of painting or sculpture or music is always apparent. Artistry is necessarily a subjective process and the artist may not always be concerned with what is the most effective way to communicate to others what insight he or she has achieved. Rather the artist is searching for the best sensual referent or concrete expression for what has been a thoroughly personal experience. The artist's principal concern may not be the extent to which others comprehend that experience.

The point is that writing poetry, like any art, is not easy or simple or a matter of an inherent gift, and – more to the point at hand – neither is *art* of the reading of poetry, for so I call it. With almost any art, the audience must be trained to understand the depth of thought underlying the beguiling surface of expression. Perhaps virtually anyone can appreciate the blatant beauty of Michelangelo's 'The David', Hayden's 'Messiah', Sophocles' *Oedipus Rex*, Rumi's Ma<u>th</u>naví, Wright's 'Falling Water' or the majesty of a medieval cathedral, the Greek Acropolis or the Roman Forum. But it takes a bit more energy and training to appreciate the atonality of Sternberg, Eliot's *The Waste Land*, Becket's *Waiting for Godot* or Joyce's *Ulysses*.

In other words, the good artist does not talk down to the audience, does not 'dumb down' the art. The good artist assumes that there may be a few who (if not now, then in the future) will have the wit, the time, the energy, and the interest to gain access to the veiled or concealed window on reality which the art has provided. The artist may further presume that, having discovered this window on reality, we might somehow be better people for our efforts – that we will have learned something we did not know before, or at least not as well, or perhaps not in this particular way. On the other hand, the artist may take such delight in the existential act of creating art that communication is the farthest thing from the artist's mind.

So poetry is not usually profitable. Poetry books rarely sell well. Most people are not aware of the works of the masters of poetry, let alone those who presently struggle among us to provide those windows into the world of ideas. Later, often centuries later, we may observe how incisively the artist perceived what was going on in his or her age, how accurately the artist portrayed what was happening beyond the awareness of the populace at large. But that appreciation, that 'success', is almost always in retrospect as we lament how tragic it was that the poet met with disdain and ridicule for the radical vision he or she espoused or the unusual methods the artist employed.

Poetry that is Culturally Based

The critical reader will notice that our examples of art so far are of western or middle eastern origin. We have not alluded to myriad types of art of the indigenous peoples throughout the world or the great wealth of oriental art. That is because we ourselves as writers and thinkers are most familiar with the art of our own culture. Naturally, we can study the art of other cultures and we may discover in that art music that speaks to us, beauty that stirs our hearts, magic and mystery in the whole environment in which that art was fashioned. But all art, however universal it tries to be or is, is necessarily culturally based.

True, we can take a play like *Macbeth* and translate it into another language so that Wagner can render it into a magnificent opera. Or we can take the dactylic hexameters of Homer's epic *The Odyssey* in the original Greek and translate it into English rhyming blank verse as did Chapman. But these are not really translations – they are works of art in their own right in which a second artist (the translator) has attempted to convey the sense of the original.

The problem is this. The original artist has already used an indirect method of speaking to us – the artist has translated the literal into the figurative. But almost inevitably, those figures, those artistic equivalents of thought, derive from some experience that is culturally based – the common or shared experiences of a people. For example, we have to know or have access to a compass to appreciate Donne's analogy in 'Valediction'.

Stated more categorically, art can rarely be fully appreciated until the audience learns something about the cultural context in which the art was produced, regardless of how 'universal' the message might be. Otherwise we might wonder why Hamlet did not simply call the police or a private investigator when he suspected his uncle of murdering his father, or why a samurai can consider killing himself as an honourable thing to do when the Catholic Church has strictly forbidden self-slaughter. Or if we see a Chinese painting with a hundred cranes, it helps to know what those cranes symbolize in order to appreciate why this is an expression of happiness and not simply a portrait of a rather monotonous aviary.

But let us discuss the particular problem of translating poetry. With the visual or auditory arts, we may greatly benefit from studying the cultural context which produced the art, but at least we are not prevented from seeing what we see or hearing what we hear. The sensual impact is immediate. Of course, with poetry sound effects are integral to meaning and we can hear the beauty of rhythms and sounds even with a language we do not understand. But beyond the sound effects, we are faced with either learning the language and the culture or else trying to translate the poetry into our own language. The former requires years and years of study. Clearly, then, a translation of a poem is a much easier way for the ordinary person to appreciate the poetry of another language.

This sounds simple enough but in fact this process is fraught with almost insurmountable problems. First of all, while we have discussed poetry as a technique of translating the ineffable into symbols, metaphors and other veiled or hidden or coded messages, a fair amount of the impact of poetry is auditory – rhythm or what might be called sound on sound (rhyme, assonance, alliteration, euphony, cacophony, etc.). But rhythm or metre can be based on patterns of syllabic stress or on length, and some languages lend themselves to qualitative metre, while others are best suited to quantitative metre. Likewise, some languages lend themselves easily to rhyme, while others (English in particular) are very difficult to rhyme.

Now, assuming we can translate the words from one language to another, what do we do about all the sound effects we have just lost? We could try to create the same patterns of rhythm or rhyme but because each language has its own peculiar strengths, its own special beauty, the best we can do is find a metrical scheme or a pattern of sound on sound that feels similar to the sound effects of the original. In short, the best we can expect is a new type of rhythm and metre that produces something like the emotion and feeling of the original.

Since translating the sound is virtually impossible, many translators forgo any attempt at translating the sound and form and focus on trying to convey the thought, a task which seems much easier. One simply has to translate as accurately as possible what the poem says, possibly with some creative line breaks to make the new creation feel like a poem.

But the translator will soon discover that what may sound simple is hardly simple at all. The translator is immediately faced with two rather immense problems. If the translator is quite literal, changing perhaps only the syntax (because meaning in English sentences is based on word order, not word endings), the poem is likely to make no sense whatsoever.

Why? Because the poet has clothed his ideas in the garment of figurative language and, as we also have noted, figurative language is almost always culturally based. What sense would it make to translate Donne's image of the twin compasses into a language of a people who have neither seen a compass nor have any knowledge of how one works. Of course, the translator could try in various notes to give the background to what a compass is and why such an image in the context of a love poem was such a radical shift from the proverbial images of overused Petrarchan conceits, but simply to give the image in its literal form without some assistance would accomplish almost nothing.

A second alternative for the translator is to interpret the image for the reader. This practice is absolutely necessary for idiomatic expressions but it is a more troublesome process with the metaphor, the symbol and the allusion. For example, let us deal with Donne's image of the 'stiff twin compasses'. The original says the following about the unity of two souls of the lovers:

> If they [our souls] be two, they are two so
>   As stiff twin compasses are two;
> Thy soul, the fixed foot, makes no show
>   To move, but doth, if th' other do.
>
> And though it in the centre sit,
>   Yet when the other far doth roam,
> It leans and hearkens after it,
>   And grows erect, as that comes home.
>
> Such wilt thou be to me, who must
>   Like th' other foot, obliquely run.
> Thy firmness makes my circle just,
>   And makes me end where I begun.

Now what Donne seems to mean here is that he and his beloved are so united that when he departs from her physical presence they are still joined together (at the top – hence a higher intellectual or spiritual conjunction). Thus, as he roams away, she, like the pointed leg of a compass, will incline towards him (implying some sort of spiritual communication). Furthermore, if she remains fixed (stays at home and is faithful), he will make a 'just' or perfect circle by returning to the point where he started.

We can argue whether the speaker here is simply trying to give a rational justification to his wife as to why he must go to Paris and leave her in London but the fact is that this conceit is hard enough to understand in English. So the translator may simply give a parallel statement of what the image means instead of forcing the poor reader to figure out the analogy: 'I love you so much that when I have to leave, your thoughts will still be with me, and if you remain faithful to me, I will return home – I promise I really will.'

Now what have we lost? We have lost the rhyme, the metre and the conceit. In effect, while the translator may have given us a sense of what the translator thinks the poem means, in no sense has the poem as such been translated – it has been interpreted. Furthermore, there is hardly any poetry left in it. It would be more accurate to say the poetry has been translated *out* of the poem.

What, then, is the solution to these several ostensibly insurmountable problems? There is only one solution I am aware of and even it is rather limited. The translator must have two precisely different sorts of skills – skills which, unfortunately, are almost never found together in the same personality. The translator must be a true scholar of the language, the history and the culture and, in some cases, of the personal circumstances of the poet that have brought forth the original art and the translator must be a poet in his or her own right because the process we are describing is not really a translation – ultimately what we are talking about is bringing forth a new work of art that attempts to imitate the essential meaning, feeling and other poetic characteristics of the original, a work that, ideally, is capable of standing on its own merits.

The end result may be quite inferior to the original. It may be superior. The point is what we have is a new creation, not really a translation *per se*, yet neither is it an interpretation, not if the translation is done right. The most important point, however, is that what we need for this process is either a most rare individual who combines the talents of scholarship with the artistry of the poet or else we need two people working together.

Now while there have been a few individuals capable of doing both these jobs, very few works of distinctly different cultures have been translated successfully. One of the best jobs of combining both tasks with which I am familiar is the recent work of poet professor Coleman Barks who, over the past decade or so has successfully translated a great deal of the poetry of Rumi into English. Indeed, his most recent collections *The Essential Rumi* and, more recently, *The Glance*, has met with tremendous critical acclaim and public response.

The process by which my former colleague at the University of Georgia achieved this success was to utilize a scholar in Middle East studies to provide him with the raw materials from which he could then create a quality of verse that captures exquisitely the tone, the humour, the imagery, the 'feel' of Rumi's work. It is his work that inspired us to attempt the same sort of process with the poetry of Ṭáhirih.

But Ṭáhirih's poetry is particularly challenging. She is writing from the point of view of a convert to the Bábí Faith and so a knowledge of the history of the beginnings of this religion in Persia is essential. She is using mostly Persian poetic modes, so a knowledge of Persian literature and poetry is essential. She also uses Arabic, so a knowledge of Arabic is likewise necessary. She employs traditions from Sufi mystic verse but also alludes to various philosophical traditions, from Platonism to Gnosticism. She further alludes succinctly to Quranic verses, ḥadíth, Old and New Testament scripture and to events from her personal experiences.

So it was that we began a collaboration similar to that with which Barks began his work with John Moynes. The end result has been the evolution of a process that has been challenging, exciting, energizing and rewarding. Indeed, we feel the success of this project warrants the application of our combined talents to further translations of other early Bahá'í poets, like Varqá. We think we have produced a volume that is accurate and well researched, which also conveys something of the rather remarkable intellect, artistry and character of Ṭáhirih but a volume that is also capable of standing on its own merit as poetry.

Some Background to a Study of Ṭáhirih's Art

Whether we are reading poetry in its original language, translating it into another language or simply trying our best to understand the abstractions to which the poet has given artistic form in the medium of language, we must go through more or less the same process. We must ask ourselves questions about what the poet assumes we know or assumes we are capable of discovering in order to achieve understanding of what is being communicated.

But since poetry, particularly the various forms of lyric mode, are so varied, each poem creates its own rules – each poem requires us to 'go to school' in the language, style and forms that the artist chooses to employ in any given work. Therefore, any extensive generalizations one might apply to the study of one poet might prove more or less useless with another.

The work of Ṭáhirih, whether read in Persian and Arabic or in our translation into English, requires various kinds of information and skills for the proper appreciation of her work. While we will leave it to future scholars to unearth all of the related branches of learning related to the hidden meanings in her verses, we will here share with the reader a few related areas of study necessary to understand her work, with more specific information in our notes.

The most obvious and immediate assistance is some degree of knowledge of Ṭáhirih's life, especially since many of her poems allude to personal feelings and experiences. The previous chapter may provide sufficient information for most readers to begin to discern these relationships.

A second thing the reader needs to understand is that often Ṭáhirih as a historical figure is deceptively absent in her poetry. Instead, she has chosen to employ various personae – fictional first person narrators. Some of these may be based on her experiences but many are either a totally distinct narrative point of view or else some hyperbolic presentation of her perspective. The voice may be that of the mystic seeker, the wayfarer, the dervish. The voice may be that of the heart-stricken lover searching for the Beloved. The voice may be that of the steadfast believer praising God for having revealed Himself to humankind through the Prophets. The speaker may be the spiritual leader, a source of authority bestowing guidance on her followers. The voice may be that of an astute theologian and philosopher. The first person speaker may be the voice of the Prophet Himself or even the voice of God. In any case, we cannot approach her art assuming that what we are reading is a personal confessional verse or even that the voice is that of Ṭáhirih at all.

Another thing the reader needs to understand is that Ṭáhirih assumes her audience is aware of, or willing to become aware of, religious history and traditions. Her poems are particularly thick with images of and allusions to concepts and passages from the Qur'án and various ḥadíth. Thus, with a single word or phrase in Arabic from the Qur'án she may allude to an entire religious belief or concept. For example, the word *Ṭúr* alludes to Mount Sinai where Moses received the word of God. And yet, she assumes the reader also is familiar with the traditions of the fire from God revealing the commandments in stone, the mountain trembling and it turning to dust. She may thus refer to her own body as *Ṭúr*, meaning that the revelation has had a similar effect on her. Or take the simple word *lá* ('no' or 'not'). In some poems she will employ this word to allude to the mystic concept that the loftiest stage of spiritual ascent is the state of individual nothingness (i.e. the individual identity is integrated into or merged with the divine spirit).

The poems of Ṭáhirih are strongly based in the reader's ability to understand both the concept of the historical revelation of God through a succession of Prophets (progressive revelation) as well as several other key theological, cosmological and ontological concepts. For example, she often alludes to the fact that on the one hand the Prophets are for human beings tantamount to God on earth. Consequently, to enter their presence (either literally or through their utterance) is the equivalent of being in the presence of God. At the same time, she also alludes to the fact that the Prophets are utterly submissive to and humbled before God and, further, that the Prophets of old are humbled before the new Prophet.

Likewise, she often alludes to the eternality of God and creation itself. For while she alludes to this earth as having a beginning and a spiritual evolution, she also often alludes to the eternality of God, the eternality of creation itself and the existence of other worlds and realities which likewise reflect divine attributes.

Certainly among the most critical philosophical/theological concepts she presents in her verse is the idea of the human soul as a divine emanation (a 'dancing particle' in the light emanating from God's face). But the soul of the Prophet comes as the source of all illumination – something Ṭáhirih alludes to as the light beaming or flashing from the Prophet's face (the moon-faced one) or else by alluding to the Prophet as the Friend, the Beloved, the face of God Himself. Thus Shoghi Effendi in *The Dawn-Breakers* translates a verse from Ṭáhirih as follows:

(1)

The effulgence of the Abhá Beauty hath pierced the veil of night;
behold the souls of His lovers dancing, moth-like, in the light that
    has flashed from His face![24]

Yet translated literally, these same lines would read something like this: 'The sun of Abhá became manifest and the lives (souls) of the lovers/ in the air of His countenance are dancing like particles.'

We see in this that Shoghi Effendi has captured the essential intent of the original, retained the meaning of the essential metaphor at work, then translated the entire couplet into another poem. We might well ponder, therefore, is this translation or interpretation or inspired poetry? The answer is that it is all this and more. But the answer also means that without an intimate knowledge of the poet's intent and point of view, the translator is merely guessing.

One final philosophical/theological belief that should be mentioned is what will be perceived by some as the neo-Platonic notion of all created things having the capacity to reflect divine attributes (Plato's concept of 'forms' or 'ideas'). In fact, the Qur'án itself alludes to this same concept, as do other Prophets. But it is a particularly dear point to Ṭáhirih – that when the Prophet appears all created things reflect to some degree the attributes of God, each according to the *Qadar* or 'measure' of capacity with which God has endowed that created thing. According to this same idea, man (unique among creatures on the earth) has the free will to recognize this relationship and to react appropriately by putting 'Adam's wish' into action (combining insight with service).

A third area of background with which the reader needs to be familiar is the notion of mysticism and Arabic and Persian concepts of love as they relate to mysticism. To any western student of literature familiar with the so-called courtly love tradition (beginning with the French Provençal poets of the 12th century), these traditions will sound very familiar. This is probably no coincidence, but is, in fact, the real source of these western European poetic conventions. Indeed, C. S. Lewis in *Allegory of Love,* Denis de Rougemont in *Love in the Western World*, and various other scholars theorize that the Arabic-middle eastern poetic tradition may well be a possible source of courtly love in the medieval romances, particularly in the Arthurian works. Scholars also noted the relationship between the mystic longing for transcendence, even death (also a form of 'nothingness'), and the inevitable tragedy that is the end result of the courtly love relationship.

Without going into the complexities of such a discussion, well worth a book or two on its own, suffice it here to note that Ṭáhirih in her poetry plays off both traditions. She assumes the reader is quite familiar with the formulaic nature of the intensity of the love relationship depicted in middle eastern verse, the fundamental ingredients of which are as follows: love at first sight contracted through the eyes, possibly in a single glance; the 'malady' of love, a lovesickness that involves the inability to eat or sleep or have any sort of peace of mind; an almost insane longing for the nearness of the beloved; the conflicting emotions of the lover towards the beloved – the beloved is simultaneously the source of all joy and all sorrow and all pain; the lover is at the beck and call of the beloved and thus feels utter despair in remoteness from the beloved – in courtly love because the beloved is married to someone else, in Petrarchan love because the beloved is aloof, in middle-eastern tradition because the beloved is capricious or cruel.

Of particular interest in Ṭáhirih's work are certain specific Persian and Arabic allusions that are not common in western courtly love. The arch of the eye brow is a particularly provocative feature of the beloved, as are the scent of the lover's tresses, the tresses themselves (which are likened unto a snare or lariat) and the beauty spot (which is often compared to a seed that captures the bird of the heart). Thus, instead of the Petrarchan conceits of teeth like pearls, breasts like globes and eyes like stars, we have different conceits representing how the beloved captures the heart of and tantalizes the lover.

As we have already noted in the Preface, the student of Ṭáhirih's poetry has to be familiar with a good many of the historical events surrounding the beginnings of the Bábí Faith and the Bahá'í Faith, since her poems are replete with allusions to that history and, especially, to her part in that history as a Letter of the Living. Ṭáhirih consulted with Bahá'u'lláh and Quddús in the planning of the conference at Badasht in which they revealed to the assembled believers that the teachings of the Báb constituted not a reform movement in Islam but an entirely new Revelation. This information they imparted through a dramatic subterfuge in which Ṭáhirih and Quddús pretended to be arguing this very point – Quddús taking the position that they should abide by Islamic law and Ṭáhirih espousing the more radical view that this was the Day of Resurrection foretold in Quranic scripture and that she was the Trumpet heralding that day, for the Báb Himself was the promised Qá'im.

Ṭáhirih also assumes the reader has some familiarity with mysticism in general and with Sufism in particular. Thus, while we have explained most of the specific allusions within the poems, we should mention several general observations about the theory of mysticism. The object of the mystic (regardless of era, religious background or culture) is union with the divine (with God or with divine reality). The means by which this union (or reunion) is attained varies among the several branches of mysticism. It usually involves some specific method or 'path'. Most often that procedure or path involves prayer, chanting, meditation, mantras, sensual deprivation and other forms of asceticism – in many cultures the experience is assisted with various forms of hallucinogens. The whirling dervishes (founded by Rumi) achieve a meditative state by a steady whirling dance.

But regardless of the path, there are several definable stages in this journey towards a sense of nearness to the divine perspective, stages which a number of more intellectual mystics have tried to describe. Most often these stages are described in terms of sensual indices. For example, the first stage is the search for the path itself, something alluded to in Sufism as discovering 'the Friend', the 'Beloved' – who possesses wisdom, selflessness and a multitude of divine attributes. This stage is described as a process of intense ardour for a glimpse or scent of the fragrance of the Beloved, much as an animal wishing to mate searches for a musky scent.

Once the Beloved is identified, the seeker experiences intense love, a love which is most often expressed in the metaphorical terminology of a romantic human love relationship such as we have described regarding courtly love. The lover cannot eat or sleep. The lover endures untold 'calamity' in trying to attain the presence of the Beloved, a calamity which may be internal or, in the case of many, actual suffering and persecution for their beliefs. The Beloved or the Friend – by his very nature of being self-sufficient, stable, calm, implacable or imperturbable – thus seems aloof or cruel or remote.

Another stage is that of intellectual perspective. The seeker or mystic has, or feels he or she has, an intense sense of understanding eternal verities. In particular, the lover senses an understanding of how divine order pervades and unifies all creation. This stage may be typified by the articulation of actual dictums or verities or universal laws, but more often than not, this insight defies words and can only be hinted at through poetic metaphors or abstruse allusions.

The final stage involves a feeling that the individual self is merging with or being subsumed by the divine reality. This stage is usually alluded to as an intense awareness of one's own insignificance compared to the ultimate unity of all creation. But this is by no means a sense of unimportance or loss of self. Rather it is a sense of ecstasy at having achieved a feeling of total belonging to and union with the divine reality. This stage is therefore described in terms of individual nothingness, as intense ecstatic delight in having become part of some plan or purpose or reality grander than self.

What the mystic then does with this total experience is completely dependent on the individual. Some believe in sharing this experience that others might also enjoy this path to wisdom and ecstasy. Others believe in returning from this state of vision and wonderment to work in the world. Others simply try to return to the sensation of ecstasy as often as possible. In short, for some, the mystical experience becomes the goal itself, while for others it becomes a temporary refuge, a source of reinvigoration whereby one is enabled or empowered to participate more fully in assisting human society.

The Forms of Ṭáhirih's Verse

While the introductions to each section and to the individual poems discuss what Ṭáhirih has done with particular poetic forms, let us mention here some of the variety one will encounter with her verse.

Some poems are brief prayers or panegyrics to God. Others are lengthy meditations. As we have already noted, she often employs various personae (first person speakers) to suit the purpose of the poem. Most often she employs the couplet, though on occasion these will be grouped together in quatrains, as in 'Rebuking the King's Desire'. In 'The Realm of Ecstasy' she employs five-line sections (two couplets and a fifth line that functions as a poem unto itself). In the 'Song of the Captive Heart' she uses six line sections – two couplets and then a third couplet which functions as a series of spiritual verities apart from the narrative progress of thought in the first two couplets.

We have in about half the poems stayed close to the original, translating line for line and couplet for couplet. However, with a substantial number of poems we have found it necessary to translate the couplets into quatrains, either because the line in the original is too long and cumbersome to translate into a single line in English or else because there is a purposeful caesura (or break) in mid line that lends itself to better poetics in the form of a quatrain.

We have not tried to imitate the metrical pattern or rhyme scheme used by Ṭáhirih, though in several poems we have employed a refrain or repeated word used by her. We have attempted to capture the meaning and feeling of the original without translating the poetry out of her rhetorical devices. By doing this, we feel, we have better captured the tone, the spirit and the overall sense of the piece than had we attempted to imitate poetics alone.

Whatever changes or liberties we have taken with the original are explained in our notes. Since there is no authoritative collection of her original verse, we have at times had to correct errors in transcription or to make choices among variant readings in the several extant versions of a poem. As regards the capitalization and punctuation, we have followed our own instincts, capitalizing some nouns and pronouns when they seem to represent God or the Manifestations, though no doubt some reader will perceive this as imposing our own interpretation on the work. Certainly, the reader is free to ignore this since there is no such distinction in the original. The same goes for punctuation, which can sometimes make major differences in how a couplet is read or interpreted.

Perhaps the most important thing we have discovered in these poems is that all are very meticulously formulated. Almost always, even among the most abstruse allusions and ostensibly disconnected thoughts, is a plan, a theme, a progression of thought, a unifying purpose if the reader has the patience to discover it. While in many cases we have in the introductions or in our notes attempted to hint at what we believe some of those themes to be, we certainly do not presume that our opinion is anything more than our personal sense of what is going on.

We leave it to future readers and scholars to determine with ever greater accuracy the authentic canon of her work, to discover further allusions and meanings we have missed. Our purpose is to make a beginning by sharing with the English-speaking audience, and Persian readers as well, a sense of the art of this remarkable woman so that she may become for us a little less mythical and, thereby, even more heroic.

Finally, we have grouped her poems according to what seem to us similarities of theme and genre and style. In some cases, we have made an attempt to order the poems within these groups according to some logical order. We do not imagine that our grouping is authoritative or final but rather a useful structure for the purposes of this volume.

The Problem with Sources

We have included an extensive bibliography and we have also included the sources for the poems, though much more needs to be done in the future to authenticate poems attributed to Ṭáhirih and to add to her canon poems that she wrote which we have not yet discovered as the work goes to press. For example Dr Vaḥíd Ra'fatí sanctions Bayḍá'í's belief expressed in *Ta<u>dh</u>kari-yi-Shu'ará-yi-Qarn-i-Awwal-i-Bahá'í* that of the eight poems mentioned in Fáḍil-i-Mázandarání's *Ẓuhúru'l-Haq* as Ṭáhirih's poems ('Arise!', 'Daybreak', 'Behold the New Day!', 'The Love of Bahá', 'This Longing for You', 'The Burning Heart', 'Behold the Face of God', 'Fire in the Eyes of the Friend') only three are actually hers: 'Arise!', 'Behold the Face of God!' and 'This Longing for You'.[25] Dr Ra'fatí traces three of the eight poems ('Arise!', 'The Love of Bahá' and 'This Longing for You') in Fayḍ-i-Ká<u>sh</u>ání's collection and intends to discover the author of the other two poems ('Behold the New Day!' and 'The Burning Heart') which, according to Bayḍá'í do not belong to Ṭáhirih. Also, Dr Nuṣrat'ulláh Muḥammad-Husseiní's recent scholarly work on Ṭáhirih clarifies many issues regarding the authenticity of poems attributed to Ṭáhirih.

According to Bayḍá'í, Ṭáhirih would write down and memorize the poems she came across that she was fond of and she would recite them at special occasions or in her state of ecstasy. Some of her companions, hearing these poems from her or finding them in her handwriting, not knowing the true source, would assume that these were her own.

Considering Bayḍá'í's analysis of the reason why some poems are wrongly attributed to Ṭáhirih, the disputed poems which we have included as hers should at the very least tell us something about Ṭáhirih's interests, her state of mind and her thinking. Furthermore, Ṭáhirih could have applied a poem in a way not intended by the original author. For example, Ṭáhirih might have employed the term *Bahá* as an allusion to Bahá'u'lláh even though the word in the original poem was used in its denotative sense of 'glory', 'light' or 'splendour'.

Chapter Three

The Day of Resurrection

O ye great ones, the Creator of the Age
has fashioned the universe into a paradise!
This must be the Day of Resurrection
when morning light shall drive away
all traces of darksome night.

Ṭáhirih, 'Daybreak'

Ṭáhirih was well aware from her spiritual intuition and from her study of the works of S͟hayk͟h Aḥmad and Siyyid Káẓim that the advent of the promised Qá'im was at hand. As is also indicated, her capacity and certitude was such that she recognized the station of the Báb as Qá'im without even having to meet Him.[26] What is more, she was also well aware that the Day of Resurrection would see not one Revelation but two. Therefore, early on she is aware of the stations of both the Báb and Bahá'u'lláh (as was Quddús). Or stated another way, she was aware that these twin Revelations were part of one process that was the Day of Resurrection. Thus, where the Báb alludes to the completion of what He has announced as the 'Latter Resurrection',[27] Ṭáhirih alludes more commonly to the Quranic reference to the same event as the twice sounding of the Trumpet mentioned in the Qur'án. The first would cause people to become unconscious and the second would bestow life so that those unconscious ones would arise and behold the truth alluded to in the Qur'án (39:67–9):

> And there shall be a blast on the trumpet, and all who are in the Heavens and all who are in the Earth shall expire, save those whom God shall vouchsafe to live. Then shall there be another blast on it, and lo! arising they shall gaze around them:
>
> And the earth shall shine with the light of her Lord, and the Book shall be set, and the prophets shall be brought up, and the witnesses, and judgement shall be given between them with equity . . .

The poems in this section thus take us through the several emotions related to this long-awaited advent. Sometimes the emotions are

Ṭáhirih's own, but most often she speaks not for herself alone, but for all the faithful souls who were attuned to the imminence of this 'hidden secret' and who in their hearts longed for the Day of Resurrection promised in the Qur'án when the faithful would be rewarded, the 'dry bones' would be resurrected and the world would be judged.

Clearly Ṭáhirih viewed this event as a time of rejoicing, a time of the earth's renewal, the long-awaited dawn of a new age when the earth would be transformed into a united family. However, the fundamentalist views of other religions awaited this same event with trepidation and consternation, fearing that the eschatological images of resurrection and judgement at the 'time of the end' portended the end of the world and not the true beginning of human civilization based on spiritual principles.

It is in this vein that Shoghi Effendi in *God Passes By*[28] alludes to how the dawning of the Revelation of Bahá'u'lláh fulfilled many religions' prophecies, traditions and scriptural allusions to this Promised Day of God. Of particular interest to these poems, however, is Shoghi Effendi's equally astounding explication of how the advent of the Báb fulfilled Quranic and Muslim expectations of the incomparable event of the advent of the Qá'im:

> The Báb, acclaimed by Bahá'u'lláh as the '*Essence of Essences*', the '*Sea of Seas*', the '*Point round Whom the realities of the Prophets and Messengers revolve*', '*from Whom God hath caused to proceed the knowledge of all that was and shall be*', Whose '*rank excelleth that of all the Prophets*', and Whose '*Revelation transcendeth the comprehension and understanding of all their chosen ones*', had delivered His Message and discharged His mission. He Who was, in the words of 'Abdu'l-Bahá, the '*Morn of Truth*' and '*Harbinger of the Most Great Light*', Whose advent at once signalized the termination of the '*Prophetic Cycle*' and the inception of the '*Cycle of Fulfilment*', had simultaneously through His Revelation banished the shades of night that had descended upon His country, and proclaimed the impending rise of that Incomparable Orb Whose radiance was to envelop the whole of mankind. He, as affirmed by Himself, '*the Primal Point from which have been generated all created things*', '*one of the sustaining pillars of the Primal Word of God*', the '*Mystic Fane*', the '*Great Announcement*', the '*Flame of that supernal Light that glowed upon Sinai*', the '*Remembrance of God*' concerning Whom '*a separate Covenant hath been established with each and every Prophet*' had, through His advent, at once fulfilled the promise of all ages and ushered in the consummation of all Revelations. He the 'Qá'im' (He Who ariseth) promised to the Shí'ahs, the 'Mihdí' (One Who is guided) awaited by the Sunnís, the 'Return of John the Baptist' expected by the Christians, the 'Úshídar-Máh' referred to in the Zoroastrian scriptures, the 'Return of Elijah' anticipated by the Jews, Whose Revelation was to show

forth '*the signs and tokens of all the Prophets*', Who was to '*manifest the perfection of Moses, the radiance of Jesus and the patience of Job*' had appeared, proclaimed His Cause, been mercilessly persecuted and died gloriously. The '*Second Woe*', spoken of in the Apocalypse of St. John the Divine, had, at long last, appeared, and the first of the two '*Messengers*', Whose appearance had been prophesied in the Qur'an, had been sent down. The first '*Trumpet-Blast*', destined to smite the earth with extermination, announced in the latter Book, had finally been sounded. '*The Inevitable*', '*The Catastrophe*', '*The Resurrection*', '*The Earthquake of the Last Hour*', foretold by that same Book, had all come to pass. The '*clear tokens*' had been '*sent down*', and the '*Spirit*' had '*breathed*', and the '*souls*' had '*waked up*', and the '*heaven*' had been '*cleft*', and the '*angels*' had '*ranged in order*', and the '*stars*' had been '*blotted out*', and the '*earth*' had '*cast forth her burden*', and '*Paradise*' had been '*brought near*', and '*hell*' had been '*made to blaze*', and the '*Book*' had been '*set*', and the '*Bridge*' had been '*laid out*', and the '*Balance*' had been '*set up*', and the '*mountains scattered in dust*'. The '*cleansing of the Sanctuary*', prophesied by Daniel and confirmed by Jesus Christ in His reference to '*the abomination of desolation*', had been accomplished. The '*day whose length shall be a thousand years*', foretold by the Apostle of God in His Book, had terminated. The '*forty and two months*', during which the '*Holy City*', as predicted by St. John the Divine, would be trodden under foot, had elapsed. The '*time of the end*' had been ushered in, and the first of the '*two Witnesses*' into Whom, '*after three days and a half the Spirit of Life from God*' would enter, had arisen and had '*ascended up to heaven in a cloud*'. The '*remaining twenty and five letters to be made manifest*', according to Islamic tradition, out of the '*twenty and seven letters*' of which Knowledge has been declared to consist, had been revealed. The '*Man Child*', mentioned in the Book of Revelation, destined to '*rule all nations with a rod of iron*', had released, through His coming, the creative energies which, reinforced by the effusions of a swiftly succeeding and infinitely mightier Revelation, were to instil into the entire human race the capacity to achieve its organic unification, attain maturity and thereby reach the final stage in its age-long evolution. The clarion-call addressed to the '*concourse of kings and of the sons of kings*', marking the inception of a process which, accelerated by Bahá'u'lláh's subsequent warnings to the entire company of the monarchs of East and West, was to produce so widespread a revolution in the fortunes of royalty, had been raised in the Qayyumú'l-Asmá'. The '*Order*', whose foundation the Promised One was to establish in the Kitáb-i-Aqdas, and the features of which the Centre of the Covenant was to delineate in His Testament, and whose administrative framework the entire body of His followers are now erecting, had been categorically announced in the Persian Bayán. The laws which were designed, on the one hand, to abolish at a stroke the privileges and ceremonials, the ordinances and institutions of a superannuated Dispensation, and to bridge, on the other, the gap between an obsolete system and the institutions of a world-encompassing Order destined to supersede it, had been clearly formulated and proclaimed. The Covenant which, despite the determined assaults launched against it, succeeded, unlike all previous Dispensations, in preserving the integrity of the Faith of its Author, and in paving the way for the advent of the One Who was to be its Centre and Object, had been firmly and irrevocably established.[29]

It is to this event and to these prophecies that some of the poems in this section allude with understandable joy as Ṭáhirih admonishes the peoples of the world to awaken to the new reality that had dawned.

And yet some verses also allude to the second trumpet blast and the advent of Bahá'u'lláh, which Shoghi Effendi described even more elaborately in *God Passes By*.[30] Within this most remarkably researched catalogue of allusions to the advent of Bahá'u'lláh made by various religious traditions are the specific Islamic prophecies that Bahá'u'lláh fulfils:

> To Him Muḥammad, the Apostle of God, had alluded in His Book as the '*Great Announcement*', and declared His Day to be the Day whereon '*God*' will '*come down*' '*overshadowed with clouds*', the Day whereon '*thy Lord shall come and the angels rank on rank*', and '*The Spirit shall arise and the angels shall be ranged in order*'. His advent He, in that Book, in a súrih said to have been termed by Him '*the heart of the Qur'án*', had foreshadowed as that of the '*third*' Messenger, sent down to 'strengthen' the two who preceded Him. To His Day He, in the pages of that same Book, had paid a glowing tribute, glorifying it as the '*Great Day*', the '*Last Day*', the '*Day of God*', the '*Day of Judgement*', the '*Day of Reckoning*', the '*Day of Mutual Deceit*', the '*Day of Severing*', the '*Day of Sighing*', the '*Day of Meeting*', the Day '*when the Decree shall be accomplished*', the Day whereon the second '*Trumpet blast*' will be sounded, the '*Day when mankind shall stand before the Lord of the world*', and '*all shall come to Him in humble guise*', the Day when '*thou shalt see the mountains, which thou thinkest so firm, pass away with the passing of a cloud*', the Day '*wherein account shall be taken*', '*the approaching Day, when men's hearts shall rise up, choking them, into their throats*', the Day when '*all that are in the heavens and all that are on the earth shall be terror-stricken, save him whom God pleaseth to deliver*', the Day whereon '*every suckling woman shall forsake her sucking babe, and every woman that hath a burden in her womb shall cast her burden*', the Day '*when the earth shall shine with the light of her Lord, and the Book shall be set, and the Prophets shall be brought up, and the witnesses; and judgement shall be given between them with equity; and none shall be wronged*'.[31]

We have arranged the poems relating to these issues according to the logic of the parts of this event to which they seem to relate. There is first the waiting, the longing for the event to occur. Then Ṭáhirih, having recognized that the event has occurred, seems to plead with the Báb that He unveil His station so that the world will become aware of what has transpired. The poems then shift to a tone of joyous advent and announcement but also to the necessity of Bahá'u'lláh revealing Himself to complete the process of reformation and resurrection.

In these pieces Ṭáhirih exhorts humankind to awaken and arise. She announces that the Promised Day has at last arrived. She affirms everything for which the peoples of the world throughout the ages have been longing – peace, justice, equity – will now occur.

These poems employ images of the day dawning, the Beloved Friend appearing and the Presence of God being accessible through the person of the Prophet. Ṭáhirih thus blends common imagery with specific allusions to mystic terms and allusions as well to Old and New Testament passages regarding this day when the earth would be recreated. The tone of the last pieces is thus uniformly energetic, joyful and celebratory.

This Longing For You

(2)

This poem is beautifully rhythmical, with the second half of most couplets (which we have rendered into quatrains) fully in Arabic (numbers 1–7 and number 11). The first half of all quatrains (except for the sixth) is in Persian. The poem thus alternates between Persian and Arabic sentences. In other poems of Ṭáhirih, except for 'For the Love of Bahá' which is fully in Arabic, Persian dominates, though Ṭáhirih often employs Arabic words, phrases and sentences.

Structurally, this poem is divided into two distinct parts. The first – stanzas one through seven – describe the lovers of God who patiently wait 'behind the veils' for the Beloved (the Prophet) to unveil Himself to them. Because of Ṭáhirih's unique position as one of the 18 Letters of the Living yet one who also recognized the station of Bahá'u'lláh and worked with Him, these lines could allude either to those awaiting the unveiling of the Qá'im (the Báb) or to those Bábís who eagerly awaited 'Him Whom God will make manifest' (Bahá'u'lláh – the promised Manifestation mentioned throughout the writings of the Báb).

The second section begins with stanza eight in which the persona (possibly Ṭáhirih herself) beseeches God or the Manifestation on behalf of the waiting souls to unveil Himself in the plentitude of His beauty and grandeur. The last three stanzas give three sorts of effects that will be produced by such an unveiling. Each of these three contains a paradox, much in the vein of Rumi's work.

O Thou Opener of Gates,[32]
open the portal of reunion!
Can't you hear how
the friends of God are knocking?

What harm could it do
if they find their way to your side?
So many have been waiting
and watching behind your door.

How long must they patiently wait
to attain your presence?[33]

Your remoteness is prolonged
and still they linger behind the veil.

How long must your lovers endure
this anguish from behind the curtain?
At least bestow upon them
a glimpse[34] of your unveiled beauty.

They ask nothing more from you
than your presence.
There is no reward for them
except meeting you.

They became drunk with ecstasy[35]
in desire for you – then sober again –
for there is no respite,
no sanctuary for them but you.[36]

By piercing the veils
they have abandoned the causes;
by rending the veils,
they have surpassed the means.[37]

Cast aside the clouds to show them
the sun in its full splendour
by removing the veils
from the beauty of your face

so that the wise ones
will become astonished with wonderment
and those whose brains have withered
will be replenished with wisdom,

so that the self deluded ones
will be brought to their senses
and those who are sober and wise
will become crazy with intoxication,[38]

so that the slave and the master
will become so intermingled
that no distinction between them
can be found.

The Voice of God's Command

(3)

Here we have one of the clearest examples of how Ṭáhirih shifts personae (narrative perspective) in her poems for imaginative effect. In this verse the first person narrator is God the Creator speaking with authority, commanding humankind in no uncertain terms to pay heed to the new Revelation.

The imagery is succinct and relatively commonplace but no less effective. Humanity is commanded to cast off the old garments (the laws and traditions of the previous Revelation) and receive the new Revelation (the new apparel). Each of the four couplets (rendered here as quatrains) is thus a distinct command from God: 1) a new Revelation has occurred – accede to the binding commandments it brings; 2) lay aside the trappings of the old Revelation; 3) cut yourself loose from the temptations of worldly desires; 4) become aware of your true nature and submit to the will of God.

Behold, my resistless Faith[39]
has once more become manifest;
It is the binding commandment,
the subduing verses.[40]

Cast off the garments of old laws,
of outworn traditions!
Immerse yourself in the sea
of my bounteousness!

How long in this world,
rabid with passion and corruption,
will you remain so remote from your true
purpose,
so pitifully far?

From but two letters, *B* and *E*,[41]
Our Faith has appeared again.
You need only respond: 'from God'
and 'to Him shall we return'.[42]

The Announcement

(4)

This is one of several poems stating in utmost simplicity and clarity the concept of renewal and revelation that is the cornerstone of Islamic, Bábí and Bahá'í belief – the idea that God reveals Himself incrementally throughout history by sending 'Angelic Messengers' or Prophets – what Bahá'u'lláh designates as 'Manifestations'. More than that, Ṭáhirih alludes here to the idea that the purpose of those endowed with spiritual insight is to reveal to others how the signs of God are concealed within all created things, a theme to which Ṭáhirih will return in numerous poems. In this poem, Ṭáhirih seems to be sharing with us the exhortation she has received from God, that it is her duty as one of those with insight to help others penetrate the veils of semblance in order to discern the signs of God in whatever form they appear. The speaker may thus be Ṭáhirih or the voice of Divine Command charging her with the duty of announcing these verities.

He came with reflections of the Eternal One.
He made manifest the countenance of Aḥmad.[43]

Yet the learned ones remain heedless
of the ecstatic melodies of the Holy Spirit.

Verily, it is Aḥmad who has descended with Holy
verses
as a blessing from the heaven of grandeur.

He has ignited the whole world with sparks of fire
and He has turned humankind completely into
light.[44]

O Ṭáhirih, tear away the veil from their midst
that the hidden mystery may become revealed.

Give thanks that He, the Most Beauteous[45] Lord
on High,
did indeed shine down with such astounding[46]
adornments.

Arise![47]

(5)

This poem is a sterling example of the religious lyric at its best. It is succinct, memorable, musical, imagistic and finely chiselled. It bears many readings and produces many levels of meaning. It is first and foremost an announcement to humankind that a new Revelation has occurred, that the time for indolence, sadness and lethargy has suddenly ended and the time of revival and rejuvenation has appeared.

And yet the poem does not come off as homiletic or as polemical. Because the speaker/persona addresses an individual, the poem speaks to the individual heart and humankind only implicitly. And yet, the careful reader will note that the individuals being addressed are not the same person from couplet to couplet. The 'sleepers' might symbolize those who have been spiritually dead. The 'heartsick lovers' are those who are spiritually awake but who have longed for some further relationship with God through a new Revelation, the Promised Prophet. The sick ones might be those who have suffered injustice or who have felt cut off from spiritual sustenance because of the decline of the previous Dispensation. The 'half-drunk' ones might be those who have gained great spiritual insight and love of God through a previous Manifestation and who now long for even more understanding and insight.

The poem concludes with the image of the new season, the new day, the new Revelation which will bring the solace that will bring benefits to everyone. For as the new year causes nature to put on new 'clothing' or a new 'body', so the new Revelation will have a new institution through which to channel the Holy Spirit to humankind.

The speaker throughout is nameless. The narrator does not seem to be Ṭáhirih as an individual, nor the Prophet, but a nameless herald of the new day, the very role that Ṭáhirih herself acts out at the conclusion of the conference at Badas͟ht.

O sleeping one, the Friend has arrived! Arise!
Shake off that earthly dust! Arise!

Behold, O heartsick lover of the Friend,
He who was aloof has turned kind and benevolent!
Arise!

O frail and broken-hearted one,
the consoling physician has come to your bedside!
Arise!

O thou, half drunk with intoxication for the
Friend,[48]
the choice solacing wine is here! Arise![49]

O thou who art sick with separation,
the season of reunion with the Friend has arrived!
Arise!

O thou whom autumn made melancholic
now spring really has come! Arise![50]

Behold the new year teaming with new life!
Cast off that dead flesh! Become reborn! Arise![51]

Behold the New Day!

(6)

Almost a continuation of the theme and tone of the previous poem, this poem is a more specific catalogue of the glorious effects that will result from the New Day (the long-awaited 'Day of Resurrection'). This poem, too, is totally positive and celebratory in tone. Furthermore, because Ṭáhirih here alludes to a complete reformation of society, we can presume she foresees not merely the results of the advent of the Báb but also the ultimate results that will be achieved during the dispensation of Bahá'u'lláh, even though the New Day has only 'begun to dawn'.

Ṭáhirih does not allude to herself, nor does she dwell on her adoration of the Manifestation as the means by which this reformation of human society will take place. However, as is so often her custom, Ṭáhirih mocks the pretentiousness and hypocrisy of clerics and kings alike. The poem is equally divided between listing those negative things that will be abolished and those positive forces that will cause this transformation and resurrection.

Behold, the morn of guidance has begun to dawn!
The whole world has become illumined, from *áfáq*
to *anfus*![52]

No more will the Shaykh occupy the throne[53] of
hypocrisy.
No more will the mosque be a marketplace for
piety.[54]

The chin strap of turbans[55] will be severed.
No Shaykhs, no haughtiness, no deceit will remain.

The world will be freed from vain fancies and
superstitions.
Humanity will be relieved of all confusion and
doubt.

Injustice will be convicted by the power of justice.
Ignorance will be defeated by the power of
thought.

Everywhere the carpet of equity will be rolled out.
Everywhere the seeds of amity will be scattered.

The reign[56] of disunity will be vanquished from all
regions.
The diverse peoples of the world will become one
nation.[57]

Daybreak

(7)

As with the poem 'Arise!', this poem heralds the dawn of a new Revelation and a new age. But where 'Arise!' speaks to the individual, this poem articulates more directly the effects that this new Revelation will have on society as a whole: e.g. the advent of 'Justice, Law, Order' and the banishment of unjust political and religious systems.

Furthermore, where 'Arise!' dwells on the sheer joy of the new Revelation, this piece specifically indicts those who have until now held the reigns of power (the monarchs and Shaykhs). Consequently, in this poem we have a clearer sense of the probability that the speaker is Ṭáhirih herself because so often in her poems (as in her life), she is utterly disdainful of the so-called learned ones of her society, represented in this poem by the 'Shaykhs'.

Of further interest in this poem is the stanzaic form. Here the original eight couplet form does not work well translated line for line because of the line lengths and the amount of information imparted. But instead of quatrains, the couplets seem to fall naturally into five line stanzas.

Lovers! O Ye Lovers!
The face of truth has become manifest!
Lo, the veils have at last been removed
through the power of *Rabbu'l Falaq*,
'The Lord of the Dawn'![58]

Arise, each one of you!
In Bahá the face of God can be seen![59]
Look! See how that face,
bright like sun at daybreak,
shines with compassion and delight!

O ye great ones,[60] the Creator of the Age[61]
has fashioned the universe into a paradise!
This must be the Day of Resurrection
when morning light shall drive away
all traces of darksome night.

The time for rectitude has come!
Perversity is in retreat!
Indeed, everything you longed for
– Law, Order, Justice –
has at long last appeared!

Injustice and iniquity
have vanished from our midst.
Now is the age of charity[62] and munificence.
All feebleness and frailty have been replaced
with sustenance and power.

True knowledge has unveiled itself.
Ignorance has been banished from our
councils.
Go! Tell the Shaykhs[63] of this age[64]
to arise at once
and revise[65] all their texts!

For ages the world's order
has been turned upside down
through vain imaginings of the learned.[66]
Now milk shall flow instead of bloodshed[67]
if you but set aright the order of the world.[68]

For though the King of all kings has
appeared
in the manner and custom of a single nation,
He will, through the mercy of the Eternal
One,
deliver all the peoples of the world
from their burdens and their bondage.[69]

Praise God for this Promised Day![70]

(8)

More a hymn of praise, this poem is unlike almost any other poem except 'The Love of Bahá' in its use of repetition and refrain. Clearly this piece is meant to be chanted, sung or intoned in such a way that these repeated phrases become antiphonal to the incremental progression of thought. Ṭáhirih even alludes to the singing of these praises in the poem itself.

Thus what might at first glance seem to be a paucity of meaning is, in reality, the gradual progress of very profound statements glorifying God for having fulfilled the promised Day of the Lord alluded to in all the scriptures of past religions. The power of this psalm of praise, therefore, lies in the celebratory nature of its tone and the exaltation of praise that the long-awaited Day of Resurrection has at last arrived, and in the driving rhythm. Possibly the only equivalent poetic tone would be in the Afro-American spirituals which, through supreme irony or divine inspiration, were being composed at precisely this same period under the oppression of slavery. Certainly the enigmatic joy of the Afro-American spiritual would be explained were these enslaved peoples attuned to the birth of a new day, even if that birth was occurring thousands of miles away. Because of the celebratory spirit of this piece, we have deviated somewhat more liberally from an exact translation of the original couplets.

Finally, we should note that the Centennial publication version of this poem includes an additional verse which does not appear in Afnán's version adopted by us.

Begin the festival for the Promised Day!
Praise God for this Blessed Day!
A new Apostle has appeared at last!
Praise God for this Promised Day!

The Divine celebration has now begun!
Delight in the joy of your own hearts!
Glad tidings have descended from the realm
on high:
'Praise God for this Promised Day!'

This joyous time has come at last
descended from Paradise on high,[71]
The peerless time has come at last!
Praise God for this Promised Day!

Everything will be made new,[72]
For the joyous time has come.
The Divine light has been unveiled at last
Descended from realm above.

This is the Day foretold in sacred texts,
Welcome to the Blessed Day![73]
Humankind has come alive through Thy will
alone,
Welcome to this Blessed Day!

Rejoice! Rejoice! there is happiness today!
Sing praises for this wondrous revelation
today!
Hearts are longing and searching today!
Welcome to this Blessed Day!

Humankind has become enriched through
You!
Lo, some have even become worthy through
You!
Such splendour and such light have emanated
from You!
Welcome to this Blessed Day!

O Thou whose Essence has no beginning,
For You life and death are the same,
Through your coming the darkness at long
last has passed,
Welcome to this Blessed Day!

I am astonished by the wine of Thy cup!
I am filled with joy from your name!
At last I am at peace in your days, O Lord.
Welcome to this Blessed Day!

Rejoice, my friend! Rejoice!
for your soul no longer doubts!

Rise up, rise up, sing praises now!
Sing 'Welcome to this Blessed Day!'

Arise, my friend, and be joyful!
Become a follower of Bahá![74]
Escape from all bonds of distinction!
Sing, 'Welcome to this Blessed Day!'

These guests at Your mighty feast
Have brought to You their hearts and souls!
Gabriel himself will chase the flies away!
Welcome to this Blessed Day!

Each moment sing this with glee, my friend,
with music pitched high and low:
'All my pain was cured through You!
Welcome to this Blessed Day!'

O Qurra,[75] at each moment cry out
with a heart finally free from grief,
with joy in your heart from the face of the
King:
'Welcome to this Blessed Day!'

An Ode to the Báb

(9)

These verses state in emphatic language the essential nature of what the Revelation of the Báb has accomplished. They do not employ the imagery of the mystic love relationship, nor do they delve into the more esoteric aspects of theology. Here again Ṭáhirih alludes to the idea that all created things express some divine attribute and that the Revelation of the Báb explains this essential harmony or unity underlying all creation. The couplets break naturally into quatrains, which we find here a more suitable form for this piece.

One noteworthy point concerns her use of the concept of the 'veil' in the last quatrain to allude not to the negative barriers (as she does in the first quatrain with 'shadows of vain imaginings' that conceal or distort true reality) but to the intensity of the light that constitute the 'veils' of God's grandeur (*jalál*) and Divine Beauty (*jamál*) which can also blind one, even though these are positive forces.

The shadows of vain imaginings[76]
have disappeared in the clear light of learning.
Our minds have become sober again
through Divine Revelation.

In the Bayán You embraced
every distinct path and form.[77]
Indeed, You removed every limitation
from our midst.

You disclosed the concealed unity
among all created things.
You expelled from the earth
all discord and enmity.[78]

The veils concealing *Jalál*
have been rent asunder.
Indeed, every *Jamál*
has now become manifested.[79]

The Dry Bones

(10)

These two brief couplets which we have translated into free verse contain a compressed allusion to the beginning of the Báb's Revelation. He is here both the 'Primal Point' and the 'Pen', as alluded to frequently in the works of Bahá'u'lláh. The first couplet thus states that the process of revelation has now begun and that the Báb is beginning to reveal the divine utterance (the point of the pen is beginning to move across the pages).

The second section alludes to the prophecies regarding the advent of a day in which all the knowledge that was hidden would become revealed and all those that were dead would be resurrected. For example, the Prophet Ezekiel prophesied the following:

> The hand of the LORD was upon me, and he brought me out by the Spirit of the LORD, and set me down in the midst of the valley; it was full of bones. And he led me round among them; and behold, there were very many upon the valley; and lo, they were very dry. And he said to me, 'Son of man, can these bones live?' And I answered, 'O Lord GOD, thou knowest.' Again he said to me, 'Prophesy to these bones, and say to them, O dry bones, hear the word of the LORD. Thus says the Lord GOD to these bones: Behold, I will cause breath to enter you, and you shall live. And I will lay sinews upon you, and will cause flesh to come upon you, and cover you with skin, and put breath in you, and you shall live; and you shall know that I am the LORD.' (Ezekiel 37:1–6)

The notes to this poem reveal further allusions for the 'dry bones' and for the concept of 'eternal Mysteries' and the overall theological perspective that Ṭáhirih assumes here. But from the subject of this poem as an announcement, similar to that which she made at the conference at Badasht, we can assume this would be an early work.

Behold!
The Most Great Sea
has begun to stir
and the Primal Point,
motionless ere now,
has begun to move![80]

This is that Pen
you prayed for
to teach you about
the mystery of eternality,[81]
to fulfil your desire
that all the dry bones[82]
may at last become
resurrected.

The Hidden Secret

(11)

In the Centennial publication, this poem is at the opening of a letter written by Ṭáhirih to a believer called Qurratu'l-'Ayn encouraging her to rise and support the Faith and educate the believers. The content and language of the letter leads one to believe that this poem is in fact part of the letter. What is written on the back of the source indicates that this letter should be delivered to Qurratu'l-'Ayn. It also includes a short note addressed to Qurratu'l-'Ayn indicating that Ṭáhirih has sent her letters from the friends in Qazvín including Bihjat's letters and asking her to read these letters but to keep them hidden. The author of the Centennial publication indicates in the notes to that volume that this letter is apparently written to 'Izzíyyih Khánum.

The six couplets of this poem take their meaning from a variety of sources – from ḥadíth, from biblical prophecy and from traditional poetic terms in the works of Rumi and others.

The idea of the poem seems clear and relatively simple in light of the information we have discussed in the introduction to this chapter. Ṭáhirih seems to appeal to Bahá'u'lláh (who is referred to in the Báb's writing as Qurratu'l-'Ayn – 'Solace of the Eyes') to emerge from obscurity and to manifest Himself so that the dead souls may be resurrected, an event consummate with the second Trumpet blast. In couplet four Ṭáhirih alludes to the souls that have fallen 'unconscious into their graves', the result of the first Trumpet blast (the Revelation of the Báb). In couplet five, she calls out to Bahá'u'lláh to reveal Himself that the effects of the second Trumpet blast will be effected: the dead will be resurrected and the world will be united.

These allusions thus seem to place the work after the declaration of the Báb as Ṭáhirih longs to see Bahá'u'lláh reveal Himself instead of remaining a 'hidden secret'. In short, the poem is a succinct and elliptical statement of twin revelation.[83]

O Thou the Eternal, the Self Subsisting

O, Qurratu'l-'Ayn,[84] begin singing
the melodies of the songs of the flute[85]

so that the fire of Ṭúr[86] will flash from your face
and attract by its light all the moth-like souls.[87]

O, my Precious One, arise with ecstasy and delight!
Look! Behold with your omniscient eyes[88]

how all the souls,[89] once so full of promise,
have fallen unconscious into their graves.[90]

O Light of my eyes, arise from your abode, gaze on
them,
and resurrect them through your power!

How long will You remain remote, lowly and subdued?[91]
How long must You remain a Hidden Secret?

Chapter Four

The Ecstasy of Nearness

Seeing His face makes all the poor ones
drown in the Sea of nothingness.

It is not only I who praise his face;
He is praised by every particle in the universe.

Whosoever becomes aware of His *illá*
would in this station make himself *lá*.
Ṭáhirih, 'Attaining the Presence of God'

Ṭáhirih is most often considered by those who have not studied her work in depth as a poet writing in typically Persian forms in a typically mystical framework. Her work is thus often compared to that of the classical Persian poets such as Rumi. If this volume shows nothing else, it demonstrates the variety of her poetic modes, themes and personae she employs in her verse.

And yet she did indeed also employ the terminology and context of the mystic poetic tradition and the entire theme of the mystic quest for the Friend and, through the Friend, the state of nearness to God. This sense of union or reunion caused by the nearness to the Beloved (whether to the Friend or to the Prophet as Friend, or to the presence of God) by following the path of the Friend is the goal of the mystic and Ṭáhirih often portrays immersion in the joy of spiritual nearness in mystic terminology.

We will leave it to the reader to decide whether these experiences are autobiographical or whether in a more general way she is translating what should be the true believer's sense of priorities in this quest for truth: love of the newly-discovered Beauty and devotion to the path of the Beloved. Possibly it is both.

The poems in this section thus portray the emotions and reactions of the mystic believer in terms with which anyone will be familiar who is aware of the 'courtly love' traditions of the medieval European romances, the 'Petrarchan love' traditions of the sonnets or the Persian and Arabic mystic-love traditions (from which both of the former derive).

The lover is attracted through the eyes and face of the beloved. The lover becomes lovesick and cannot abide a moment's separation from the beloved. The lover experiences calamities in the path of quest to attain the presence of the beloved, the malady of love itself being the most obvious of these. The lover complains about the remoteness of the beloved – and the implicit cruelty or aloofness of the beloved. The lover finally realizes that the ultimate union or reunion with the beloved will only occur in some form of death. In the case of Ṭáhirih, these allusions to death are at least twofold: she anticipates her own martyrdom and looks forward to that event with excitement because she is confident of the more felicitous reality that awaits her; and she also knows – especially after the martyrdom of the Báb – that her ultimate reunion with her Beloved can only occur in the next life.

Thus, while many of these poems employ traditional images of intoxication, love longing, calamity and suffering, they are, in the context of the deeper levels of Ṭáhirih's meaning, filled with allusions to both historical events and to an understanding of spiritual reality that renders them more than mere imitation of ancient traditions. Indeed, the last few longer poems in this section are certainly among the finest verses she penned.

For Love of My Beauty

(12)

The cleverness and power of this brief poem lies in the outlandish hyperbole of the several images and in the probability that the point of view or persona employed by Ṭáhirih is not the poetess herself but that of the Prophet – hence the title. Most immediately it reminds the Bahá'í reader of the statement by Bahá'u'lláh in the Kitáb-i-Aqdas that the goal of the believer is to 'Observe My commandments, for the love of My beauty':

> The Tongue of My power hath, from the heaven of My omnipotent glory, addressed to My creation these words: 'Observe My commandments, for the love of My beauty'. Happy is the lover that hath inhaled the divine fragrance of his Best-Beloved from these words, laden with the perfume of a grace which no tongue can describe. By My life! He who hath drunk the choice wine of fairness from the hands of My bountiful favour will circle around My commandments that shine above the Dayspring of My creation.[92]

Of course, since every Prophet states that His power and attraction derive from the capacity to manifest the attributes of God, the frank confession of His attracting power is naught but praise of God – the source of all beauty (or 'forms' of beauty, as Ṭáhirih states in another poem).

If I blandish my tresses
so that the wind extracts their fragrance,
I will capture
the gazelles of the plains.

If I line my eyes
with collyrium,[93]
I will distract the whole world
with my beauty.

Each morning heaven
brings out its golden mirror
only that it might
observe my face.

If one day by chance
I should pass by the church
I would convert to my Faith
all the Christian girls.

Attaining the Presence of God[94]

(13)

This poem is very rhythmical, possessing a musical quality and terminology that reminds one of the ecstatic chants of whirling dervishes and the joyful poems of Rumi. The structure of this poem is unlike the majority of Ṭáhirih's work in that the couplets are closed – each couplet is a complete statement.

The poem has an obvious clear thematic unity – the appearance of the 'face of God' and its effects on those who behold that face. Doubtless this is an allusion to the appearance of the Prophet of God, or what Bahá'u'lláh describes in the Kitáb-i-Íqán as 'attaining the Presence of God'.[95] Of particular interest is the fifth couplet where we find what would seem to be not so much an allusion to the whirling dance of the dervish (though it could be that as well) as it is a reference to the martyrs. It brings to mind Ḥájí Sulaymán Khán, who literally danced through the streets with 'lighted candles thrust into holes driven into his flesh'.[96]

The Monarch of Love is raising the call,
Summoning all to the path of the Beloved.

The pen of attributes trembles in shame
in daring to describe His face of lights.

Whoever becomes informed of His mysteries
would doubtless sacrifice his life for Him.

In this, the Day of Illumination, His face
is the sun filling the world with the light of
His glory.

Whosoever desires reunion with Him,
will gladly dance towards His calamity.[97]

Consider His face like unto a mirror
in which are manifested the lights of *illá*.[98]

Seeing His face makes all the poor ones[99]
drown in the Sea of nothingness.

It is not only I who praise His face;
He is praised by every particle in the
universe.[100]

Whosoever becomes aware of His *illá*
would, in this station, make himself *lá*.[101]

Fire in the Eyes of the Friend

(14)

Nothing is simple or obvious in this powerful lyric. Virtually every phrase is symbolic or allusive, playing off traditional mystic imagery, but in Ṭáhirih's own special style. We have left the images intact so as not to take the poetry from the poem and also to give the reader the sense of brevity with which these symbols convey their meaning. However, we have conveyed the essential meanings of these images in the notes because without some sense of the background for these figures, the reader might be utterly lost. We have also retained the couplets as couplets, all of which (like the previous poem) are 'closed' except for the last two.

With an understanding of the traditions behind these allusions, the poem can be seen to contain possible allusions to the Prophet in traditional terms of Sufi verse. In particular, we can detect the admixture of masculine and feminine traits of beauty in the images of the Friend that might seem alien to the western image of the hero – an image of mostly masculine physical prowess and rugged individualism. And yet a study of the heroic images in medieval English poetry reveals a strikingly similar mixture of masculine and feminine imagery, derived in part from the fact that the courtly love image of the beloved is strongly influenced by (if not originating in) the Persian and Arabic poetic traditions of the same period.

Perhaps the most important crux of the poem is the ambiguity about whose eyes and whose heart are being alluded to as having power. Is Ṭáhirih referring to her own heart which, having been transformed, is now endowed with power? Is the 'Majnún heart' her own or the Prophet's heart. The poem works well with either interpretation.

Those intoxicating eyes have shattered creation;
all who beheld them fell, twisted and writhing.

Each glance of those roving eyes
has transfixed everyone possessing insight.

But what is this power pouring forth from this Majnún
heart[102]
that has razed so many tents[103] in Laylí's pavilion?

It is the sparks from the tent of the fire sitters[104]
that have ignited every veil with blazing flames.

If this conflagration be not the same fire Moses saw,[105]
then why is the whole earth consumed and in such a
frenzy?

I need in my cup only one sip of wine from the
Cupbearer[106]
to tell you the secret of what this is that God now hath
wrought.[107]

Lo, if you but study us[108] carefully with judicious eyes,
you too will observe the face of God unveiled,

a countenance descended from the heavenly realm,
a face luminous and bright as midday sun.

The Burning Heart

(15)

This is a fairly typical poetic use of mystical longing translated into terms of a human love relationship and longing. The piece is thus a melodious, soft flowing lamentation (plaint) of a suffering lover addressing the beloved. It is rhythmic and musical in its structure but it does not attempt to startle the reader with vigour and vitality as do pieces 'Arise!' and 'Daybreak'.

And yet the poem is more than this surface expression of adoration. After beginning simply, the poem soon turns to esoteric concepts: the shadowy nature of physical reality, the soul as divine emanation and the desire of the lover to escape the bonds of physical reality in order to achieve union with the beloved in the realm of the spirit. The reader should also note that here, as in several other pieces, 'calamity' in pursuit of the beloved is medicinal for the soul of the wayfarer on the journey of the spirit to union (reunion) and ultimately to annihilation (selflessness). We have with this piece translated the couplets into quatrains.

O Thou with beauteous Face, this heart is perpetually
day-dreaming about You, contemplating only You.
O Thou most Noble One, this heart can speak
of nothing else but Your incomparable elegance!

With such wondrous and bewitching charm[109]
You have revealed Yourself to me
that this aching, sigh-blown heart
watches endlessly in the madness[110] of love.

The sole object of this heart's desire
is the exquisite comeliness of Your face,
the Tartar musk scent of Your hair,
the sanctuary[111] of the pavilion[112] of Your abode.[113]

If You call this heart into Your presence,
and bestow on this heart the bounty of Your
    countenance
with Your grandeur, Your pomp, and Your majesty,
then, only then, will this heart find its home.

This heart has become so entranced by thy moon-like
beauty,
so engulfed in the flames of Your love
that never again can this heart
be content with mere shadows.[114]

Through Your benevolence and grace,
through Your compassion and mercy,
free me from all vain imaginings
so that this heart might become truly leonine.[115]

Only when, with a taste of Your calamity,
You pluck this heart from me
and place it into Your own bosom,[116]
only then will this heart be steadfast.

But behold how sparks fly from this heart,
descended as it is from Your own fire![117]
Why, then, does this burning heart bring forth
neither sweet peace nor solace?[118]

Song of the Captive Heart

(16)

This poem is unique in that it combines two different rhythms, as a composer might combine two melodies in a single piece. After each section a portion of the theme of the succeeding section appears. Thus, if one were to combine the sections we have put in italics, one would discover a separate poem that is, thematically, a virtual précis of the poem as a whole. In this sense, these couplets are 'prefrains' (as opposed to 'refrains').

The poem taken as a whole is an impassioned expression of deep love and affection for the Friend (the Prophet in this case), filled with some traditional imagery from the mystic vein. The images, however, are fresh, light-hearted and even humorous in their praise of the Beloved.

The persona here is not Ṭáhirih the herald, Ṭáhirih the martyr, Ṭáhirih the rebuker of authority or Ṭáhirih the theologian philosopher. This is Ṭáhirih the joy-filled lover indulging herself in praise and glorification of her heart's desire. Among her poems in this vein, this is among her very finest works. Certainly it contains some of her most inventive and remarkable imagery.

Finally, we should note here that the Centennial collection of this poem includes three additional verses but lacks three verses of Afnán's version. We have used Afnán's version here but we have made a few corrections to it based on the Centennial version.

1

I have this secret dream about you
from whence derives all my happiness and delight:

I am at your banquet, without any rivals for your
  affection –
I alone have become your acquaintance, O Dear Heart.

O, my beauteous one with your musk-scented hair,
O my king, you and only you are my friend.

2

O my beloved, because you now occupy my heart's throne,
The vanishing of your face has proven to be but a fable.

Hidden beneath the snare of your tresses was a seed;[119]
with that tiny seed you trapped the bird of my heart.

Admit me into your company, O friend,
That I might not be humiliated before my rivals.

3

O Monarch of the winsome ones, estrangement from your face
has vexed the world, like the tangles of your hair.

How like an anxious child I attend every festive gathering
on the mere chance that I might hear stories about you.[120]

If only once my name would cross your lips,
I would cast a hundred lives at your feet.

4

O beauteous moon of the friends,[121] the malady of my love for you is so fatal
that bewildered physicians, knowing no antidote, flee from my presence.[122]

Though there are rivals for your affection, happy is that moment
when I alone drink the choice wine from your chalice.

O Thou who hast ravished my heart, I have nothing but you;
O my crown-adorned King, may my life be sacrificed for you.

5

O thou who art majestic and stately as a cypress, truly I am mad for you,
and for those two intoxicating narcissus eyes of yours.

Because of the captivating power of your face
I have become a slave to your eternal love.

Desiring only you, I die in the court of your nearness;
I have no desire except reunion with your countenance.

6

Even if the fiery pain of your love sears through to my bones,
I will still utter no name but yours.

For the one who will escort me but once near your abode,
I will offer my life a hundred times.

In one instant you delight me with reunion;
In the next you slay me with separation.

7

O Thou heart-ravishing one, I am so warm with the wine of your love,
That I am oblivious to any desire for eternal paradise.

I am that bird who, having left its nest,
now knows no sanctuary but nearness to you.

Return to me! Observe my wounded heart!
How long must you keep me waiting?

8

Each hair of your tresses has become for me a lariat
that has bound me to your love.

O majestic hunter of my heart,
the arrows of your seductive glances have slain me.

Your elegant gait – a walking cypress;
Your lariat locks – my Tartar musk.

9

Such pearls have poured down from the clouds of eternity[123]
that the beauty of the wet hyacinth is hardly worth noting.

And what value have musk and ambergris
when the fragrance of your hyacinth is near?

O my chevalier![124] *Though you be like a mighty king,*
now and then cast a glance at me, your captive thrall.

The Realm of Ecstasy

(17)

The one ineffable experience to which the mystic poet inevitably alludes is the ecstatic delight of attaining a sense of union or reunion with the divine world or, more especially, with the Friend who has led the poet to this state of spiritual proximity to God or to the divine reality.

While many of Ṭáhirih's poems allude to this state of nearness and her longing to attain that condition, this poem is perhaps the best example of her attempt to describe this experience without merely resorting to traditional images. As in other poems, she relies heavily here on allusions to the calamity or suffering that the seeker must endure at the hands of the Beloved in order to attain this state.

On the one hand, this suffering is the sense of remoteness the believer feels from the spiritual realm and yet it also clearly alludes to the very real earthly calamities that befall the believer, as indicated in Bahá'u'lláh's well-known Arabic Hidden Words 50 and 51:

> O Son of Man! If adversity befall thee not in My path, how canst thou walk in the ways of them that are content with My pleasure? If trials afflict thee not in thy longing to meet Me, how wilt thou attain the light in thy love for My beauty?
>
> O Son of Man! My calamity is My providence, outwardly it is fire and vengeance, but inwardly it is light and mercy. Hasten thereunto that thou mayest become an eternal light and an immortal spirit. This is My command unto thee, do thou observe it.

Each section of this poem is composed of five lines. The first four lines form a pair of couplets (which rhyme with each other in the original).[125]

This poem is symphonic in structure, rhythmic, full of enthusiasm and energy but it also possesses a melodious and soothing quality, its energy and power gradually heightening as we get closer to the end and as the plaints and descriptions of ecstasy turn into an ardent desire for sacrifice. Finally, this poem describes about as well as a poem can the state of bewilderment, joy and delight that typify the mystical state of ecstasy.

1

O thou whose curled tresses have kindled my passion,
separation from you is the source of my anguish

and the rubies that are your lips are my sweet delicacies.
Your love has wholly enveloped me.

I no longer exist – you have replaced me.

2

Though the cup of your sorrows has brought untold grief,
I have gladly drunk cup after cup of your calamity.

Though I am frozen in sadness, my heart is singed by your fire.
Though I have died from grief, my heart is yet vibrant

since your messiah lips have resurrected me.

3

I am a jewel – you are the jeweller.
I am silver – you are the mine owner.

I am a seed – you are the husbandman.
What is in this body of mine if you have become me?

If you have displaced me, what is this corporal form of me?

4

From the sun of your being I descended nimble as an atom;[126]
I became drunk from the cup of your wine

when my hands stroked the strands of your tresses.
So long as you have replaced me, then I can worship myself,

because my body has become only an altar for
worshipping you.

5

But if this heart has become your own, why do you make
it bleed?
And if it is not yours, why do you make it insane with
desire?

Moment by moment you have increased the fire in this
heart.
At last you have burned away all the self within it

so that you yourself now reside inside my frenzied heart.

6

When the fire of your love burst into flame,
its conflagration consumed the essence of all that I was;

it purged me, cleansed me of my infidelity and my
Islam.
Now I prostrate myself only before the arch of your
brow;

For me there is now no distinction between a church
and the Ka'ba.

7

When the Pen of Eternity first touched the page of
creation,
when Tablet and Pen first embraced each other,

creation had not yet been fashioned from non-existence.
As soon as the breath of God was blown into the body of
Adam,[127]

your love took its existence in my delirious heart.

8

When the hand of destiny moulded the clay of Adam,
planted your love in the soil of my heart,

your love became my destiny.
Now I am oblivious to either heaven or hell –

my sole desire has become you alone.

9

Though mortal, I have become eternal through
remembrance of Him;[128]
truly, I am a drunkard when it comes to that sacred
wine;

I am athirst in the valley of wonderment.
I am a wanderer in the desert of affliction.

Who can know what will happen next to my
emboldened heart?[129]

10

No sooner had I approached the heart's door and said,
'Show thyself to me!'[130]
than He appeared before me in the midst of that
nearness.[131]

From all sides I became surrounded by the warmth of
that ecstasy.[132]
He became completely I, and I became completely He –

I, the heart and He, the beloved of my heart.

11

My Ka'ba is the earth of your nearness.
Your face is the torch that illuminates the world.[133]

The curls of your tresses are the chains of my soul.
The arches of your two eyebrows are my heart's Qiblih;
your ringlet is my cross in the monastery.

12

I am in love with His Holiness, the Lord Most High.[134]
I am in love with the face of the Cherished Beloved.

I am the wanderer in the desert of His love.[135]
I have forgotten all else and ask only for you.

Every member of my body is filled with your love.

13

For how long, O for how long should I heed advice?
For how long should I conceal the bubbling of the wine?[136]

For how long must I keep my silence about my remoteness from you?
For how long should I feign piety before family and friends

hoping that someone might become interested in my wares?[137]

14

I will cast out the clock and the prayer rug!
I will splash wine into the crystal goblet!

I will illuminate the desert of Ṭúr!
I will throw heaven and earth into consternation!

The place for me is at the tavern door.[138]

15

At my lowly hovel love planted its banner.
At my door my beloved called on me.

The wine of God was poured into my goblet.
I am estranged from the world and from myself.

My sole aspiration[139] is to attain the presence of God.

16

When at the banquet of '*Am I not*?'[140] the lord of the eternal tavern
with the hand of power poured the wine to the brim of every cup,

then all uncreated[141] atoms became created.
Wine itself became existent and drunk through us,

so intoxicated were we by this wine of my love.

17

Thus it is that love calls out each moment,
its voice echoing throughout all existence,

calling out to all who venture on our path:
'In no way can a soul avoid the waves of calamity

who paces beside the shores of my sea!'

18

I am the servant one who beats the drum.[142]
I am the wandering bird who has fallen into your snare.

I am the wise owl who calls out in your night.[143]
I am the one who has become nothingness,[144] who is alive only in your name –

whose pain and self alike have become entirely obliterated.[145]

The Cupbearer

(18)

Among the longest and best of Ṭáhirih's poems, 'The Cupbearer' is of *sáqí námih* genre. According to E. G. Browne, this poem is 'a mat͟hnaví of the kind known as *sáqí náma*, or invocations to the Cupbearer, such as Háfiẓ and other Sufi poets have written',[146] a mat͟hnaví being a type of poem in which only the two halves of each couplet rhyme with each other. The couplets themselves do not rhyme with each other but have the same metre. This relative freedom of rhyme enables the poet to compose long poems with ease.

But who or what does the 'Cupbearer' symbolize? The *sáqí* or 'cupbearer' is employed by Rumi variously. He uses the term *sáqí-i-ján* or 'cupbearer of soul' to refer to God. He uses *sáqí-i-alast* to refer to 'the cupbearer of "Am I not (your Lord)?"' – i.e. for God who in the ancient eternity poured the wine on creation.[147] Furthermore, the wine of 'Am I not' in gnostic terminology refers to the manifestation of God's attributes at the time of ancient eternity. The poet Aráqí states in one verse: 'From the wine of "Am I not" of the day of union,/ my drunken heart is still intoxicated.'[148] In the *sáqí námih* genre, the poet normally complains about the impermanence of life and encourages the cupbearer to bestow wine to take away life's sorrows. The cupbearer in Sufi terms refers to the bestower of spiritual insight, the beloved who quickens the hearts of the lovers by disclosing the mysteries and revealing the truth. The term has also been used to refer to God, who bestows the wine of His love to the lovers of truth, making them annihilated (i.e. unconscious of the self).[149] It also refers to God's names and attributes that generate ecstasy and attract the lovers to His Beauty.

As it is normally the case with her poems, Ṭáhirih alludes to multiple layers of meanings in this poem. In addition to the traditional images and meanings associated with the *sáqí-námih* genre and the image of the 'cupbearer', she unfolds in this poem a spectacular drama which reflects the sorrows and joys of her own particular age. In the midst of the heartbreaking events that encompass the Bábí community, Ṭáhirih foresees a joyful, spiritual season and she portrays the coming of the Promised One of all ages and the fulfilment of the dispensation of the Bayán. She portrays an auspicious and festive time in which the stars and celestial bodies are summoned to join together with the angels on earth to celebrate the coming of Bahá'u'lláh, the cupbearer whom she begs to reveal Himself by bestowing the choice wine of truth to a sorrow-stricken humanity.

The 'cupbearer' in this poem thus conveys various meanings: God who by manifesting His names and attributes brings the universe into existence; the Primal Point or the divine aspect of the Manifestations of God that reveals itself at various ages to humanity; and, in particular, Bahá'u'lláh, who is the purpose and fruit of all the religions of the past.

One further allusion in the first couplet should be explained (though many other terms are explicated in the notes) – the 'Royal Falcon'. The falcon (*s͟háhbáz*) is the noble bird a king would take with him for hunting. Often the king would carry the bird himself on his arm. Rumi alludes to the reality of the Prophets or their divine aspect which has been hidden from the eyes of the people of the age in which they appear as royal falcons who perform at the command of God's voice.[150] Ṭáhirih is here using the image of the royal falcon in the same vein – the Prophet as the Cupbearer of God and as the Royal Falcon of God. Though the central symbol of the cupbearer will change its specific meanings throughout the poem (from God, to the Manifestations, to the Báb, to Bahá'u'lláh), the victorious Royal Falcon seems more exactly an allusion to Bahá'u'lláh as the One whose Revelation will fulfil the expectations of the past and inaugurate this auspicious age.

The structure of this poem is largely associational, proceeding from thought to thought and image to image but always sustained and driven by the figure of the cupbearer and the delight of the persona in the wine of the new Revelation. All of these figurative devices are intertwined with allusions to Ṭáhirih's own thoughts and emotions as she considers the power and wonder of the divine Revelation and rejoices in her total rapture and joy in being allowed to participate in this process. For while the unifying image is wine and intoxication, the perspective is much broader than that of an individual believer in the midst of emotion. It encompasses some of the grandest themes of Ṭáhirih's work and some of the more esoteric verities of the Bábí and Bahá'í religions – the divine nature of creation and the cosmos, the eternality of the divine world and of the creative process itself.

While at every turn the poem echoes the strains of a mystic in the throes of ecstasy caused by a personal sense of nearness to or union with the divine world, there is humour here as well as theological and philosophical matter. Most importantly, we sense here (possibly more clearly than in any other piece) the complex personality of this gifted and remarkable woman.

He is the Beloved!

Come, O Cupbearer, O Victorious[151] Royal Falcon,
Grant me a cup of thy heavenly wine![152]

Grant me another cup of that wine
To burn to ashes this body!

Come, O Cupbearer, and bestow a cup of wine
to banish entirely yesterday's grief.

Pass your cup to the disconsolate ones
that you may resurrect these dead souls.

Since I am a salamander in this fire,[153]
Grant me, O Cupbearer, a draught of that pure wine.

Cast away the veil from thy moonlike[154] face!
Step through the door! Bestow a cup of that wine!

Fill my cup to the brim with that pure draught;
Enlighten my soul through the Friend.[155]

Overpower me as you did Moses who swooned at thy
light.
Shatter my body like Ṭúr, which turned to dust at thy
call.[156]

Let thy fire consume my body from head to toe
that I may become oblivious to both realities.[157]

O Cupbearer, bring the solace of wine to this sorrowing
one.
Let me not remain dishevelled like the beloved's
tresses.[158]

For though I have a hangover from last night's wine,
quell my consciousness with yet another draught.[159]

O Cupbearer, since I set my affection on your tresses,
I have escaped the limitations of both worlds.

From the Ancient Eternity[160] I have had no other belief
or faith;
no religion exists for me except my love for you.

I will be steadfast in this eternal covenant –
I will always prove faithful, always choose your love.

Since I have accepted the religion of your love,
Do give me now a cup of thy wine – do not keep me
weary.

From one moment to the next, grant me then thy cup
lest I drown in the sea of this sadness.

Since a single cup will never suffice me,
Lead me, O Cupbearer, beside His sea.[161]

For I would plunge into those vast waters
that I might drown all traces of myself.[162]

Then might I shatter this shell that is my heart,
hold in my palm the pearl that is my soul.[163]

Come, O Cupbearer! Spring has appeared in the
universe!
The earth with its verdure has become like an emerald.

It is springtime and the array of flowers has blossomed,
has unrolled a festive spread[164] in thy garden.

The musician is playing the flute, the harp, and the viol,
wringing out winsome melodies for heart-weary lovers.

O Cupbearer, divest yourself of earthly attire;
Dress yourself in ethereal robes.[165]

Get ambergris from the trimmings of angels' hair
and burn them in the gold scattering censer.

Open the gate of delight for all who dwell in paradise!
Shed your radiance on all the denizens of heaven!

Summon to the earth from the eternal paradise
every *ḥúrí* and *qilmán* and bid them render service.[166]

When the moon shines on this banquet,
The rosy cheeked ones will dance about in joy.

Venus will ascend in the celestial sphere to catch a moonbeam;
Saturn and the moon will gaze at each other across the vault of heaven.

Spread such a banquet on the earth that
the heavenly angels will send their greetings.

O Cupbearer, give glad tidings to the people of the world
that the night of sorrow has ended and the joyous morn has appeared.

Bestow the cup of delight to the grieving ones!
Cry out to the heart-sick lovers:

'The sun of the Ancient Eternity has appeared!
The Divine face has become manifest!'[167]

'It is fitting that I offer up my life for such glad tidings!'[168]
These glad tidings have delighted *Rabb-i-A'lá'*,[169] the Exalted Lord!

The light of God has become manifest!
The whole world has become His Ṭúr!

Give me now a cup of thy wine
that in this age I may loose my tongue in praise of this King.[170]

Even should he reject my praise, what path is left for me
since adoration of Him has become my addiction?[171]

From the dawn of the ancient eternity this gift was bestowed on me.
My wet nurse suckled me with the milk of this love.

O King, what should I compose in praise of you?
All creatures and all creation exist but to proclaim your
Beauty.

You are the Creator of the entire universe!
O God, you are both *Qá'im* and *Qayyúm*.[172]

Too lowly am I even to utter 'God'!
Those raised to the station of Lordship[173] were but your
servants.

Those who have proclaimed 'I am God' are but your
servants.[174]
Those who have performed God-like miracles are but
your obedient servants.

By your command every atom was created.
You are the Primal Point, the Pre-Existent.

When the light of your countenance became manifest
in His benevolence, the Lord of the Bayán called you its
fruit,

even as it is said, 'The purpose of the tree is naught but
its fruit,
for the tree becomes fulfilled by its fruit.'[175]

Through you the Bayán became fulfilled;
through you the hidden secrets of God were unveiled.

Nor would there be a Bayán if you yourself did not
exist;
nor would any sign of faith remain in the world.

Through you the Cause of God is proclaimed
and Godly grandeur is made manifest.[176]

You have been the goal of religion in every age,
and in every age you made yourself manifest.

Since you are pre-existent, I can hardly call you 'First';
since you are eternal, how can I call you 'Last'?

In the universe you are both First and Last[177] –
the signs of your essence are engraved on every atom.[178]

Because you are the guide to the true path for every
nation and creed,[179]
all the peoples of the earth worship you.

All prostrate themselves before but one of your infinite
names,
for in your presence all become meek and humble.

It is your light that illumines both church and shrine.
You are the manifestation of the Essence, the
countenance of Pre-Existence.

O Venerable God, who am I even to utter your names?
How can non-existence allude to Pre-Existent Essence?

My understanding of your divine unity is mere idolatry,
For you are sanctified far beyond my knowledge and
praise.

Yet, if I be but a blasphemer, a polytheist,[180] am I not
your creation?
And if I be but a negligent sinner, am I not still yours?

After all, it is the nature of a thrall to falter and fail,
but is it not the master's nature to be benevolent and
kind?[181]

O Venerable Cupbearer, in your benevolence grant me
a cup of your grace to burn away my shortcomings.

Grant me but a cup of the wine of your love!
Though I am annihilated, bestow existence upon me.[182]

Chapter Five

In Praise of the Abhá Beauty

> The effulgence of the Abhá Beauty hath pierced the
> veil of night;
> behold the souls of His lovers dancing, moth-like,
> in the light that has flashed from His face!
>
> *Ṭáhirih*[183]

While some of Ṭáhirih's allusions are directed to the Báb, the herald for the advent of Bahá'u'lláh, she clearly sees the twin Manifestations as a single great event in the history of humankind. The poems in this section allude to Ṭáhirih's understanding that Bahá'u'lláh was the promised Manifestation to whom the Báb referred as Mustag͟háth ('He Who is Invoked'), 'Him Whom God will make manifest', the 'Blessed Beauty'. Even some of the poems in Chapters Three and Four may well be referring to both the Báb and Bahá'u'lláh, for as we noted in Chapter One, she was aware of the 'twin Revelation' that had been discussed in full in the writings of S͟hayk͟h Aḥmad-i-Aḥsá'í, just as she was well aware that this prophecy alluded to the synthesis of the Bábí and Bahá'í Faiths.

Consequently, when studying her central role in all that occurred in the early history of the Bábí and Bahá'í religions, one needs to pay careful attention both to her clear prophecies about what would transpire after her death and to the following statement by Nabíl:

> The hour which Ṭáhirih had fixed for her deliverance found her already securely established under the sheltering shadow of Bahá'u'lláh. She knew full well into whose presence she had been admitted; she was profoundly aware of the sacredness of the hospitality she had been so graciously accorded. As it was with her acceptance of the Faith proclaimed by the Báb when she, unwarned and unsummoned, had hailed His Message and recognized its truth, so did she perceive through her own intuitive knowledge the future glory of Bahá'u'lláh. It was in the year '60, while in Karbilá, that she alluded in her odes to her recognition of the Truth He was to reveal. I have myself been shown in Ṭihrán, in the home of Siyyid Muḥammad, whom Ṭáhirih had styled Fata'l-Malíḥ, the verses which she, in her own handwriting, had penned, every letter of which bore eloquent

> testimony to her faith in the exalted Missions of both the Báb and Bahá'u'lláh. In that ode the following verse occurs: 'The effulgence of the Abhá Beauty hath pierced the veil of night; behold the souls of His lovers dancing, mothlike, in the light that has flashed from His face!' It was her steadfast conviction in the unconquerable power of Bahá'u'lláh that prompted her to utter her prediction with such confidence, and to fling her challenge so boldly in the face of her enemies. Nothing short of an immovable faith in the unfailing efficacy of that power could have induced her, in the darkest hours of her captivity, to assert with such courage and assurance the approach of her victory.[184]

The poems that follow leave little doubt about her recognition of the station of Bahá'u'lláh before His experience in the Síyáh-Chál[185] – an event which transpired shortly after Ṭáhirih's death.

What is all the more remarkable about this recognition is that she indicates not merely a certitude that Bahá'u'lláh is the figure who will fulfil this promise; she also indicates in these poems a clear understanding of exactly what effect this further revelation will have on the transformation of human society.

Him Whom God Shall Make Manifest[186]

(19)

This poem, while employing some difficult terms, clearly describes the status of Bahá'u'lláh in relation to other Prophets. For while all the Manifestations have the same capacity and are ontologically the same, Bahá'u'lláh's task (according to Bahá'í scripture) is to fulfil the promises of all previous religions (including that of the Báb) by bringing about a global civilization based on spiritual principles. Therefore, in this poem Ṭáhirih notes how all the previous Prophets become humbled before this long-awaited advent, something Shoghi Effendi discusses in great detail in Chapter Six of *God Passes By*.

Thus, in the second couplet, Ṭáhirih states that since the Prophet has now become manifest, the essentially unknowable (God) can be understood through the attributes of the Prophet and His illumination of physical reality. Here, as at the conference at Bada<u>sh</u>t, Ṭáhirih becomes the herald, the trumpet call proclaiming the advent of the Day of Resurrection.[187]

This poem appears in quatrains in Martha Root's book and in couplets in Afnán's collection. We have preserved the quatrain form and have managed for the most part to have each line in the quatrain correspond to the same half line that appears in the original.

O concourse of the realm on high,
Proclaim with joy the cry of reunion,
For the matchless beauty of the beloved's face
has appeared and is disclosed.

Since the veil has been lifted
from the face of Him whom we 'did not know',[188]
Let your melodies be heard from every quarter:
'Light has subdued night's darkness!'[189]

A Persian *Ṣanam* who is an Arab *Ṣamad*
has arrived with legions of ecstasy[190]
and raised the sun in Western skies.
Hasten towards His presence!

Fire surges from the land of *Fá*!
Light radiates from the city of *Ṭá*!
The spirit takes flight from the realm of *Há*,
becomes exalted and glorified.[191]

The birds of darkness desisted.
The Doves of Bahá intoned sweet melodies.
The cock of the morning adorned itself
with splendour and great glory.

By that Manifestation of the Lord of Lords,
that Full Moon,[192] calling, 'Am I not your Lord?'
all the heavenly concourse became ecstatic!
In melodious voices they reply: 'Yes! Yes!'

Such a sea has been churned up
and loosed upon the earth's expanse[193]
that each moment two thousand Karbilá deserts
are transformed into verdurous planes.[194]

From the arc of that joyous countenance;
from the snare of that mutable moon,[195]
Two thousand divisions and sects
are dispersed, trembling.

Every Moses from that sanctified realm,
every exalted Christ,
every single beloved one
becomes stupefied and humbled.

Two thousand Muḥammads[196] have trembled
before the lightning of that Immaculate King,
have gone into hiding,
cloaked and covered with clothing.[197]

From one glance of His magnificence,
the ocean of existence began to stir;
the lethargic twilight hastened
that it might soon behold the dawning sun.[198]

O beneficent Moon, O King of hearts,
the sorrow of their grief of separation from you,

has made the bodies of your lovers so slim
that they have become spirits – ethereal and
porous.

Beside his face, forms of beauty dwindle;[199]
beside his height, summits are diminished.
Beside his might, the mightiest of kingdoms
become humbled and abashed.

How my heart longs for that moon-like face
and but two strands of that jet black hair!
On the path of His earthly footsteps
My very blood has been shed![200]

By the resplendent beauty of your face,
by your luminous tresses,
assist me now, even at this very instant,
speedily to attain the bounty of your presence![201]

The Footsteps of Bahá

(20)

This brief tribute to Bahá'u'lláh by Ṭáhirih was provided to us by Shukúh Riḍá'í. It is presumed to be verse written about Ṭáhirih's experience at the conference of Badasht. The conference, planned by Bahá'u'lláh in consultation with the Báb but executed by Bahá'u'lláh with the explicit assistance of Ṭáhirih and Quddús, was a dramatic contrivance to provide the full impact of the Báb's claim to be the Qá'im and His Revelation to be a new religion and not a mere reform movement in Islam. To carry this out, three tents or pavilions were rented in three separate gardens. In this poem, we are to imagine that Ṭáhirih hears the footsteps of Bahá'u'lláh outside her pavilion. Fully aware of Bahá'u'lláh's station, she speaks of this sound as causing a rapture in her heart. It is an image very similar to that created by poet Robert Hayden in his poem 'Bahá'u'lláh in the Garden of Ridwan' in which he portrays Bahá'u'lláh stepping among the sleeping believers at night.

The sound of footsteps
I hear from afar
suddenly enraptures
the essence of all that I am –
I recognize it!

Oh, it is the sound of
His footfall!
It is His graceful gait
as He treads the pathway
outside my pavilion!

Salutation and Praise

(21)

This poem has some complicated language and difficult allusive terms, though the general meaning is discernible. Because the verse celebrates the advent of a new Revelation, the tone is happy, vibrant and exciting. In this sense, 'Salutation and Praise' is similar to the previous two poems but with even more vitality.

It begins with an allusion to both the Báb and Bahá'u'lláh and goes on to celebrate the advent of the twin Revelations of the Bábí and Bahá'í Faiths. After celebrating in very elliptical terms the human capacity to unveil the hidden attributes of God, Ṭáhirih invites others to join in with those who have recognized the undisclosed countenance of the Qá'im.

Praised be Thee, O Joy of Fars![202] All Praise!
Praised be Thee, O Delight of Tehran![203] All Praise!

Greetings! O Ye Drop of spring rain,
illuminated in these mirrors.[204] All Praise!

When your exaltation was commanded by *'Amá*,
You were transformed from *Há* to *Abhá*! All Praise![205]

Every created particle is stirred by His spirit![206]
Praise to you who have discovered this Hidden
Treasure![207] All Praise!

Descended as you are from God Almighty,
without any doubt[208] an unequalled Essence, All Praise!

Indeed, behold this face from the glorious province of
Fars,
but hidden from the world. All Praise!

O friend, come sing with us in joyful praise
that you, too, may discover the secret of certitude. All
Praise![209]

The Blessed Beauty[210]

(22)

This celebration of the station of Bahá'u'lláh as the Manifestation whom the Báb had foretold in all of His writings will not seem strange to anyone aware of the station of Ṭáhirih and her close association with Bahá'u'lláh, as we have already mentioned. As we have noted, she and Quddús conferred with Bahá'u'lláh to plan the dramatic semblance of confrontation at the conference at Badasht to teach the Bábís the nature of their new religion. Earlier, Bahá'u'lláh had rescued Ṭáhirih from Qazvín where she was under house arrest and she stayed at Bahá'u'lláh's home in Ṭihrán where she conferred with Bahá'u'lláh, Vaḥíd and others about what course of action they should follow.

In this brief eulogy, Ṭáhirih succinctly articulates and honours the importance of Bahá'u'lláh's station, though no doubt only a few would have understood the ultimate significance of her allusions in this piece until years later when Bahá'u'lláh formally declared His station to the Bábís in 1863. We have translated the couplets into quatrains and the two italicized lines are praises of God (prayers) in Arabic.

Since the appearance of that unknowable King
So lofty is his glorious station[211]
took place with nobility in the realm of the soul,
So beauteous and honoured is His word,

all the souls of both man and djinn[212]
have been sacrificed at His feet,
and, consumed with adoration, lovers have
laid down their lives in the path of reunion with
Him.

Bahá has dawned and glistened;
Bahá has appeared, adorned with splendour,
And the summits of existence
have flowed towards His beauty.[213]

Countless verses, one after the other,
have descend from His honeyed tongue.
Countless prophets of God speed forth
to bask in the beauty of His presence.

The Riddle of the Twin Revelation

(23)

The following verses are not like those poems in which Ṭáhirih has grouped pairs of couplets. The lines of the original are so long that we have chosen to form the couplets into quatrains. But several features of the poetics make this poem quite special. First, this poem was composed after a debate Ṭáhirih had with two clerics (Mullá Muḥammad-i-Kaní and Mullá Muḥammad-i-Andarmání) in the house of the Kalántar in Ṭihrán where she was imprisoned before she was executed.[214] After this interview, which took place by order of the prime minister, the two clerics sent a letter to the king asking for her execution.[215]

Second, this is one of several poems distinctive for its cleverness and wittiness. The poem focuses on pairs of objects or pairs of observations wherein, like many haiku, the first line (or the first two lines in the case of this translation) makes what seems to be an enigmatic or else disconnected statement. The second line then explains the first statement in terms of a puzzle, a clever analogy, a pun or a joke (much like the 'riddle poems' of the Anglo-Saxon poetic tradition). Some of these are quite challenging.

In the original, each line of the poem ends with the word 'two'. The humour thus plays off the number two, sometimes with a wry, almost brazen wit in the case of her condemnation of the 'learned ones'. At other times she employs delightful conceits, as in the case of her allusion to the Prophets of God as the Beloved (not unlike the imagery in Petrarchan sonnets).

In one sense, then, the poem comprises a series of nine different poems. Yet all the couplets play off the number two and all ultimately reveal Ṭáhirih's awareness, albeit in a veiled manner, that both the Báb and Bahá'u'lláh are integral parts of one Revelation which will bring about the transformation of human society.

But one beauty spot at the corner of the mouth
surrounded by two musk-coloured tresses;[216]

Woe be unto that bird of the heart –
there is one seed but two snares![217]

I converse with two – an officer[218] and a Shaykh;
Between us is a discussion about love.

Why should I bother to refute them –
but one of us is cooked – the other two are raw.[219]

The Moon-like faces
surrounded by the lariat of tresses;

never before has the world witnessed
two nights with one morning.[220]

Wine drinkers surround the cask
made pregnant by the maiden[221] of the vineyard;

Behold this foundling child;[222]
it has one father but two mothers.[223]

O my moon-face Cupbearer,
why do you sit so heedlessly?

Bring us wine and give us drink;
one for now and the second for later.[224]

Those two heart-rending eyes are drunk,
like a goblet brimming with wine;

Observe in the palm of that drunken Tartar;
a single vintage but two vessels.[225]

Thousands like me were slain
by the sword of your eyebrows;[226]

Nations are captivated by the spell of your eyes;
one *M* and two *L*s.[227]

You promise union
but you do not kept your word.

Never have I observed in this world
an honourable man with two opposing words.[228]

At one time call me but a dog at your gate;
at another call me your lowly thrall.

It matters not to me;
the same servant with two names.[229]

Behold the Face of God

(24)

In this piece, one senses an outburst of joy and thankfulness for the blessings of the new Revelation. In spite of its complicated language and abstruse terms that need to be deciphered, its rhythmic tone generates feelings of joy in the reader's heart.

These brief six couplets, which we have translated into quatrains, are thus a sort of panegyric in praise of the fact that the Revelation is no longer concealed and that the time of rejoicing has come. In this sense it responds to the longing for the opening of the doors alluded to in the poem 'Him Whom God Shall Make Manifest' as concealing or veiling the Revelation from the waiting lovers of God.

Of even greater interest to some will be what seems to be Ṭáhirih's clear allusion to future events – Bahá'u'lláh's redemption of the fallen Bábí community during His ten-year exile in Baghdád (1853–63), a period after Ṭáhirih's own execution in 1852. Here, as in several other poems, she also clearly demonstrates her awareness that Bahá'u'lláh is the promised Manifestation alluded to in the writings of the Báb and that both Manifestations are inseparable parts of one divine process – the twin Revelation alluded to in the previous poem.

O Ṣabá,[230] go on my behalf
and impart to the beloved of Há[231]
all that is fitting
for the face of Bahá.

The cloud of his mercy
rains down drop by drop,
anoints the bodies prostrate
from having gazed on the mystery of Há.[232]

His reviving breeze blows
abundant mercy from Iraqi shores[233]
bestowing vitality and solace
on the separated and fallen ones.[234]

Thus did the West Gate[235] become
the opener of all gates![236]

Thus is his bounty pouring down
as befits the mercy of *Ṭá*.[237]

O Bábís, followers of the light,
all of you come forth!
Come out from behind the veils of
grandeur![238]
Behold this one from *Fá*![239]

From behind the veils of grandeur
the face of God is suddenly manifest![240]
O, believers, you need no longer heed:
'You shall not see me!'[241]

Behold the Worlds of God

(25)

This piece is very deceiving in its ostensible simplicity. The connotatively loaded terms she uses (several of which we have chosen to leave in Arabic) imply a meaning quite beyond what seems to be a personal panegyric to the power and grandeur of Bahá'u'lláh and God. Indeed, this verse may well be as mysterious and veiled as the truths she states she longs to share.

For example, in the fourth couplet she states what 'Abdu'l-Bahá discusses in the *Lawḥ-i-Aflák* – that since God is infinite, the worlds of God must necessarily also be infinite. In other words, we should not be so limited in our understanding of God as to imagine that this is the only world of God set in motion to achieve the state of Bahá (perfection).

Similarly profound is the allusion in couplet nine to the speaker being like the sun. This would seem to allude to the sequence of dispensations and the speaker seems to be asking how many Prophets must come and go before humankind finally understands the concept of Divine Unity underlying this process, as well as how long before the speaker can boldly proclaim the secret of Divine Unity so that everyone will finally understand that the only true paradise is proximity to God.

We have kept this very literal, except in several couplets where we have reversed the lines to make for better English syntax. We will leave it to the reader to decide whether Ṭáhirih is here speaking from her own station and perspective or is speaking as part of the heavenly concourse serving at God's behest to educate humankind.

Because in the Bayán all imaginings have been shattered,
nothing can now be seen in the created universe save Him.

Because the *Furqán*[242] of God was revealed
The name *A'lá*[243] became established in the kingdom of names.

His station is *A'ẓam*[244] and *A'lá* – the Greatest Lord on High;
He is *Rabb-i-Akbar*,[245] the Garden of Paradise.[246]

So many are the mysteries in the celestial realm,[247]
So many kingdoms[248] with the station of *Bahá*.[249]

O Alláh, Alláh, Perpetual and Eternal,
Omnipotent, Pre-Existent, Benevolent, Peerless,

grant but a glance with Your Merciful eyes
to resurrect all the dry and dusty bones[250]

So that I may venture out with the sun at its zenith,[251]
may disclose and proclaim Your hidden secrets.[252]

There is no goal in creation except You!
There is no object of worship except exaltation of You!

How long should I cycle in the sky like the sun?[253]
Make manifest the secret of Divine Unity,

O Lover of the love of the Beloved Bahá,[254]
Absorb this love-sick servant.

At Your feast of Grandeur and Unity,
bestow bounty without limit, without measure.

The Love of Bahá[255]

(26)

The only fully Arabic poem attributed to Ṭáhirih, a forthright expression of love and devotion, this poem is based on typical imagery for such a piece: the spiritual love expressed in terms of secular romance (love at first sight, the secretive nature of the love, the 'malady' of love, especially when separation must occur). Even the idea that the lover slaying the beloved with a glance and making the lover drunk with the wine of his eyes is traditional. However, unlike some of her other couplets, these are closed (complete statements unto themselves), so while there is some continuity, each couplet can stand by itself.

The image of the nighttime worker or traveller feeling solace as he sees the approaching dawn and knows his patience and endurance have brought him to his long-sought goal is a bit more imaginative, especially given the obvious symbolic nature of the nighttime as symbolic of a period of spiritual darkness and ignorance. Naturally, the reader is also struck by the fact that where most love poetry, even devotional poetry expressed in terms of love imagery, is based on hyperbole – the overstatement of the affection to make the point clear – this poem ends with Ṭáhirih alluding to her literal death. Consequently, the poem reads not so much as hyperbolic but as an accurate depiction of her fidelity and heroism.

O my companion, the cock has crowed![256] Arise!
Intone a verse for me and grant me a cup of joy!

Even a moment's separation from my beloved[257] is
  unbearable!
Will a stolen glance at him reveal my secret passion?

It is a facile thing to sacrifice my soul for his love –
a traveller in the night becomes still as dawn
  approaches.[258]

Without a sword he has slain me with a single glance.
Without wine his eyes have made me drunk.

A single glimpse of him was sufficient
from my Bahá at morn or in the eventide.

But how did it happen that my heart fell in love?
Why does my soul follow him wherever he goes?

The very thought of him will not leave me for a moment!
He is forever in my restless heart.

If he wishes to burn my heart to ashes with his leaving, he may.
Or he may simply slay my heart outright – death by his hands would be fitting.

Chapter Six

Let Deeds Be Our Adorning

> You can kill me as soon as you like, but you cannot stop the emancipation of women.
>
> *Ṭáhirih*[259]

> Cease idly repeating the traditions of the past, for the day of service, of steadfast action, is come. Now is the time to show forth the true signs of God, to rend asunder the veils of idle fancy, to promote the Word of God, and to sacrifice ourselves in His path. Let deeds, not words, be our adorning!
>
> *Ṭáhirih*[260]

In several poems it is clear that Ṭáhirih is speaking in her own voice about her own experience. These poems may also fit into the category of the mystic lover in that they employ some of the terminology from that tradition. But unlike the poems we included in Chapter Four: The Ecstasy of Nearness, the poems in this chapter seem to allude very specifically to Ṭáhirih's own life.

So far as we are able, we have arranged these verses in a rough chronological order according to the events to which they seem to allude. These begin with what is probably her best known poem, 'Face to Face', a touching and enchanting series of images portraying her devotion to the Báb, though as with a few other pieces we have included, there is scholarly debate as to whether or not this poem was actually composed by Ṭáhirih. While this piece has obvious spiritual implications, it may also allude to the fact that she never did meet the Báb 'face to face' and possibly contemplates in this piece how intensely she longs for such an encounter, whether in this world or the next.

The next two poems are in much the same vein, though these also serve to teach her fellow believers by her example that whatever exalted status she may have in their eyes, she is happy to consider herself as but an integral part of a grand divine plan. Through these pieces Ṭáhirih exemplifies the quality of humility one must have before God and His Prophets.

The rest of the poems allude to specific events, most of them surrounding the approach of her martyrdom and her awareness of and longing to attain that station. There is superb irony in her comparison of herself to an impatient bride and as a lover of the Friend, especially since at her death she dresses herself in wedding apparel and yet she boldly rejects the literal offer of marriage from the king, Náṣiri'd-Dín Sháh. Here we see her defiance of traditional authority, together with her total rejection of worldly vanity and what she considers to be the emptiness of worldly position and possessions. The last poem in this section may well be one of her last poems as it consists of a series of vows that testify to her fidelity and dedication.

Face to Face[261]

(27)

This is perhaps the most widely known of Ṭáhirih's poems. It is a melodious and lyrical expression of love for the face of the beloved that may be understood to imply Ṭáhirih's adoration of the Báb. The scholar Dhuká'í Bayḍá'í believes the poem is not by Ṭáhirih, perhaps because its style is more imagistic and regular in pattern, quite unlike some of her other work which is very complicated in language and filled with deep philosophical and religious allusions that could not be understood by the ordinary reader. A few other scholars also believe this poem is not by Ṭáhirih and, instead, attribute it to the Bahá'í Ṭá'ir of Isfahan. As we have already noted, however, it is slim evidence to question the attribution of a poem to Ṭáhirih if based solely on style since, as the reader will discover in this volume, Ṭáhirih was a poet capable of a wide variety of styles, themes and personae.

The emphasis in this poem on the face of the beloved as a manifestation of divine attributes reminds one of some traditional images from Sufi terminology. Many of these same images (ambergris-scented hair, the beauty of the eyebrow, the adoration of the face in general, the beauty of the eye, the beauty spot and the beauty spot as compared to a seed attracting the bird of the heart) we have already observed in Ṭáhirih's verses in Chapter Four. Because Ṭáhirih does employ an unusual parallel construction within every couplet, we have found it poetically useful to translate the couplets into seven line stanzas.[262]

If ever I should behold you
face to face,
eye to eye,
I would be bold to recount
my heart's plaint
point by point,
verse by verse.

Like Ṣabá[263] the east wind,
I have searched everywhere
for your countenance
from house to house,
door to door,

alley to alley,
from quarter to quarter.

Bereft of your visage,
my two eyes have wept
such bloody tears,
Tigris after Tigris,
stream upon stream,
spring after spring,
brook upon brook.

Your bloom-like mouth,[264]
your face enveloped
with ambergris hair,
blossom to blossom,
flower to flower,
tulip to tulip,
fragrance to fragrance;

Your perfect brow,[265]
your eyes, your beauty spot
have preyed on the bird of my heart,
sense to sense
and heart to heart,
feeling to feeling
and mood to mood.

My desperate heart
has knitted your love
to the very fabric of my being,
string by string,
thread by thread,
warp by warp,
and woof by woof.

Ṭáhirih has searched
every layer of her heart
but found only you there,
sheet by sheet,
fold by fold,
cover by cover
over and over again.

The Ka'ba of Your Face[266]

(28)

This poem is very traditional in Ṭáhirih's expression of love in terms of the hyperbolic use of divine love as expressed through both the analogy of a love poem about earthly love and the analogy of the mystic's love of the Friend. The occasion for this piece is not evident. One might infer its allusion to death would indicate it to have been composed shortly after the martyrdom of the Báb but it is more likely she is anticipating her own death. Certainly the humour in the first quatrain would seem to confirm this speculation.

Since she seems to be referring to her own death, we would naturally assume the persona is Ṭáhirih and the 'you' to whom she is speaking is Bahá'u'lláh, since the Báb would have already been executed by this point. However, she may well have talked about her death before the Báb's martyrdom.

The couplets here, as in other pieces, break very naturally into quatrains and the imagery, though mostly proverbial, is very effective in conveying a feeling of a personal relationship between Ṭáhirih as an individual and Bahá'u'lláh, which, as we know, she actually had.

Prostrating myself before your face
is a law for me in my prayers.
I would worship you methodically,
even if you were *Lát* and *Manát*.[267]

But don't chastise me for being drunk!
Look at your own eyes in the mirror!
See the beauty of your face?
Need you ask me why you are astonished?

Because of my adoration of the Ka'ba of your face
I have no need to go on pilgrimage to your holy
places;
the Euphrates is flowing forth
from the springs that are my eyes.

May the Lord of the world and humankind,
the Educator of all things,

bestow on you a kind heart
or else relieve me from my sadness.

My life derives not from my soul,
nor does my dying come from my death;
Union with you is my life,
and separation from you is my death.

At the moment of death[268] you moved
your sweet lips to inquire about me,
so that I would remain[269] a life newly fashioned
by the breath of God.[270]

A Shameless Servant Am I[271]

(29)

As with 'The Ka'ba of Your Face', this poem breaks very naturally into quatrains because of line length and, primarily, because it has a natural pause, a caesura, in the middle of each line. We have included the poem here because Ṭáhirih refers specifically to herself and to her own suffering. Therefore, while this could refer to the hardships she endured at any point in her life as a believer, it seems more appropriate to that period when she is under house arrest and is 'bereft of all companionship'.

Several of the couplets in this poem establish a contrast between the first two lines (which exalt the station and beauty of the Beloved) and the second two lines (which confess and contrast the lover's lowly station and complete obeisance). Furthermore, the structure of this piece is very precise. Each quatrain portrays a very specific aspect of the total love and affection the lover has for the Beloved.

One additional point is worth noting. Each quatrain in the original begins with the phrase 'I am'. For poetic purposes, we have placed the phrase at the end of the lines and translated it into English syntax as 'am I'.[272]

O Beloved, infatuated with calamity am I
in the quest for your affection;
how much longer will you disdain me –
too familiar with the pain of your remoteness
am I.

Alienated from every created thing am I –
my face covered and concealed,
grief-stricken with calamities,
bereft of all companionship am I.

You are milk and sugar;[273]
you are the branch and the fruit;
You are the sun and the moon;
a mere atom, a fleck of dust am I;[274]

You are the date palm and the date;
you are the adored one with honey lips;

You are the master, so elegant and refined;[275]
a shameless servant[276] am I.

You are the Ka'ba, the idol,
You are cloister and shrine;[277]
You are the revered heart breaker;[278]
the pitiful lover am I.

The beauteous[279] and brazen heart ravisher
says:
'Approach me with a heart freed
from all arrogance and hypocrisy –
The Ensign of Grandeur am I!'

Ṭáhirih is but sand beneath your feet,[280]
drunk with the wine of reunion and
longing,[281]
patiently awaiting your gift –
confessor of my transgressions[282] am I.

Rebuking the King's Desire

(30)

According to some accounts, 'before her execution was ratified, Ṭáhirih was taken before Náṣiri'd-Dín Shah'[283] who proposed marrying her if she would recant her beliefs. This poem may well have been written as a disdainful rejection of his offer (and of him) as well as a condemnation of anyone whose single goal in life is earthly power and possessions.

In contrast, Ṭáhirih exalts her passion for her true beloved (the Báb or Bahá'u'lláh – or both). Perhaps her final act of defiance in light of this proposal was to dress herself in wedding attire in preparation for her martyrdom. In effect, the reunion she longs for as alluded to so often in her verse is about to take place, and this is her true marriage in its most meaningful sense, an image not unlike the early Christian concept of the soul of the true believer being wedded to Christ.

This poem piece consists of groups of two couplets (as are the two poems that follow in this section) which are not to be confused with quatrains – we have kept the original form. Structurally, it is divided into two clearly distinct parts. First she addresses the Beloved before turning her attention to the king and his proposal. The obvious irony in the contrast between these two parts is that she is faithful to the Beloved even though He seems to bestow on her nothing but calamity in the path of love, whereas she utterly disdains the temporal ease the king offers.

The raptures of yearning for you have constrained
with the chains of sorrow and calamity

all the broken-hearted lovers,
who gladly give up their lives in the path of your love.[284]

And if out of caprice or cruelty
my Beloved be intent on slaying me, stainless though I
be,

I will be patient under his sword,
and indeed I will content myself with whatsoever
contents him.

At dawn that cruel charmer of mine
deigned to approach my bed,[285]

and when I saw his face,
it was as if the morning itself had dawned.

No musky scent in all Khotan
can match the fragrance of his tresses![286]

No infidel in all Khatá possesses
such seditious eyes as those of my beloved![287]

But you, O King,[288] ignorant of wine's ecstasy and love's longing,
can but pace behind the pious ones, the ascetics.

And what can I do when you doubt or disdain
the holy motives of the sanctified ones?

You desire only a woman's dangling ringlets,
the well-bred steed, the silver studded saddle.

Your entire life you have been ungrateful to the poor,
have abhorred the destitute in your midst.[289]

For you there exist empires only – Alexander's pomp and glory;
for me, the ways and the habit of the dervish suffice.

You adore kingdoms? Take them.
As for me, this chastisement is bounty enough.[290]

So pass beyond this interlude[291] – this notion of 'I' and 'we';[292]
dwell in your kingdom of nothingness.

When you enter therein,
you will indeed have attained your heart's desire.[293]

The Impatient Bride

(31)

This powerful lyric, while clearly alluding to Ṭáhirih herself, also appears to have a general applicability, something true with so many of Ṭáhirih's poems, as we have noted earlier. Here she seems to be writing in the first person from her perspective as a believer who, like so many Bábís and Bahá'ís, was suffering for her beliefs.

Her personal plaints are cast in the image of a pining lover who has been abandoned or whose Beloved seems capricious. On another level, the poem speaks from the point of view of any believer who, having realized his or her true nature, longs to leave the physical realm and attain the presence of God, as is stated in an oft-quoted verse from the Qur'án 2:151: 'Verily we are God's, and to Him shall we return.'

Structurally, the poem achieves resolution as the speaker considers the joy that will inevitably occur at leaving this reality. Like the previous poem, the verses are set in pairs of couplets, with each four lines being more or less a complete and a somewhat self-contained statement, though the poem as a whole has an obvious continuity.

I have been abandoned in the land of your love
nor do I find kindness from a single soul.

Regard my solitude,
O you who rule this realm.

Is this my sin, O my beloved – this secret and
  incessant love of mine?

Is this why time after time you leave me,
slay me, and punish me for my heinous crime?

At long last my patience and resilience are gone.
How long must I yet abide this separation from
  you?

Like a reed flute, every joint in my being
intones this song of my longing for you:[294]

'The mind is incapable of comprehending Him;
The people have lost hope of grasping His
perfection.'[295]

Can anyone find a path to your divinity?
And yet all paths lead but to you alone.

When Ṣabá the breeze reaches you,
brings to you tidings of your suffering lovers,

images of dejected faces with tear-filled eyes,
what harm would it do to show a little mercy?

If in your magnanimity you should
suddenly approach my bed at dawn

I would fly in the atmosphere of your nearness –
My two hands would become two wings.

When you release me from this nether world
and draw me into the realm of the placeless,[296]

I will happily cast away this life and all that is
therein,
since you are life itself and the life-giver to all
creation.

Meditation on My Death[297]

(32)

Like the previous two poems, this piece is written in pairs of couplets but unlike 'The Impatient Bride', these are not closed sections (i.e. self-contained). Rather there is a narrative flow to this piece that may well portray the love of Ṭáhirih for the Báb, and by implication, the love of a believer for the Creator.

The poem focuses on how, by responding to the call of the advent of the new Manifestation from God, Ṭáhirih invites calamities upon herself. She foresees her own martyrdom and envisions herself dying on the battlefield and her beloved rushing to her side. She pleads for total annihilation (cf. 'true poverty and absolute nothingness' in *The Seven Valleys*) and the unity of her own heart with that of the 'Friend'. The call to the Beloved's feast of love is then raised by chosen angels and Ṭáhirih ponders whether she will be able to attain that eternal realm.

We have entitled the poem 'Meditation on My Death' because Ṭáhirih clearly indicates here (as she does in other pieces) foreknowledge and proximity of her own martyrdom. As in other allusions to her death, she is fearless and she also describes a relentless longing to attain the eternal realm, a joy and happiness which, according to several accounts, accurately portray her demeanour until her death.

The dawn of your face shone above the horizon;
the rays of your countenance beamed forth.

Why not drum out: 'Am I not your Lord?'[298]
The drum of our hearts would reply, 'Verily, Thou
art!'[299]

Contrapuntal to the drum of your 'Am I not?'
do our hearts[300] in their love beat out 'Yea, verily!'

Now beside the gate of my heart do they pitch
their tents,
these troops of sorrows, these armies of
adversity.[301]

Truly the love of that beauteous Moon suffices me,
He who, when God called to Him 'Yea, verily!'

became filled with laughter and delight,
calling out boldly, 'Behold, I am the martyr of
Karbilá!'

When He heard the lamentation at my death,
He went to retrieve my meagre possessions,

Then He hurried to my side and cried for me
and with a loud and piercing voice.

Why not strike the summit of the Ṭúr of my heart
with the blazing fire of wonderment?[302]

Have you not already excavated and pounded it,
levelled it and trembled it?

The angelic hosts of cherubim call out each night
hearkening all to His love feast,

trumpeting this Divine Command:
'Hasten forth, O sorrowing friends!'

You, who are but a speck[303] on the leviathan of
wonderment,[304]
do you dare speak about the sea of existence
itself?[305]

At every moment be like Ṭáhirih – remain still and
listen,
hear the whale roar: 'There is no God but God!'[306]

The Arc of Ascent[307]

(33)

This poem is an orison in praise of the believers (explicitly the Bábís but there are also allusions to Bahá'u'lláh and therefore would include those who became Bahá'ís). It is particularly touching because it is a forthright expression of Ṭáhirih's deep and sincere affection and admiration for the more than 20,000 Bábí martyrs who detached themselves from the world and sacrificed their beings for the sake of the Beloved, as well as those who may not have been executed but who endured or risked torture and deprivation (calamity) simply by refusing to recant their belief in the Báb.

The poem ends with Ṭáhirih's plea that she, too, may attain such a spiritual height and thereby become acceptable to God. We have titled this verse according to a central theme in this piece, the idea that by recognizing the truth revealed by the Báb, the believers have achieved the heights of understanding because the writings of the Báb (and Bahá'u'lláh later) unveil all those mysteries that the scholars of the Qur'án had struggled with for 12 centuries. We have changed the couplets into quatrains to retain the mood of the original with its succinct language but incredibly reverent tone.

O most kind Lord,
O Thou the most compassionate,
I beg You to come rescue me
with Your perfect benevolence.

I beg of You by those countless souls
who came and who kept on coming,
who became deserving of sacrifice
in your quarter,

by those who found
that Hidden Treasure manifest
through the concealed kindness
of Your assistance,

by those who ascended to
the heights of the sun of *A'lá*,

and thereby became deserving
of the signs of 'or even closer',[308]

by those who divested themselves
of any concerns other than You,[309]
by those who surpassed all
which is not of God.[310]

O Powerful *Qayyúm*,[311]
O Thou Omnipotent Lord,
O Helper, Beloved,
O Thou Living, Helping Lord,

What is this world
that became manifest through You?
All the secrets of the mysteries
have now been disclosed!

All Your beloved friends,
O Lord of the Bayán,
have become entirely detached
from all created things.[312]

They have closed their eyes
to all earthly affairs.
They have released themselves
from the hint of vain imaginings.

Because of their silence,[313]
these souls have descended
to the depth of depths
waiting for Your assistance, O Living Helper.

O God, bestow on me a glance
of Your favour and benevolence
that I may become cleansed
of the gore oozing from my wounds[314]

so that I, too, might ascend
to the tree of Abhá[315]
and become deserving
of being a sacrifice for A'lá

As God is My Witness: Ṭáhirih's Farewell

(34)

Reminiscent of Socrates' farewell speeches to his followers in Plato's dialogues the *Crito* and the *Phaedo*,[316] Ṭáhirih in this amazingly powerful profession of faith is clearly nearing her execution. She is beseeching those who have regard for her and her life to take note of this sequence of quasi-doctrinal or credal assertions or pledges.

At the heart of all these is her observation that if you love or respect or admire me, then look to the one for whom I have sacrificed all (Bahá'u'lláh) and follow Him as I have. Otherwise, she seems to say, my sacrifice and suffering have been for nothing.

Here as in only a couple of Ṭáhirih's other poems she employs a refrain, though for the sake of English poetics and syntax, we have chosen to place the refrain up front rather than at the end of the couplet where it is in the original. We have translated the couplets into quatrains partly because of the caesura but primarily because the lines would otherwise become too long to convey the poetics of the original in English.

As our notes indicate, several allusions in this piece clearly bring to the fore questions about the spiritual station of this remarkable figure, a station which, like the Prophets of God, she does not hesitate to acknowledge or describe.

As God is my witness,
I sacrificed my life for nearness to Him.
As God is my witness,
I am steadfast in my loyalty to Him.

As God is my witness,
the first day that I arrived
at the station of the Eternal,
I put aside everything except Him.

As God is my witness,
from the ancient eternity
and the revolution of ages,
I have been steadfast in my loyalty to Him.[317]

As God is my witness,
He looked on me with eyes of acceptance.[318]
By God, there is no other object of my
affection
than acceptance by Him.

As God is my witness,
look at Qurratu'l-'Ayn with her immaculate
heart!
Who is the object of her affection?
Naught but Bahá'u'lláh!

As God is my witness,
I beg from the magnanimity
of the Self-Sufficient God
that my blood might be shed for
Bahá'u'lláh.[319]

As God is my witness,
all the hardships I have endured
in the passing of these days,
was but in the path of His companionship.

As God is my witness,
any speck[320] of purity in me
has been made possible
through His bounty and favour alone.

As God is my witness,
would that He could create me anew
that yet again I might
sacrifice my life for Him.

Chapter Seven
The Voice of God's Command

> Undeterred, unruffled, exultant with joy, Ṭáhirih arose, and, without the least premeditation and in a language strikingly resembling that of the Qur'án, delivered a fervid and eloquent appeal to the remnant of the assembly, ending it with this bold assertion: 'I am the Word which the Qá'im is to utter, the Word which shall put to flight the chiefs and nobles of the earth!' Thereupon, she invited them to embrace each other and celebrate so great an occasion.
>
> On that memorable day the 'Bugle' mentioned in the Qur'án was sounded, the 'stunning trumpet-blast' was loudly raised, and the 'Catastrophe' came to pass.
>
> *Shoghi Effendi*[321]

In spite of the statements we cited in Chapter One about the life of Ṭáhirih, the reader may be tempted to view her as a figure of delicate beauty who wrote lyric poems and died romantically in a wedding dress as a symbol of her imminent reunion with her Beloved. What is overlooked in such an impression is the remarkable intellect of the woman, as well as her brazen and defiant courage. For while she may have been selfless in her service to her beliefs, she was anything but meek and retiring when it came to articulating those beliefs and rejecting the authority of anyone who tried to prevent her from pursuing them, whether it was her husband, her father, the clerics or the government.

According to Jináb-i-Adíb, a former university professor who founded the famous Tarbíyat School in Ṭihrán, Ṭáhirih's brother, when asked about the 'learning and perfection of Ṭáhirih' made the following observation:

> Know verily, that in a meeting where she sat neither I nor anyone else could say a word. It was as if all the former and future books were with her. She used to explain a subject by bringing forth demonstrations and proofs from the learned books, page by page, so that no one had the power to deny. Ḥájí Mullá Taqí, who was assassinated, was heard to say many times, 'When the signs of the promised One appear, the Zindíq [Heretic] of Qazvín will also appear, and the words of the Zindíq will be the words of a woman's religion! Now this

> woman and her religion have appeared.' In fact her talks and explanations were the true witnesses for her. Since then, the clergy have prevented all women from studying lest they should become believers like Ṭáhirih.[322]

In other words, what may have been most misunderstood about Ṭáhirih – there being little of her words translated into English – is the truly remarkable insight Ṭáhirih possessed about the most esoteric matters of theology, cosmology, ontology and philosophy.

We have in our notes tried to make a decent beginning towards communicating to an English-speaking audience some of the depth of her thought. But this last group of poems shows as well as anything can how aware she was of the totality of the divine process at work, not only in human history but in the laws of physics and in the process of creation itself.

Very similar in some respects to Bahá'u'lláh's *Lawḥ-i-Ḥikmat* or 'Abdu'l-Bahá's *Lawḥ-i-Aflák*, these poems address questions put to her – primarily by Bihjat, an intermediary between herself and her followers. According to Fáḍil Mázandarání, Ṭáhirih and Bihjat used to correspond with each other in poems. In the space of a relatively few lines, she speaks of such matters as how divine attributes are infused into every particle of creation, how creation is without beginning or end, how the worlds of God are without number (hence the number of worlds in which a process similar to that we are experiencing on this planet is occurring). She alludes both to the 'twin Revelations' of the Báb and Bahá'u'lláh, as well as the foundational law underlying all revelations and all human progress: the capacity to comprehend abstract knowledge and then translate that knowledge into creative action through the use of free will.

Thus, while she alludes to the fact that she will not live to see the total fulfilment of the unity of humankind, she clearly is aware of what Bahá'u'lláh will reveal and how it will result in world fellowship and global governance. She anticipates the essential verities of both the Kitáb-i-Aqdas and the Kitáb-i-Íqán. Indeed, the profundity of her thought leaves us pondering – as well we should – what exactly was the spiritual station of this unique and amazing figure.

The Primal Point

(35)

The lyric mode is capable of compressing an amazing amount of thought and feeling into a handful of words, something we observed in our discussion of poetry in Chapter Two. In the two quatrains of this poem (originally two couplets), Ṭáhirih has alluded to a central symbol of the divine process by which creation takes place – the 'primal point'. From a single point on a page, the word is generated and from the simple command 'Be' God creates the universe through the agency of His Prophets.

This verse, which seems to celebrate the power unleashed through the Báb and Bahá'u'lláh, alludes most obviously to the Shí'í tradition cited by Bahá'u'lláh in the Kitáb-i-Íqán regarding the importance of the Báb as fulfilling the expectations espoused by Muḥammad regarding the Qá'im: 'Knowledge is twenty and seven letters. All that the Prophets have revealed are two letters thereof. No man thus far hath known more than these two letters. But when the Qá'im shall arise, He will cause the remaining twenty and five letters to be made manifest.'[323]

Thus, whether the 'point of *bá*' alluded to here refers to the Báb (the Primal Point), to Bahá'u'lláh or to both as parts of a twin Revelation, the ḥadíth cited by Bahá'u'lláh (particularly the allusion to a 'veil' not as a source of obfuscation or concealment but as the overwhelming effect of knowledge) becomes a very important image. Here 'veil' alludes to light or the power of knowledge, such as the ḥadíth cited by Bahá'u'lláh in The Four Valleys: 'His beauty hath no veiling save light, His face no covering save revelation'[324] or Bahá'u'lláh's observation in the *Lawḥ-i-Ḥikmat*: 'At the time when We were hidden behind countless veils of light thou didst commune with Me and didst witness the luminaries of the heaven of My wisdom and the billows of the ocean of Mine utterance.'[325]

One final point, as the notes explain, the term *Aḥmad* – a title for Muḥammad – here alludes to *Núr-i-Muḥammadí* ('Muḥammadan Light') or to *Rúḥ-i-Muḥammadí* ('Muḥammadan Spirit'), the reality of the Manifestation of God that appears at different ages to illumine humankind. A parallel expression of this ongoing process is the illumination of humankind through the Islamic Dispensation, which Ṭáhirih is saying has occurred again, only with even greater potency.

From the Eternal Veil[326]
have radiated
infinite manifestations
of Aḥmad:[327]

From the point of *bá*[328]
the countenance of *há*,[329]
concealed ere now in its Essence,[330]
has now become entirely manifest!

Am I Not Your Lord?[331]

(36)

There is a special tone of power and authority that pervades this majestic piece. To some extent, this power derives from Ṭáhirih's use of particularly powerful Arabic and Persian phrases. But even more important as regards the lyric mode of this poem is that it is written entirely from the divine perspective.

Some lines seem to be the voice of God, others employ the point of view of the Báb, or at least a persona of similar authority and knowledge. But the result is a rather amazing effect. That Ṭáhirih (or any believer) would have presumed to pen such a poem and do it convincingly is indicative of immense poetic power and sublime spiritual station that only a figure like Ṭáhirih or Quddús would have presumed to assume during the Bábí Dispensation.

As with a number of other poems we have translated, the four line groupings are not quatrains; Ṭáhirih has employed pairs of couplets. But unlike some of the other uses of this form, this poem contains enjambment from one section to another (sometimes the sentence carries over from one section to another).

Glad tidings be unto you, O countenance of
 Holiness!
The Beauty of God has become manifest to all!

O Ṣabá,[332] call out to the grief-stricken multitudes!
Invite them into His presence!

Say: O you waiting tribes of the earth,
by the grace of the Omnipotent King,

The once concealed Moon[333] has now become
 uncovered,
glorious, and wondrously adorned![334]

The Eternal Countenance has last unveiled
 Himself
that He might hoist high the banner of the Bayán.

His sanctified abode[335] is far beyond the ken
and vain imaginings of the peoples of the world!

On the throne of grandeur and honour and
loftiness
that traceless King has dwelled

until He raised this call to the sufferers:[336]
'O ye who profess love for me,

When one follows the path of my love,
I will proclaim to him this fateful warning[337] –

whosoever falls in love with my beauty
shall not be withheld from suffering and calamity.

And whosoever has obeyed me not,
whosoever has not clung to the cord of my
covenant,

him will I drive forth from the Court of my
Presence.
Angrily I will subject him to the wind of
destruction.[338]

I am the Perpetual! I am[339] the Eternal!
I am the One who comes from the realm of the
Placeless!

I have come for those whose hearts are quickened!
Hasten unto me! Indeed, approach my presence!

From the fire of my Mighty Will fly forth these
sparks:
'It is I – Am I not your Lord?'

Enter the presence of the holy ones
and hear their reply: 'Yes! Yes!'[340]

I am the Lord of Dominion!
I am the Ark of Salvation!

I am reality without existence!
Lo, I have appeared before you immaculate,
flawless!

I am the eternal Tree of Life.[341]
I am the seen and the unseen fruit.

Throughout the universe I am the King of kings,
and through me was the Bayán exalted.

O ye who have glimpsed[342] my bloodied face,[343]
Hasten towards the province of my abode!

Sacrifice your heads and bodies for me,
for I am the King of Karbilá!'[344]

God the Creator

(37)

These verses might at first seem to be another panegyric about the loftiness of God, with several allusions about how the Prophets reveal the attributes of the essentially unknowable Deity. But like so many of Ṭáhirih's poems, this piece is structured around a rather precise logical discourse or argument.

The theme is the continuity and infinity of God's love. It begins and ends with allusions to Moses and the light of Paran, thus discussing the concept that the force operant early in religious history is the same force presently revealing itself through the Báb and Bahá'u'lláh. But the focus is not on the Day of Resurrection. Rather Ṭáhirih speaks of the eternality of God in time and space: His light embraces the constellations and sets them in motion physically and spiritually.

In short, she implicitly asserts that our planet is not the only 'world' going through a process of spiritual evolution. As soon as the human temple (human physical evolution) is capable of receiving divine guidance, the secrets of the hidden world are revealed. Thus, the same essential truth is revealed in every world of God that was revealed in the Wilderness of Paran. By the same token, at every age in human history the same light which is manifested to Moses will manifest itself to humanity but in a different manner.

While some of the line lengths and mid-line pauses in these verses would seem to warrant breaking the couplets into quatrains, the dignity and power of these lines require that they be left as they are in the original couplet form. Our translation thus follows the original line for line. Because of the specific difficulties of this poem, however, we have taken more liberty by way of deviating from an exacting word for word translation.

From behind the veils of grandeur
The face of God has appeared with honour and nobility.

From bright beams of light
The form[345] of God has appeared with perfection and
    glory.

Lo, when He spoke of the ecstasy of the Most
    Beneficent,
He unlocked all the closed portals.

Indeed, His reviving call of 'hasten unto me'[346]
has dissolved the rust of doubt, superstition, and
wavering.

Indeed, in this very age has every veiled allusion
become unveiled through Him.

The fire of Sinai is manifest in this age;
The light of Paran[347] is shining on you.

The Greatest Name has appeared in earthly form
and made every cherubim ecstatic with delight.

The Greatest Name has illumined every other name
and led the way to the banquet of the Nearness[348] of
God.

O God, O God, what benevolence and bounty this is
That Thou hast been so clearly manifested through the
attributes of Bahá![349]

What preeminence, what esteem, and what distinction
this is
That Thou hast been made to appear through the
words 'Be! and it is!'[350]

Neither roots nor branches can be assigned to Him,[351]
Neither can there be imagined a dawning nor a setting
for Him.[352]

Verily He was a firm root from the day of eternity,
so sanctified was He from all causes and limitations.

The bounty of God is manifest in the holy scriptures
where He is revealed as the One,[353] the Eternal.[354]

He made the moon shine forth in the world of
existence[355]
and it traversed the constellations of the heavens.

As the moon arrived at each constellation,
it discovered a new reality and perceived its special
attributes.[356]

Once the body of the Prophet was created from the four
elements,
achieved maturity, God revealed to Him the secrets of
Bahá.[357]

Verily, in this revelation of divine beams of light can be
seen
that same sparkling ecstasy that was Paran's fire![358]

The Prophet Noah

(38)

This is one of at least four poems addressed to Bihjat, who, according to Dhuká'í Bayḍá'í, was Karím Khán-i-Máfí, a famous Bahá'í from Qazvín. As noted in other poems where he is mentioned or addressed, he served as an intermediary between Ṭáhirih and her followers. This poem is straightforward and relatively simple, though no less profound. Ṭáhirih alludes to Noah as a Prophet who stood firm in the midst of adversity and the taunting of those to whom He appeared as a Prophet, a story told in the Old Testament, in the Qur'án and in Bahá'u'lláh's Kitáb-i-Íqán. While the Kitáb-i-Íqán was not revealed until ten years after Ṭáhirih's death, she seems to allude here to what Bahá'u'lláh states regarding Noah that appears in neither the Old Testament nor the Qur'án: that God tested the people by changing His promises.[359]

The reason Ṭáhirih cites this particular story from among the stories of past Prophets might have to do with the judgement alluded to by Muḥammad that would occur on the Day of Resurrection. Still more likely is the possibility that she is trying to encourage the Bábís in the midst of their persecution and despondency after the execution of the Báb that all would succeed as God had promised (i.e. Bahá'u'lláh would revive and lead them) and that they, like the followers of Noah, though few in number, would be those to achieve salvation and the new knowledge unveiled by 'Him Whom God will make manifest'.

Hearken to me, O Bihjat, that you may hear of
God's mysteries
and bear witness to my utterance.

By God's command do I intone[360] for you
The nature of things past and how they came to
be.

After revealing the new[361] message from God,
Noah stood firm through the power of Divine
Authority,

delivered to all the message of the oneness of God,
pulled to the shore of salvation all those worthy of
Unity,

disclosed the mysteries hidden in their vain
imaginings,
opened for them the portal of the lights of true
knowledge.

The Twin Duties
for Bihjat

(39)

Like Bahá'u'lláh's Tablet the *Lawḥ-i-Ḥikmat*, this poem is addressed to a devoted follower in answer to a specific question. Bahá'u'lláh's Tablet responded to Nabíl-i-Qá'iní about creation. Ṭáhirih here seems to respond to questions posed by Bihjat about how to attain spiritual development. Her fundamental answer is that all the Prophets bring the same essential requirement that Adam Himself brought: to recognize the Prophet and to follow His guidance.

Consequently, this poem, though beautiful in its own right, is filled with obscure philosophical and theological notions deserving a great deal of meditation and study. In her response, Ṭáhirih in the fourth and fifth quatrains (translated from couplets) provides a synopsis of what she plans to say throughout the poem. She refers to the 'wish' of Adam and the fact that in this age we also need to make the mystery of Adam's wish manifest – i.e. to identify or understand the names and attributes of God and to make these spiritual abstractions manifest in the material world, 'the Kingdom of Names'.[362] She points out that this is not only a mystery of the beginning of the creation but also the mystery of today – the 'time of the end'.

In the sixth quatrain she begins her treatment of the subject by discussing the question of free will as it is symbolized in the story of creation or the beginning of the world. She concludes the poem with the twin duties incumbent on the people of this and every age:[363] to employ our free will to recognize the Manifestation and then to employ that same power to be faithful to the guidance that forms the Covenant of that Prophet. The poem ends abruptly with this point.

Lo, look around you, O my Bihjat,
study everything so that you
may discover manifest the face
of the Sign of God on earth.[364]

You have asked us about the secrets
of the divine mysteries
that you might might attain
the hidden stations of the spirit.

O my dear Bihjat,
O light of Ṭáhirih's heart,
you who come to us
with splendour and veneration,

Say: What was the wish
of His Holiness Adam?
Let us make His hidden mysteries
manifest in the world of existence.

Indeed, hearken to the ecstasy
of our[365] oneness that you may
discover the mystery
of the beginning and the end.[366]

It is for this reason
that the Venerable, Omnipotent God
has endowed each thing with capacity
according to a pre-ordained measure[367] –

that in this world of existence
He might fashion free will
by placing One in these regions
who undergoes unrelenting torment.[368]

From the very dawn of eternity
the Beloved, the Friend, the Eternal,
has endowed everyone
with the power of free will.[369]

Since there was nothing in existence,
except for God Himself,
The Cause and Creator of free will,
God made the first free-willed ones with
fire.[370]

Therefore, though I am one with free will
living at the dawn of this new age,[371]
for Him there is no beginning
and there is no end.

O Bihjat, understand these my words,
these matchless verities
that I have poured forth
into the delicate cup of thy search.

Lo, make the concealed mysteries of Adam –
Both the first and second of these –
manifest in the world
by your elucidation of the Bayán:

The first truth is to discern in the Bayán
the revelation of the Divine Beauty;
The second truth is to manifest your insight
with an appropriate portion of service.[372]

A Prayer for Bihjat

(40)

This poem could possibly be an envoy to the previous poem, 'The Twin Duties', but most likely it is not. Certainly it alludes strongly to that poem in this poetic prayer by Ṭáhirih that Bihjat understand the depth of thought she is trying to convey to him. But since she has several such poems to him, she might be referring to any one of these.

Even in its brevity, these three quatrains (translated from couplets) are fascinating for two reasons. First, the poem seems to indicate that she has purposely revealed the answer to Bihjat's question in a veiled language. In effect, like the good teacher she is, Ṭáhirih is forcing Bihjat to meditate on the deeper implications of what she has noted about free will and the twin duties incumbent upon humankind. Second, this poem gives further insight about the concept of *qadar* or 'measure'. For though we explained this term in the notes to the previous poem as alluding to the concept of free will and how it is each person's responsibility to utilize free will according to the measure of capacity God has bestowed upon him, this deeper context of the term seems to refer to the entire history of the philosophical debate about whether it is possible for there to exist simultaneously an omniscient God and free will.[373]

O Lord, assist Bihjat
at this very moment
that he might discover
the mystery of the true path.

May not one letter[374]
of this senna leaf[375]
remain concealed or hidden
from his understanding.

O God, verily you are my witness
that with your help and majesty
I have delivered to him
the secret of the signs of *Qadar*.[376]

The Prophecy of the Latter Resurrection[377]

(41)

This relatively long poem of some 27 couplets, also addressed to Bihjat, contains a degree of obfuscation that might indicate an intentionally secret or 'coded' message to Ṭáhirih's followers or close associates. This speculation is based on the fact that she entrusts the 'message' of the poem to Bihjat, the intermediary between Ṭáhirih and her close companions, and also on the fact that the piece is an extremely compressed and allusive image of virtually the entire history of the heroic age of the Bahá'í Faith.

That is, Ṭáhirih alludes to Quddús, to herself and the Letters of the Living, to the Báb as the 'Primal Point', to the martyrdom of the Báb and the concealing of His earthly remains, to the respite that will occur after the execution of the Báb and after Ṭáhirih's own execution with Bahá'u'lláh's experience in the Síyáh-Chál, a 'respite' that fulfils the Báb's request (as explained in the endnotes) that the Prophet of the 'Latter Resurrection' would delay revealing Himself for 'nineteen years'.[378] The poem further alludes to Ṭáhirih's own role as herald of the New Day and her longing to see the Sun of the New Day (the Dispensation of Bahá'u'lláh) in all its plentitude.

And yet, while all these allusions are difficult to discern even in retrospect, we can imagine how abstruse they would have been to anyone but the most astute, learned and faithful companions. The reason for such a technique could thus be twofold. First, if she is penning these verses from imprisonment or house arrest (which is likely), she is able to reassure the disheartened believers that the future is bright and yet no one other than they would be able to understand her message. Second, like so much of prophecy, its primary benefit is for the future followers of the religion who can then in retrospect observe the spiritual station and otherworldly knowledge that this individual possessed. Finally, if any of her poems confirms the loftiness of her station, certainly this one does.

I bestow on you, Bihjat, from the vast sea of Revelation,
gladly pour forth into your cup[379] this wisdom:

what has transpired in bygone ages soon will pass away.
He will come with the signs of the Prophets of old.

This One will be sanctified from reason and disputation;
He will come descended from the realm of *'Amá*.[380]

He will manifest naught else save the mention[381] of
God:
'Indeed I am quddús,[382] *acting as befits this age.'*[383]

Lo, listen to the unity in the ecstasy of His voice;
hear how many portentous melodies pour forth from
His mouth:

'No Creator is there in existence except Me.
I will bring into being whatsoever I willeth.'

Lo, ye who hear the words and verses of God,
Behold how the Faith of God has always come to you
through speech.

Behold those on board the ark –
the chosen[384] people, the Letters so illumined[385]

that from them are emitted sparks of fire[386]
*from Him of whom it can be said, none is changeless save
Him.*[387]

Because the Faith of God has appeared veiled in its
essence,
it illumined with its fire the four elements.[388]

We who have heard the voice of God obeyed it;
we have cut ourselves off from everything except that
which was revealed.

O hearer, regard every created thing around you
into which the great concealed mystery is infused.

Say: O God, what is this fiery ecstasy
that descended from the realm of the house of *qadar*?[389]

The reason for your power,[390] O Lord of the Bayán,[391]
is naught but the light manifest from the Point.[392]

Because this Point contains the mystery of the
beginning:[393]

Without Him, nothing would remain from what
began.[394]

O God, whosoever it was that took Him away
retrieved Him but did not forsake Him.[395]

O God, after the Primal Point, let there be a respite,
For there will be a period without guidance.[396]

O God, fill Ṭáhirih's cup
from Your bestowals of pure illumination

so that it makes manifest the Most Great Spirit[397] –
Indeed, I am a herald to the mystery, to the heavenly bestowals![398] –

and, like clouds, it will rise to the pinnacle of the sky,[399]
so that the face with the countenance of Bahá might come.[400]

I appeared so that He might come out from behind the veil,
so that I might pour from my cup the luminous drops of that cloud,[401]

Would that I might see that Sun cycling in the sky saying:[402]
'I am indeed the Lord God Omnipotent from the celestial realm!'

The Choice Wine

(42)

This poem is composed of simple words – no obscure Arabic, philosophical or Quranic terms. It has a soft flowing and melodious tone.[403]

The seven couplets, which we have translated as quatrains, are an appropriate ending to this volume because we feel they capture the spirit of this remarkable woman – her wit and courage especially. Of particular appropriateness to ending the volume is her confident closing image that in the long run – over the course of history – we will see who wins, as opposed to those who presently seem to hold the reins of power.

Of course, the conceit or analogy of love as a battlefield is a traditional one in various cultures but the application of this image to the history of the Bahá'í Faith takes on special significance in light of the slaughter of over 20,000 Bábís at the literal battles at the fort Shaykh Ṭabarsí, at Nayríz and at Zanján. Particularly powerful is the observation that this testing of those who profess love is not a game. It is thus very reminiscent of a statement made by Bahá'u'lláh which observes: 'Think not the Cause of God to be a thing lightly taken, in which any one can gratify his whims.'[404]

Another point of interest is the point of view in this piece. Here the perspective is not that of Ṭáhirih speaking her own feelings or describing her personal situation. This is a voice of rank, of intellect and authority articulating profound verities about the divine nature of human history.

What did youth bring?
The young lover.
What did old age bring?
The vintage wine.

The one brief appearance
of the young lover
bereft the heart of desire
for sleeping or eating;

The one drop
of choice wine
which the one who died did not sip
and the one who quaffed did not die

is from the same vessel
that time's cupbearer[405] gives to you,
so choice, so refined –
but to me the dregs only.[406]

Yet among the thousands
held captive by the Beloved,
only one has cleansed from the heart
the dust of worldly desires.

You see, this is no game –
going onto the battlefield of love
where only one in a hundred thousand
has emerged victorious.[407]

So let the parrot recite prayers
and let the claimant hurl accusations[408] –
at day's end we will see
who wins the field.[409]

O Thou, The Most Forgiving

(43)

We end this volume with this poetic prayer by Ṭáhirih. This poem has been found in only one published source, *The Ṭáhirih Centennial Volume*, as a continuation of her *sáqí námih*. It is clear, however, from both style and content that this is a separate and independent piece. The style, tone and language of this poem are very similar to what we find in 'A Prayer for the Martyrs'. As in 'A Prayer for the Martyrs', Ṭáhirih here expresses praise of and admiration for those believers who manifested detachment and such an exalted spiritual station that she prays to God that through their assistance she might be elevated from her human condition.

Interestingly, she never presumes in this poem that she may be elevated to their station, which she indicates is quite beyond anything she could aspire to. As such, this poem is a most fitting conclusion to this volume because it ends not with bravado or indirection – it is not clothed in the garment of mystical imagery. It is a humble prayer that she might be assisted and transformed. Of course, like all of Ṭáhirih's verse, the poem is highly compressed and allusive and it thus requires considerable thought on the part of the reader.

One final noteworthy feature of this poem is that unlike so many of Ṭáhirih's verse where couplets are 'closed' (i.e. complete statements), there is enjambment here (the thought in many cases continues from couplet to couplet) so that the reader should consider the entire sentence as containing the idea. For example, the first three couplets should be read as one poetic thought.

O Thou by Whom the light of the Beauty of the Most
Powerful[410]
Has entirely burned away the veils of the divine,

O Thou Almighty Lord of Glory, no longer does there
remain
even a minute particle of dust

from the hidden station of limitation
and from the exalted Tabernacles of Glory.

O God, O Thou Creator, I have been cleansed
by the fire of Thy Lordly flames.[411]

O My Lord, assist me through Your benevolence and graciousness
to have the honour of attaining Your Presence by attraction to Your Essence.[412]

O Thou Beauteous One, O Thou Honoured One, O Bahá,
Illumine the tablet of my heart with the manifest fire of Your will[413]

just as I have been scarred by the flames
of the deceits of the evil ones,[414] O Thou Powerful Creator.

O Thou, the Friend of the wise ones, purify
my heart from whatsoever might deter my certitude

so that I might become elevated to the realm of Justice
and detached from the trivial concerns of this world.

O God, there is nothing of import for me besides You.
My only solace comes from You alone,

O God, by all those kings of the kings
seated on the throne of manifest grace,[415]

all of whom have escaped the shackles of existence
and have become intoxicated and joyous with the One who calls '*Alast*!'[416]

those who have laid aside all transitory pleasures and delights
and have seized upon that which is fitting.

O God, behold their exalted resolve and single-minded devotion!
Praised be their endeavour in the path of God!

For them all earthly exaltations were utter nothingness
beside Your beauteous Countenance, O Lord of Existence.

By means of the loftiness of their will and the power of
Divine utterance,
they have attained unto the realm of the placeless –

so many souls seated on the thrones of honour –
that every particle of creation has been resurrected by
them

by this glorious power they received from You
through Your benevolence alone, O God.

O Lord God, would that I could but prostrate my face in
the dust
that was glorified by their glance.

Since they are foremost[417] and honoured,
They possess a lofty and exalted station.

But it was You, O God, who favoured them,[418]
trained them, protected them, and revered them,

have bestowed on them an incomparable station,
have ushered them to the abode of grandeur,

have taken away the human condition which You first
bestowed on them,
and have fashioned them into that which they have now
become.

O God, I must acknowledge my praise of them
if I myself am ever to prove worthy of being sanctified.

Should I be aided by Your fathomless grace,
I, too, might become free from this lowly existence.

O Friend, should You take from me my nothingness,
You would extract me from Your bosom, having forged
me into pure essence.

O God, by these kings among kings,
Relieve me from the condition of the base ones.

O True God, O Lord of the Worlds,
O Thou True Friend, O Thou the Most-forgiving.

Appendix
Sources of Poems

1. Shoghi Effendi's translation (translation in *Dawn-Breakers*, p. 286) from D̲h̲uká'í Bayḍá'í, *Tad̲h̲kiríy-i-S̲h̲u'aráy-i-Qarn-i-Avval-i-Bahá'í*, vol. 3, p. 131.

2. 'This Longing for You' from Afnán, *C̲h̲ahár Risálih-i-Táríkh̲í Dar Báriyih-i-Ṭáhirih Qurratu'l-'Ayn*, p. 91.

3. 'The Voice of God's Command' from D̲h̲uká'í Bayḍá'í, *Tad̲h̲kiríy-i-S̲h̲u'aráy-i-Qarn-i-Avval-i-Bahá'í*, vol. 3, p. 124

4. 'The Announcement' from D̲h̲uká'í Bayḍá'í, *Tad̲h̲kiríy-i-S̲h̲u'aráy-i-Qarn-i-Avval-i-Bahá'í*, vol. 3, p. 127.

5. 'Arise!' from Afnán, *C̲h̲ahár Risálih-i-Táríkh̲í Dar Báriyih-i-Ṭáhirih Qurratu'l-'Ayn*, p. 90.

6. 'Behold the New Day!' from Afnán, *C̲h̲ahár Risálih-i-Táríkh̲í Dar Báriyih-i-Ṭáhirih Qurratu'l-'Ayn*, p. 91.

7. 'Daybreak' from Afnán, *C̲h̲ahár Risálih-i-Táríkh̲í Dar Báriyih-i-Ṭáhirih Qurratu'l-'Ayn*, p. 90.

8. 'Praise God for this Promised Day!' from Afnán, *C̲h̲ahár Risálih-i-Táríkh̲í Dar Báriyih-i-Ṭáhirih Qurratu'l-'Ayn*, pp. 97–8.

9. 'An Ode to the Báb' from D̲h̲uká'í Bayḍá'í, *Tad̲h̲kiríy-i-S̲h̲u'aráy-i-Qarn-i-Avval-i-Bahá'í*, vol. 3, p. 122.

10. 'The Dry Bones' from D̲h̲uká'í Bayḍá'í, *Tad̲h̲kiríy-i-S̲h̲u'aráy-i-Qarn-i-Avval-i-Bahá'í*, vol. 3, p. 121.

11. 'The Hidden Secret' from Afnán, *C̲h̲ahár Risálih-i-Táríkh̲í Dar Báriyih-i-Ṭáhirih Qurratu'l-'Ayn*, p. 100.

12. 'For Love of My Beauty' from Afnán, *C̲h̲ahár Risálih-i-Táríkh̲í Dar Báriyih-i-Ṭáhirih Qurratu'l-'Ayn*, p. 94.

13. 'Attaining the Presence of God' from Nuqabá'í, *Huqúq-i-Zan*, p. 61.

14. 'Fire in the Eyes of the Friend' from Afnán, *Chahár Risálih-i-Táríkhí Dar Báriyih-i-Ṭáhirih Qurratu'l-'Ayn*, p. 93.

15. 'The Burning Heart' from Afnán, *Chahár Risálih-i-Táríkhí Dar Báriyih-i-Ṭáhirih Qurratu'l-'Ayn*, p. 92.

16. 'Song of the Captive Heart' from Afnán, *Chahár Risálih-i-Táríkhí Dar Báriyih-i-Ṭáhirih Qurratu'l-'Ayn*, pp. 96–7.

17. 'The Realm of Ecstasy' from Afnán, *Chahár Risálih-i-Táríkhí Dar Báriyih-i-Ṭáhirih Qurratu'l-'Ayn*, pp. 94–6.

18. 'The Cupbearer' from Browne, *Materials For the Study of the Bábí Religion*, pp. 344–7.

19. 'Him Whom God Shall Make Manifest' from Afnán, *Chahár Risálih-i-Táríkhí Dar Báriyih-i-Ṭáhirih Qurratu'l-'Ayn*, pp. 102–3.

20. 'The Footsteps of Bahá' source unknown.

21. 'Salutation and Praise' from Afnán, *Chahár Risálih-i-Táríkhí Dar Báriyih-i-Ṭáhirih Qurratu'l-'Ayn*, p. 101.

22. 'The Blessed Beauty' from Nuqabá'í, *Ṭáhirih Qurratu'l-'Ayn*, p. 162.

23. 'The Riddle of the Twin Revelation' from Nuqabá'í, *Ṭáhirih Qurratu'l-'Ayn*, pp. 152–3.

24. 'Behold the Face of God' from Afnán, *Chahár Risálih-i-Táríkhí Dar Báriyih-i-Ṭáhirih Qurratu'l-'Ayn*, pp. 92–3.

25. 'Behold the Worlds of God' from Dhuká'í Bayḍá'í, *Tadhkiríy-i-Shu'aráy-i-Qarn-i-Avval-i-Bahá'í*, vol. 3, pp. 122–3.

26. 'The Love of Bahá' from Afnán, *Chahár Risálih-i-Táríkhí Dar Báriyih-i-Ṭáhirih Qurratu'l-'Ayn*, p. 91.

27. 'Face to Face' from Afnán, *Chahár Risálih-i-Táríkhí Dar Báriyih-i-Ṭáhirih Qurratu'l-'Ayn*, p. 104.

28. 'The Ka'ba of Your Face' from Nuqabá'í, *Huqúq-i-Zan*, pp. 60–1.

29. 'A Shameless Servant Am I' from Ariyanpúr, *Az Ṣabá Tá Nímá (Táríkh-i-150 Sálih-i-Adab-i-Fársí)*, vol. 1, p. 132.

30. 'Rebuking the King's Desire' from Root, *Ṭáhirih the Pure*, pp. 127–8.

31. 'The Impatient Bride' from Afnán, *Chahár Risálih-i-Tárikhí Dar Báriyih-i-Ṭáhirih Qurratu'l-'Ayn*, p. 103.

32. 'Meditation on My Death' from Root, *Ṭáhirih the Pure*, pp. 126–7.

33. 'The Arc of Ascent' from an unpublished manuscript.

34. 'As God is My Witness: Ṭáhirih's Farewell' from Afnán, *Chahár Risálih-i-Tárikhí Dar Báriyih-i-Ṭáhirih Qurratu'l-'Ayn*, p. 99.

35. 'The Primal Point' from Dhuká'í Bayḍá'í, *Tadhkiríy-i-Shu'aráy-i-Qarn-i-Avval-i-Bahá'í*, vol. 3, p. 121.

36. 'Am I Not Your Lord?' from Momen, *Selections from the Writings of E. G. Browne on the Bábí and Bahá'í Religions*, pp. 461–2.

37. 'God the Creator' from Dhuká'í Bayḍá'í, *Tadhkiríy-i-Shu'aráy-i-Qarn-i-Avval-i-Bahá'í*, vol. 3, pp. 123–4.

38. 'The Prophet Noah' from Dhuká'í Bayḍá'í, *Tadhkiríy-i-Shu'aráy-i-Qarn-i-Avval-i-Bahá'í*, vol. 3, p. 125.

39. 'The Twin Duties' from Dhuká'í Bayḍá'í, *Tadhkiríy-i-Shu'aráy-i-Qarn-i-Avval-i-Bahá'í*, vol. 3, pp. 125-6.

40. 'A Prayer for Bihjat' from Dhuká'í Bayḍá'í, *Tadhkiríy-i-Shu'aráy-i-Qarn-i-Avval-i-Bahá'í*, vol. 3, pp. 126–7.

41. 'The Prophecy of the Latter Resurrection' from Afnán, *Chahár Risálih-i-Tárikhí Dar Báriyih-i-Ṭáhirih Qurratu'l-'Ayn*, pp. 101–2.

42. 'The Choice Wine' from Root, *Ṭáhirih the Pure*, pp. 129–30.

43. 'O Thou, The Most Forgiving' from *Ṭáhirih Qurratu'l-'Ayn Bi-yád-i-Ṣadumín Sál-i-Shahádat-i-Qurratu'l-'Ayn Nábighiy-i-Dawrán*: Ṭáhirih Centennial Volume,pp. 31–2.

Bibliography

Sources of the Poems Selected

An anthology of Bahá'í poems. Provided by Mr and Mrs Ashchi. Handwritten manuscript.

Afnán, Abu'l-Qasim, compiler. *Chahár Risálih-i-Táríkhí Dar Báriyih-i-Ṭáhirih Qurratu'l-'Ayn*. Wienacht, Switzerland: Landegg Academy, September 1991.

Ariyanpúr, Yahyá. *Az Ṣabá Tá Nímá (Táríkh-i-150 Sálih-i-Adab-i-Fársí)*, vol. 1. Tehran, 1971.

Bayḍá'í, Ni'matu'lláh Dhuká'í. *Tádhkiríy-i-Shu'aráy-i-Qarn-i-Avval-i-Bahá'í*, vol. 3. Tehran: Bahá'í Publishing Trust, 126 BE.

Browne, E. G., comp. *Materials for the Study of the Bábí Religion*. Cambridge: The University Press, 1961.

Momen, Moojan. *Selections from the Writings of E. G. Browne on the Bábí and Bahá'í Religions*. Oxford: George Ronald, 1987.

Nuqabá'í, Husám. *Huqúq-i-Zan*. Klosterneuburg, Austria, 1985.

— *Ṭáhirih Qurratu'l-'Ayn*. Tehran, 1983.

Root, Martha L. *Ṭáhirih the Pure*. Los Angeles: Kalimát Press, rev. edn. 1981.

Ṭáhirih Qurratu'l-'Ayn Bi-yád-i-Ṣadumín Sál-i-Shahádat-i-Qurratu'l-'Ayn Nábighih-i-Duwrán: Ṭáhirih Centennial Volume. Iran, 1949.

Reference Sources Utilized

Afnan, Soheil M. *Vázhih Námih Falsafí* (A Philosophical Lexicon in Persian and Arabic). Nashr-i-Nuqrih, n.d.

'Amíd, Ḥasan. *Amid Dictionary*, 2 vols. Sázimán-i-Cháp va Intishárát-i-Jávídán.

Baalbaki, Dr Rohi. *Al-Mawrid: A Modern Arabic-English Dictionary*. Beirut: Dar-el-ilm Lilmalayin , ninth edn. 1997.

Burúmand Sa'íd, Javád. *Zabán-i-Taṣawwuf*. Tehran: Pazhang Publishing Co., n.d.

A Dictionary of Arabic Grammar in Charts and Tables. Revised by Dr George M. Abdulmassih. Maktabat Lebanon: Librairie du Liban, 1981.

Dihkhudá, 'Alí Akbar. *Lughat-Námih 'Alí Akbar Dihkhudá*, 50 vols. Tehran: Tehran University, 1337 Shamsí.

Doniach N.S. ed. *The Oxford English-Arabic Dictionary of Current Usage*. Oxford: The Clarendon Press, 1993.

Fáḍil-i-Mázandaráni. *Asráru'l-Áthár*. Tehran: Mu'assisiy-i-Maṭbú'át-i-Amrí, 129 BE.

Farhang-i-Nuvín-i-'Arabí-Fársí (translation of *Al-Qámús-al-'Aṣrí*). Siyyid Muṣṭafá Ṭabáṭabá'i, trans. Tehran: Kitábfurúshí Islámíyyih, 1354.
Gawharín, Siyyid Ṣádiq. *Farhang-i-Lughát va Ta'bírát-i-Mathnaví*, 9 vols. Tehran: Zavvár Publishing, 1362.
— *Sharḥ-i-Iṣṭiláḥát-i-Taṣawwuf*, 4 vols. Tehran: Zavvár Publishing, n.d.
Ghadimi, Riaz K. *An Arabic Persian Dictionary of Selected Words*. Toronto: University of Toronto Press, 1986.
— *Riyáḍu'l-Lughat* (Arabic-Persian Dictionary), vols. 1–4. Toronto: University of Toronto Press, 1994–9.
Hayyim, S. *Hayyim's One-Volume English Persian Dictionary*. Tehran: Y. Beroukhim & Sons Booksellers, 1979.
— *The Larger Persian-English Dictionary*, 2 vols. Tehran: Farhand Mu'assir, 1985.
Ḥasan, 'Amíd. *Farhang-i-Fársí 'Amíd*. Tehran: Amir Kabir Publishing Corporation, n.d.
Hatcher, John S. *The Ocean of His Words: A Reader's Guide to the Art of Bahá'u'lláh*. Wilmette, IL: Báhá'í Publishing Trust, 1997.
Hemmat, Amrollah and Ehsanollah Hemmat. *'Arabí, Qava'id-i-Ṣarf va Naḥv*. Tehran, n.p., n.d.
Hemmat, Amrollah and Bijan Samali. *Learning Arabic: A Self Study Program*. 2 vols. (including six audio cassettes). The National Persian American Affairs Committee of the National Spiritual Assembly of the Bahá'ís of the United States, 1986.
Ishraq Khávarí, 'Abdu'l-Ḥamíd. *Qámús-i-Íqán*. Tehran: Mu'assisiy-i-Maṭbú'át-i-Amrí, 128 BE.
— *Raḥíq-i-Makhtúm*. Tehran: Lajniy-i-Millí Nashr-i-Áthár-i-Amrí, 103 BE.
Kamálí Dizfúlí, Ḥáj Siyyid 'Alí. *Qur'án Thiql-i-Akbar*. n.p., n.d.
Lorimer, T. Lawrence, ed. *Grolier International Encyclopedia*, 20 vols. Danbury, CT: Grolier Incorporated, 1991.
Mas'úd, Jubrán. *Ar-Rá'id Mu'jam Lughawí 'Aṣrí*. Beirut: Dáru'l-Ilm Lil-Maláyisín, 1967.
Maulana, Muhammad Ali. *The Holy Qur'án, Arabic Text, English Translation and Commentary*. Columbus, OH: Ahmadiyyah Anjuman Isha'at Islam, Lahore, Inc., 1995.
Muḥammad, Fuád Abdu'l-Báqí. *Al-Mu'jamu'l-Mufahras Lialfáẓ-il-Qurán-il-Karím*. Cairo: Dáru'l-Ḥadíth, 1996.
Mu'ín, Mohammad. *An Intermediate Persian Dictionary*, 6 vols. Tehran: Amir Kabir Publishing Corporation, 1996.
Mu'izzí, Muḥammad Kaẓim. *Mu'izzí, Muḥammad Kaẓim*. Tehran: Kitabfurúshí 'Ilmíyih Islámí, 1377.
Al-Munjidu'l-Abjadí. Beirut: Dar-el-Mashreq Publishers, 1968.
Al-Munjid Fi'l-Lughát. Beirut: Dar-el-Mashreq Publishers, 1975.
Nurbakhsh, Javad. *The Nurbakhsh Treasury of Sufi Terms*, 4 vols. n.p., 1372.
Sayyah, Ahmad. *Farhang-i-Buzurg-i-Jámi'-i-Nuvín* (Dictionary Arabic Farsi Sayyah), 4 vols. Tehran: Kitábfurúshí Islam, n.d.
Sajjádí, Siyyid Ja'far. *Farhang-i-Lughát va Iṣṭiláḥát va Ta'bírát-i-'Irfání*. Tehran: Kitábkhánih Ṭahúrí, n.d.

Scheindlin, Raymond, *201 Arabic Verbs*. Hauppauge, NY: Barron's Educational Series, Inc., n.d.
Shamissa. *Farhang-i-Talmíḥát* (A Dictionary of Allusions). Tehran: Intishárát-i-Firdaws, 1987.
Shari'at, Muḥammad Javád. *Tarjumih va Ráhnimá'-i-Mabádíyu'l-'Arabíyya*, vol. 4. Isfahan: Mu'assisiy-i-Intishárát-i-Mashál, n.d.
Shúshtarí (Mihrín), 'Abbás. *Farhang-i-Lughát-i-Qur'án*. Tehran: Intishárát-i-Daryá, n.d.
Tiflísí, Ḥubaysh. *Vujúh-i-Qur'án*. Muḥaqqiq Mahdí, ed. Tehran: Intishárát-i-Ḥikmat, 1396.
Webster's Encyclopedic Unabridged Dictionary of the English Language. Dilithium Press, Inc. 1989.

General Bibliography

'Abdu'l-Bahá. *Some Answered Questions*. Wilmette, IL: Bahá'í Publishing Trust, 1981.
The Báb. *Kitáb-i-Bayán-i-'Arabí*. n.p., n.d.
— *Kitáb-i-Bayán-i-Fársí*, n.p., n.d.
— *Ṣaḥífih-i-'Adlíyyih*. n.p., n.d.
— *Selections from the Writings of the Báb*. Haifa: Bahá'í World Centre, 1976.
Bahá'í World, The. vol. 17. Haifa: Bahá'í World Centre, 1981.
Bahá'u'lláh. *Meditations of the Blessed Beauty*. London: Bahá'í Publishing Trust, 1992.
— *Prayers and Meditations*. Wilmette, IL: Bahá'í Publishing Trust, 1987.
— *Tablets of Bahá'u'lláh revealed after the Kitáb-i-Aqdas*. Haifa: Bahá'í World Centre, 1978.
Banani, Amin. 'Chihrih-i-Ṭáhirih Qurratu'l-'Ayn az Ṣidáy-i-Khud-i-ú'. *'Andalíb*. vol. 10, no. 39, pp. 22–6.
— 'Ṭáhirih: A Portrait in Poetry'. *The Journal of Bahá'í Studies*, vol. 10, no. 1/2, March-June 2000. Ottawa: Association for Bahá'í Studies.
Bayḍá'í, Ni'matu'lláh Dhuká'i. *Tadhkarih-i-Shu'ará-i-Qarn-i-Avval-i-Bahá'í*, vol 1. Tehran: Bahá'í Publishing Trust, 121 BE.
Cobb, Stanwood. 'The Worldwide Influence of Qurratu'l-'Ayn'. *Bahá'í World, The*. vol. 1, rpt. Wilmette, IL: Bahá'í Publishing Trust, 1980, pp. 257–62.
Fáḍíl-i-Mázandaráni. *Ẓuhúru'l-Ḥaqq*, vol. 3. Tehran, n.p., n.d.
Fayḍ-i-Káshání, Mullá Muḥsin. *Díván-i-Kámil-i-Fayḍ-i-Káshání, Hamráh Bá Risálih-i-Gulzár-i-Quds Az Mu'aẓẓam Lah* with introduction and corrections by Siyyid 'Ali Shafí'í. Tehran: Nashr-i-Chakámih, n.d.
Furúzanfar, B. (Introduction) and M. Darvish (Notes). *Díván-i Kámil-i-Shams-i Tabrízí, Mawláná Jalálu'd-Dín Muḥammad Balkhí, Mashhúr bi Mawlaví*. Sázimán-i Intishárát-i Jávídán, n.d.
Gail, Marzieh. 'Stanza from Ṭahirih'. *The Journal of Bahá'í Studies*, vol. 7. Ottawa: Association for Bahá'í Studies, 1980.
— 'The White Silk Dress'. *Bahá'í World*, vol. 9. rpt. Wilmette, IL: Bahá'í Publishing Trust, 1980, pp. 814–21.
Ḥasan, Hádí. *A Golden Treasury of Persian Poetry*. M.S. Israeli, ed. Indian Council for Cultural Relations, n.p. 2nd rev. edn. March 1972.

Hatcher, John. 'A Poem'. *The Journal of Bahá'í Studies*, vol. 7. Ottawa: Association of Bahá'í Studies, 1980, p. 10.
Holy Bible, King James Version. Nashville, TN: Omega Publishing House, 1971.
Humá'í, Jalálu'd-Dín. *Tafsír-i Mathnaví-i Mawlaví*. Tehran: Mu'assisiy-i-Nashr-i Humá, 1366.
Ishaquc, M. *Four Eminent Poetesses of Iran*. Calcutta: Iran Socicty, 1950.
Khúsh-i-Há'í Az Kharman-i-Adab va Hunar 3. Presentation at Ṭáhirih Seminar, September 1991. Darmstadt, Germany: Persian Letters and Arts Society, Landegg Academy, 1992.
Láhíjí Shamsu'd-Dín, Muhammad. *Mafátíḥ al-I'jáz Fi Sharḥ-i Gulshan-i Ráz*. Tehran: Intishárát-i-Zavvár, n.d.
Lambden, Stephen. (trans.) 'Qámús Íqán, vol. 4:1875', *The Journal of Bahá'í Studies*, vol. 8, no. 2. Ottawa: Association for Bahá'í Studies, 1988, p. 34.
Maḥbúb-i-'Álam,(The Beloved of the World). Commemorative volume for the centenary of the Ascension of Bahá'u'lláh. n.p. 'Andalíb Editorial Board of the National Spiritual Assembly of the Bahá'ís of Canada, 1992–3.
Majalliy-i-Hunar va Mardum Vízhih Námih Irán va Pakistán. n.p. Vizárat-i-Farhang va Hunar-i-Ábádán, 2536 Sháhanshábí.
Mathnaví-i-Nabíl-i-Zarandí. Hofheim: Bahá'í-Verlag, 1995.
Mihrábí Mu'inu'd-Dín. *Qurrat-al-Ain freiheitsliebende und national gesinnte Dichterin Iran* (Qurrat ul-Áyn Shá'riyeh Ázádíkháh va Millí-i Irán). Koln: Nashr-i-Rúyesh, 1990.
Milani, Farzaneh. *Veils and Words: The Emerging Voices of Iranian Women Writers*. Syracuse, NY: Syracuse University Press, 1992, 1999.
Muḥammad-Ḥusayní, N. M. *Ḥaḍrat-i-Ṭáhirih*. Association for Bahá'í Studies in Persian, Ontario, 2000.
— *Yúsif-i-Bahá' Dar Qayyúmu'l-Asmá'*. Ontario: Persian Institute for Bahá'í Studies, December 1991.
Muntakhabát-i-Áyát az Áthár-i-Ḥaḍrat-i-Nuqṭih-i-Úlá. Wilmette,IL: Bahá'í Publishing Trust, 1978.
Murata, Sachiko. *The Tao of Islam*. Albany, NY: State University of New York Press, 1992.
Murata, Sachiko and William C. Chittick. *The Vision of Islam*. St Paul, MN: Paragon House, 1994.
Nabíl-i-A'ẓam. *The Dawn-Breakers: Nabíl's Narrative of the Early Days of the Bahá'í Revelation*. Wilmette, IL: Bahá'í Publishing Trust, 1970.
Nicholson, Reynold A. and B. Furúzanfar. *Mathnaví-i Ma'naví, Mawláná Jalálu'd-Din Muḥammad Balkhí*. n.p., Nashr-i-Ilm, 1374.
Niẓámí. *Laylí va Majnún Ḥakím Niẓámí Ganjí'í Bi-Taṣḥíḥ-i-Ustád-i-Sukhan Marḥúm Vaḥíd-i-Dastgirdí*. n.p., Mihr Máh-i 1333.
Qavímí, Fakhrí (Vazírí, Khasháyár). *Kárnámih-i Zanán-i Mashhúr-i Irán Az Qabl-i Islám tá Aṣr-i Ḥáḍir*. n.p., n.d.
Ra'fatí, Vaḥíd. Article on the poems attributed to Ṭáhirih. *Payám-i-Bahá'í*, no. 251, October 2000, p. 11. Paris: Assemblée Nationale des Bahá'ís de France.

Saídí, Nádir. 'Taḥlílí az Mafhúm-i Bábiyyat dar Áthár-i-Ḥaḍrat-i-A'lá.-2'. *Payám-i-Bahá'í*, no. 223, June 1998, pp. 9–12, 54–6. Paris: Assemblée Spirituelle Nationale des Bahá'ís de France.

— 'Taḥlílí az Mafhúm-i Bábíyyat dar Á<u>th</u>ár-i-Ḥaḍrat-i-A'lá-3'. *Payám-i-Bahá'í*, nos. 224, 225, July and August 1998, pp. 22–6. Paris: Assemblée Spirituelle Nationale des Bahá'ís de France.

Sandler, Rivanne. 'The Poetic Artistry of Qurratu'l-Ayn (Ṭáhirih): A Bábí Heroine'. *Bahá'í Studies Notebook*, vol. 1, no. 1, December 1988, pp. 65–7. Ottawa: Association for Bahá'í Studies.

Schimmel, Annemarie. *Deciphering the Signs of God: A Phenomenological Approach to Islam*. Albany, NY: State University of New York Press, 1994.

Shoghi Effendi. *God Passes By*. Wilmette, IL: Bahá'í Publishing Trust, rev. edn. 1974.

Stiles Maneck, Susan. 'Ṭáhirih: A Religious Paradigm of Womanhood'. *Journal of Bahá'í Studies*, vol. 2, no. 2 , 1989. pp. 40–5.

Ṣuḥbat-i-Lárí. *Díván-i-Ṣuḥbat-i-Lárí Bi Ihtimám-i-Ḥusayn Ma'rifat*. Shiraz: Kitábfurú<u>sh</u>í Ma'rifat, n.d.

Taherzadeh, Adib. *The Covenant of Bahá'u'lláh*. Oxford: George Ronald, 1992.

— *The Revelation of Bahá'u'lláh*, vol. 1. Oxford: George Ronald, 1974.

— *The Revelation of Bahá'u'lláh*, vol. 2. Oxford: George Ronald, 1977.

— *The Revelation of Bahá'u'lláh*, vol. 3. Oxford: George Ronald, 1983.

Notes

1. Shoghi Effendi, *God Passes By*, p. 3.
2. 'Abdu'l-Bahá, *Memorials of the Faithful*, p. 190.
3. This is a provisional translation of a Tablet which appears in *Rahíq-i-Makhtúm, Qámús-i-Lawh-i-Qarn* under the title 'Nuqṭiy-i-Jazbíyyih – Ṭáhirih Muṭahharih', The Point of Ecstasy – Ṭáhirih the Pure, p. 132.

   The allusion here to 'Azal' is to the half-brother of Bahá'u'lláh, Ṣubḥ-i-Azal (also called Mírzá Yaḥyá), the nominee of the Báb to lead the Bábí community after the Báb's passing. Here Ṭáhirih alludes to the fact that had Azal remained faithful, he would still have been only one of thousands of mirrors (*mir'át*) reflecting this truth.
4. 'human' in this sense alluding to beings capable of knowing and worshipping God
5. This verity can be deduced from the statements about there being no limit to the creation of an infinite creator and it is stated explicitly by 'Abdu'l-Bahá in the Tablet of the Universe.
6. 'Abdu'l-Bahá, *Memorials of the Faithful*, pp. 190–203.
7. Pronounced TÁ-heh-reh.
8. Cf. *The Dawn-Breakers*, p. 81, note 2, and p. 285, note 2. Certain lines, there translated by Shoghi Effendi, are incorporated here.
9. A forerunner of the Báb and first of the two founders of the Shaykhí school.
10. Qur'án 17:1; 30:56; 50:19; etc.
11. The sixth Imám
12. The 'Aḥsanu'l-Qiṣaṣ', the Báb's commentary on the Súrih of Joseph, was called the Qur'án of the Bábís, and was translated from Arabic into Persian by Ṭáhirih. Cf. *God Passes By*, p. 23.
13. Qur'án 3:54: 'Then will we invoke and lay the malison of God on those that lie!' The ordeal was by imprecation.
14. Qur'án 21:48; 19:37; etc. In Islam the Ṣiráṭ (Bridge), sharp as a sword and finer than a hair, stretches across Hell to Heaven.
15. Cf. *The Dawn-Breakers*, p. 276. The murderer was not a Bábí, but a fervent admirer of the Shaykhí leaders, the Twin Luminous Lights.
16. Cf. *The Dawn-Breakers*, p. 278.
17. This refers to the doctrine that there are three ways to God: the Law (*sharí'at*), the Path (*ṭaríqat*), and the Truth (*ḥaqíqat*). That is, the law of the orthodox, the path of the dervish, and the truth. Cf. R. A. Nicholson, *Commentary on the Mathnaví of Rumi*, s.v.
18. The eighteenth Letter of the Living, martyred with unspeakable cruelty in the market place at Bárfurúsh, when he was 27. Bahá'u'lláh

conferred on him a station second only to that of the Báb Himself. Cf. *The Dawn-Breakers,* pp. 408–15.

19. Cf. Qur'án 74:8 and 6:73. Also Isaiah 27:13 and Zechariah 9:14.
20. Qur'án, súrih 56.
21. A systematic campaign against the new Faith had been launched in Persia by the civil and ecclesiastical authorities combined. The believers, cut down wherever they were isolated, banded together when they could, for protection against the government, the clergy, and the people. Betrayed and surrounded as they passed through the forest of Mázindarán, some 300 believers, mostly students and recluses, built the fort of Shaykh Ṭabarsí and held out against the armies of Persia for eleven months. Cf. *The Dawn-Breakers*, chapter XIX and XX; *God Passes By*, p. 37 *et seq*.
22. On 15 August 1852, a half-crazed Bábí youth wounded the Sháh with shot from a pistol. The assailant was instantly killed, and the authorities carried out a wholesale massacre of the believers, its climax described by Renan as 'a day perhaps unparalleled in the history of the world'. Cf. Lord Curzon, *Persia and the Persian Question*, pp. 501–2, and *God Passes By*, p. 62 *et seq*.
23. Shoghi Effendi, *God Passes By*, pp. 7, 72–7.
24. Shoghi Effendi, in Nabíl, *Dawn-Breakers*, p. 286.
25. Dr Ra'fatí's article appears in *Payám-i-Bahá'í*, no. 251 (October 2000), p. 11.
26. From a letter written by Ṭáhirih in the first years after the declaration of the Báb (the year 1261 AH), it is clear that she was aware of the independence of the Revelation of the Báb and the fact that the Báb was a Manifestation of God like Muḥammad. Like the Báb Himself, however, Ṭáhirih kept this truth to herself at first (Husayní, *Yúsif-i-Bahá*, p. 66).
27. The Báb, *Selections,* p. 7.
28. Shoghi Effendi, *God Passes By*, pp. 92–100.
29. ibid. pp. 57–9.
30. See ibid. pp. 92–100.
31. ibid. p. 96.
32. The 'Opener of the Gates' (or doors) is one who gives relief and bestows success. In the Qur'án we find several allusions to opening the gates of heaven to the good people or opening the gates of hell for the evil ones. The opening of the gates of heaven (or the sky) is also mentioned as an analogy for God bestowing happiness to people.
33. *Ḥaḍrat* may signify 'nearness' or the entrance of the door. Being in the presence of important personages is symbolized by the idea of being the entrance of their door, since they themselves are above and beyond the reach of common people. The word *ḥaḍrat* is used for referring to holy people and is translated as 'His Holiness': e.g. *Ḥaḍrat-i-Bahá'u'lláh* means 'His Holiness Bahá'u'lláh'.
34. *Naẓratan*: a quick glance at something. This can also signify 'kindness', 'love' or 'pity'.
35. 'intoxicated' or 'so ecstatic that they lost their reason or wisdom'

36. 'Respite' and 'sanctuary' here derive from *ma͟tháb*, a place where people gather, a rendezvous. The word is used in the Qur'án regarding the house of God (Ka'ba) originally built by Abraham where the Muslims go for pilgrimage (see 2:125).
37. They have advanced their understanding and their spiritual perception so that they transcend the laws of cause and effect (i.e. phenomenal explanations for reality).
38. The concept of 'dead drunk' here derives from two words, one meaning drunk, the other meaning ruined and destroyed. Together they convey the meaning of being intoxicated to excess.
39. *Amr* means 'command' but has also been translated in the Bahá'í writings as 'Faith' (as in Bahá'í Faith), 'Command' as in the 'World of Command'. We have chosen 'Faith' here, though 'Command' would work quite as well.
40. *Áya*: Sign, scripture (the word 'sign' in Arabic has been used for 'verse' and 'scripture' – e.g. the verses of the Qur'án are the signs of God. In the Bahá'í writings the word 'signs' (*áyát*) also means 'signs of God' in terms of 'holy scripture'.
41. *Káf* and *nún*, the two letters that when combined make the word *kun* meaning 'Be'. It refers to the creation of man by God when God said *Kun* (Be) and there it was (*fayakún*). (Qur'án 3:52) Creation in the context of this poem is the spiritual regeneration of humanity through the advent of a new Faith. The term is seen in the Qur'án in this context prophesying the Day of Resurrection:

    > And it is He who hath created the Heavens and the Earth, in truth, and when He saith to a thing, 'Be', it is.
    >
    > His word is the truth: and His the kingdom, on the day when there shall be a blast on the trumpet: He knoweth alike the unseen and the seen: and He is the Wise, the Cognisant. (6:72–3)

    As we have noted, Ṭáhirih identifies herself as that Trumpet.

    The command 'Be and there was' is also an indication of God's power and authority. When He wants something to happen, it is sufficient for Him to say 'Be!' and that event immediately takes place: 'All obeyeth Him, Sole maker of the Heavens and of the Earth! And when He decreeth a thing, He only saith to it, "Be", and it is.' (Qur'án 2:111) 'B and E' in this poem thus indicates both the authority of God and the spiritual regeneration of humanity by God in the advent of a new religion since the word Ṭáhirih uses for 'Faith' also means 'Command'.
42. This alludes to a passage from the Qur'án: 'Verily we are God's [from God], and to Him shall we return.' (2:151) In the writings of the Báb we find: 'All men have proceeded from God and unto Him shall all return.' (The Báb, *Selections*, p. 157)
43. Aḥmad is a title for Muḥammad and means 'the most praiseworthy'. The phrase 'the countenance of Aḥmad' here thus alludes to that

which is like unto the Prophet Muḥammad (e.g. Aḥmadan, belonging to Aḥmad and Aḥmad-like).

Some scholars of Islam have made a distinction between the two names Aḥmad and Muḥammad. Muḥammad has the connotation of the divine aspect while Aḥmad connotes the human aspect. Aḥmad leads us to God's Beauty (*jamál*) reflected in the Friend and the Beloved (*ḥabíb*) of God while Muḥammad is associated with God's grandeur and the majesty (*jalál*) of God that is transcendent and separate from His Manifestation. (See Schimmel, *Deciphering the Signs of God*, p. 191) Considering this interpretation, Ṭáhirih says the Divine, Hidden and Eternal Muḥammad was made apparent and was manifested (Aḥmad). It also could be understood as follows: 'The same reality that was manifested through Muḥammad has been manifested again.' In other words, the Muḥammadan Light (*Núr-i-Muḥammadí*) or Muḥammadan Spirit (*Rúḥ-i-Muḥammadí*), the reality that manifests itself at various ages, has become manifest again. This is the meaning we have implied.

44. See 'The Twin Duties' (no. 39) in Chapter Seven for a further discussion by Ṭáhirih of this concept.
45. *Jamíl*
46. *Jalíl*. In this couplet Ṭáhirih makes a distinction between the two contrasting but complementary categories of God's attributes: *Jamáliyya* (attributes of beauty understandable or enticing to humankind) and *Jaláliyya* (attributes of power and might that emphasize the transcendent aspect of God).
47. This poem with only a minor variation is found at the beginning of a larger poem in Feyz's collection. The poem in that collection has an additional eleven verses with the last verse indicating that he is the poet.
48. *Khumár*: 'having a hangover'. After drinking wine, when you are looking for more wine – as if more wine will be the remedy for your hangover. The underlying meaning here is that you are still somewhat intoxicated because of your love for the Friend but you wish for more of it. For the Sufi background of these terms, see Nurbakhsh, *Treasury of Sufi Terms*, vol. 1, pp. 164–9: Being drunk is 'A state when love totally encompasses the lover (state of unity with the Friend)'. *Khumár* is the 'Return from the state of being drunk (state of unity) to the state of multiplicity'. Being separated from the Friend and living in the human condition. The Beloved at this state is hidden under the veils of grandeur. The cure for *Khumár* is seeing the cupbearer (having more wine).

    Khumár, then, is the lover's desperate longing for the beloved, as illustrated by this verse from Saná'í: 'Anyone who in his heart has the intoxication (*Khumár*) of the Wise,/ His lot in love would be wretchedness and infamy.' (Sajjádí, *Farhang*, p. 200)
49. The concept at work here is that the lover has become partially intoxicated by the love for the Friend and now that the Friend has

appeared, the lover can become completely intoxicated through the choice wine the Friend has brought (the Revelation itself).

50. Here the cycle of the year is being used symbolically to represent both the cycle in a person's life and, more importantly, the cycle of a dispensation. Thus, autumn is the end of vitality, the dying of the year, a time of nostalgic recollection of the fruitful times of spring and summer. Thus, the persona here is telling the believers that they have made it through the sadness of autumn and the death of winter, that the new Revelation has come to revive the earth and the hearts of humankind.
51. More literally, the line reads, 'O annihilated carcass of the past, arise!' The sense is clear and the symbolic meaning works on multiple levels. The dual symbols of body and blood in religious poetry traditionally allude to the institution of the religion and the Holy Spirit or the spiritual teachings that give life to the institution. In one sense, then, the speaker is beseeching the hearer to set aside the former religion and accept the new Revelation.
52. The realm of the earth and the realm of souls are represented by two words – *áfáq* and *'anfus*. These are used in a passage in the Qur'án (41:53) which is quoted by Bahá'u'lláh in The Four Valleys as follows: 'Hereafter We will show them Our signs in the regions of the earth, and in themselves, until it becomes manifest unto them that it is the truth.' (Bahá'u'lláh, *Seven Valleys and the Four Valleys*, p. 51) The word 'themselves' has been translated here from the phrase 'their souls' in the Qur'án.
53. The seat or 'position of authority' is an expensive carpet at the end of the room where the kings used to sit.
54. This passage implies a pretence at being holy.
55. This is an extension of the turban that the clergy used to pass under their chins to secure the turban in place.
56. *ḥukm*: also 'custom', 'method', 'law' or 'principle'
57. Literally, 'the principle of heterogeneity will be replaced with the principle of homogeneity'.
58. Quite possibly Ṭáhirih is here alluding to the Qur'án 113:1–5 wherein Muḥammad reveals a prayer to the 'Lord of the Dawn' for protection against various sorts of evil. In essence, she is saying this assistance has at long last arrived:

> In the Name of God, the Compassionate, the Merciful
> SAY: I betake me for refuge to the Lord of the DAYBREAK [*Rabbu'l-Falaq*]
> Against the mischiefs of his creation;
> And against the mischief of the night when it overtaketh me;
> And against the mischief of weird women;
> And against the mischief of the envier when he envieth.

Rumi also uses this term when emphasizing the irresistible power of God. (See Gawharín, *Farhang*, vol.5, p. 27)

59. The literal translation of the passage would be: 'with glory (*Bahá*) the face of God has become manifest'. In short, this may be an allusion to Bahá'u'lláh – something Ṭáhirih does more explicitly in other verses – or it may be an allusion to the Báb who is the 'Lord of the Dawn' as regards the 'Day of Resurrection' alluded to over and over in the Qur'án, whereas Bahá'u'lláh is the manifestation of the 'Latter Resurrection' as mentioned in the writings of both the Báb and Bahá'u'lláh: See The Báb, *Selections*, p. 7 and Bahá'u'lláh, *Kitáb-i-Íqán*, p. 229.

    Since Ṭáhirih on several occasions demonstrates her awareness of the stations of both Manifestations, this poem may very well be alluding to both (the twin Revelations) and to this period of transformation initiated by the appearance of the Báb and consummated by the appearance of Bahá'u'lláh.

60. *Muhán*: humiliated or weak person, despised. It can be also read as *mihán* meaning 'respected ones, great ones'. 'Great ones' might be more appropriate since Rumi (Gawharín, *Farhang*, vol. 8, p. 213) and Nabíl use that expression in their poetry. For example, one verse from Nabíl says: 'Become happy O great ones with God's remembrance/ Since at this time the birthday of God has arrived.' (*Mathnaví* of Nabíl, p. 8)

61. *Zamán*: 'time, age, eternity' as translated by the Guardian in relation to its meaning in the Hidden Words ('the eternal moment' in Sufi terminology; Nurbakhsh, *Treasury of Sufi Terms*, vol. 2, p. 253).

62. *Luft*: 'interacting with the others with delight and kindness, benevolence'.

63. Teacher, professor, dean, learned, an old man, a venerable man, an elder, the chief of tribe.

64. *Andar Zamán*: 'Of the age'. We see this term in another poem of Ṭáhirih ('As God is My Witness', no. 34, couplet 5) meaning 'in this age'.

65. *Bar ham zan*: literally, to 'stir' or 'disorganize'.

66. A somewhat liberal interpretation of *chand-u-chún*, meaning 'quantity and attribute, quantity and quality'. Rumi says: 'How would it fit in the narrowness of quantity and quality./ In that realm even the First Mind is bewildered.' (Gawharín, *Farhang*, vol. 4, p. 62) Hence we interpret the term in this context as implying 'people questioning what they should not question' or 'people's attachments to their own things and their own reasoning'.

67. The expression 'milk changing to blood' has been used in Rumi's poetry: 'For a while this mathnaví was delayed,/ Time is needed for the blood to change to milk' and in another verse he observes: 'Unless if your luck gives birth to a new child,/ the blood would not turn into the sweet milk, listen well.'

    In the old time, people considered the mother's milk to be her blood that at the time of giving birth turns into milk. There is a reference to that concept in the Qur'án (16:68): 'Ye have also teaching from the cattle. We give you drink of the pure milk, between dregs and blood, which is in their bellies; the pleasant beverage of them that quaff it.' (See Gawharín, *Farhang*, p. 354)

Ṭáhirih therefore seems to be saying, 'Finally, the long-awaited time has arrived for the hardship and sadness to turn into comfort and nourishment.'

68. *Ṭábaq*: The condition of people, the face of the earth (the state of the world). The word today also means 'page', i.e. one should turn the page and move on to a new chapter in the unfolding history of humankind. The word also was used for a round wooden tray with various delicacies in the different sections. People used to turn the tray around to reach for a different treat; therefore, the word might allude to a 'turn for the better'. Even more allusively, the word could allude to the ancient concept of fate or fortune as the spinning of a wheel whereby one's unfortunate circumstances might be made better.
69. *Qalaq*: 'Lock'; A bolt that fastens a door, state of being closed, tied, fastened. State of being loaded heavily, overburden.
70. Because of the simplicity of thought and language, this poem is sometimes thought to be by someone other than Ṭáhirih but, again, we have in Ṭáhirih a poet capable of employing a wide variety of styles and voices so that such an argument without other evidence to substantiate the contention is pure speculation.
71. The gnostic meaning is 'the world of the hidden' or the 'divine world'.
72. This phrase could also be understood as 'Let me say it in another way', possibly referring to the fact that the ending of the couplets changes after this to 'Welcome to this Blessed Day!'
73. This repeated phrase could more literally be translated as 'May your hearts be filled with joy!' – an equally celebratory refrain.
74. Literally, 'Become a leading cause for the letter *B*'.
75. Possibly an endearing or diminutive form of *Qurratu'l-'Ayn*.
76. Also 'superstitions'.
77. This refers to the spiritual reality that underlies and gives meaning to every object in the phenomenal world, even as Bahá'u'lláh notes that everything in creation has the capacity to reflect divine attributes and that without this capacity, phenomenal reality would cease to exist:

> Know thou that every created thing is a sign of the revelation of God. Each, according to its capacity, is, and will ever remain, a token of the Almighty. Inasmuch as He, the sovereign Lord of all, hath willed to reveal His sovereignty in the kingdom of names and attributes, each and every created thing hath, through the act of the Divine Will, been made a sign of His glory. So pervasive and general is this revelation that nothing whatsoever in the whole universe can be discovered that doth not reflect His splendour. Under such conditions every consideration of proximity and remoteness is obliterated

> . . . Were the Hand of Divine power to divest of this high endowment all created things, the entire universe would become desolate and void. (Bahá'u'lláh, *Gleanings*, p. 184)

The next two lines refer to the fact that the Qá'im (the Báb) has enabled humankind to understand that knowledge that was formerly hidden:

> Thus it is related in the 'Biháru'l-Anvár', the ''Aválim', and the 'Yanbú'' of Ṣádiq, son of Muḥammad, that he spoke these words: 'Knowledge is twenty and seven letters. All that the Prophets have revealed are two letters thereof. No man thus far hath known more than these two letters. But when the Qá'im shall arise, He will cause the remaining twenty and five letters to be made manifest.' Consider; He hath declared Knowledge to consist of twenty and seven letters, and regarded all the Prophets, from Adam even unto the 'Seal', as Expounders of only two letters thereof and of having been sent down with these two letters. He also saith that the Qá'im will reveal all the remaining twenty and five letters. (Bahá'u'lláh, *Kitáb-i-Íqán*, pp. 243–4)

The consequence of this revelation, then, is to make the unseen seen and to integrate the various paths to God into one path, thereby eliminating both limitations and separations among humankind.

78. Also: Gaps, fractures, ruptures, infirmities, violations, infractions, transgressions.

79. The heart of the meaning of these terms we have explained in the introduction but a more ample explanation may be helpful. According to the Muslim gnostics, God's names are of two kinds: the name of His grandeur (*Jalál*) and the names reflecting His beauty (*Jamál*). God's attributes and names related to His grandeur characterize Him as inaccessible to human beings and therefore are like veils that hide Him from human understanding. These are names such as 'Inaccessible', 'Mighty', 'Great', 'Majestic', and 'High King'. In contrast, His names of beauty describe God's attributes, such as 'Beautiful', 'Merciful', 'Compassionate', 'Near', 'Loving', 'Pardoner', etc. (See Murata, *Tao of Islam*, p. 9)

    Ṭáhirih says in this couplet (quatrain) that the veils of grandeur were taken away and the beauty and perfections of God were made manifest.

80. *Dawrán*: circulating or changing from one condition to another. It can also allude to an age, a generation or the cities and tribes. This sentence thus lends itself to various interpretations, though the essential sense remains the same.

81. Literally, 'The mystery of non-stop or eternality' (ceaseless mystery). The idea seems to be that one has asked the Pen to explain 'The

process of His creation hath had no beginning, and can have no end'. (Bahá'u'lláh, *Gleanings*, p. 61)

This passage alludes to the concept of progressive revelation and the fact that humanity will always be in need of God's guidance. It also could refer to the continuous and ever-present assistance of the Manifestation to the world of creation. All numerous particles are assisted by His Spirit ('Rebuking the King's Desire', no. 30, couplet 4). This is the same concept of *al khalqu'l-Jadíd* ('the new creation') or perpetual re-creation of the universe in Ibnu'l-'Arabí's philosophy.

82. In addition to the passage cited in the introduction from Ezekiel, there are in the Qur'án various passages alluding to the fact that even after people die and turn into dust, God will definitely recreate them (*khalqu'l-Jadíd*): e.g. 13:5, 32:10, 34:7, 17:49, 17:98. Also many verses of the Qur'án emphasize that God is capable of a new creation (*khalqu'l-Jadíd*): e.g. 14:19, 35:16, 50:15.

83. Refer to the discussion by Mírzá Abúl Faḍl-Gulpáygání in *Faṣlu'l-Khitáb* (pp. 164–5) on the blowing of the Trumpet.

84. While this title ('Solace of the Eyes') alludes to Ṭáhirih herself in other verses, it would not here make much sense with the pronoun 'my' unless one aspect of herself is talking to another (her spirit conversing with her intellect, for example).

But here this same appellation (*Qurratu'l-'Ayn*) is used by her to allude to the Báb and to Bahá'u'lláh. This title is used by the Báb in His commentary on the Súrih of Joseph when alluding to Bahá'u'lláh (60).

85. *Navá*: This word also appears three times in the second half of this couplet (four times in total – 'singing', 'songs', 'melody' and here as 'songs of the flute'). Repetition of the word yields plaintive and soft musical tone to the couplet. The word has the following meanings: opulence, music, tune, melody, song and singing, singing of a bird; lamentation and complaint; music in general and a specific type of Persian music which is soft and dignified – neither very happy nor very sad expressing feelings as if advising the listener. (See Mu'ín, *Qurrat-al-Ain*, 4827) The term is used in Rumi's poem to mean 'word', 'speech' and ' mention'.

Combined with the word *nay* or 'flute', the term would seem to indicate a particular sort of sound or melody, as we have explained in the notes to other poems. Rumi in his famous poem (the first line of the first poem of his Mathnaví) talks about the flute's lamentations owing to its separation from its origin on the sugar cane farm (alluding to separation of man from his origin God). The flute sound is thus a haunting or plaintive tune that alludes to stories of separation.

Nay-navá as one word is also a name for Karbilá where the Imám Ḥusayn was martyred. During His pilgrimage, the Báb was seen weeping at the shrine of the Imám Ḥusayn. *Nay-navá* also alludes to Nineveh, the capital of ancient Assyria on the left bank of the Tigris river opposite the present-day city of Mosul in Iraq. The city suffered when conquered by Nebuchadnezzar's father Nabopolassar in 612

BC. The account of this event in the Bible seems to prophesy that the city or this area will suffer great tribulations at the time of the end. (Nahum 3:7) According to some traditions, the Jews who were subdued by Nebuchadnezzar when he conquered Jerusalem knew many felicitous songs but refused to play them for the conqueror when requested by him since he had committed such atrocities.

By melodies of *Nay-navá*, Ṭáhirih could thus mean the Iraqi melodies, since the Báb had been in that region several times and since Bahá'u'lláh spent ten years there. In this sense, the allusion might thus mean that now is the time to sing the happy melodies of Nineveh that have not been played since the Jews were conquered by Nebuchadnezzar. Or she might also be alluding to the sad events associated with Karbilá (the lamentations of Nineveh) but this would not seem to be appropriate to the happy and energetic tone of the couplets that follow this first couplet.

From our relatively incomplete explication of this single word, one can begin to appreciate the possible levels of meaning in each of these pieces and the open-mindedness and creativity with which the reader must approach Ṭáhirih's work.

We can think of the following interpretations of the first couplet:

'O' My Qurratu'l-'Ayn come into singing, singing the sad music melodies of Iraq (Karbilá or Nineveh)
'O' My Qurratu'l-'Ayn become opulent by the opulent melodies of the music of the flute
'O' My Qurratu'l-'Ayn become opulent by the opulent Iraqi melodies.
'O' My Qurratu'l-'Ayn come into singing, sing the melodies of the Iraqi music.

Considering the couplet that follows, the first one makes the most sense.

86. Mount Sinai where Moses received the ten commandments. This image is used frequently as a symbol of the light of revelation which shatters former understanding of reality with the new knowledge revealed through the advent of the Manifestation.

87. *Zarrát*: plural of the Arabic *Zarra*, meaning 'particle', or 'atom', and it can also refer to particles seen when the sunlight shines through a window or opening. In Ṭáhirih's verse, this word appears frequently and alludes to the particles of dust that dance about when the rays of sun shine through a window – she likens them to the dead bodies that have turned to dust but that will become resurrected on the Day of Resurrection. Thus, Shoghi Effendi translates a similar phrase from Ṭáhirih as follows: 'behold the souls of His lovers dancing, moth-like, in the light that has flashed from His face.' (*Dawn-Breakers*, p. 286)

88. Literally 'wholesome eyes', implying 'perfect' or 'immaculate' but, as applied to the Manifestation, implying eyes capable of seeing the reality beyond outward appearances.

89. *Zarrátíyán*: the plural of *zarráti* (from the same root as the word above for 'particle' but here used to imply that which belongs to a particle.) In verses of Rumi and in ḥadíth, the term alludes to the lifeless bodies who will rise in response to the blowing of the trumpet on the Day of Resurrection.
90. *Sa'id*: 'dirt', 'earth' or 'grave'. According to the Báb in the Persian Bayán (221), the 'first unconsciousness' alludes to the severity of His Revelation which caused the majority of the people to be considered as spiritually dead and, thus, unable to come to terms with the 'second unconsciousness' (the Revelation of Bahá'u'lláh). This 'unconsciousness' happened, He says, even though God in His great mercy sent the Báb as the last gate so that people would be saved from unconsciousness.

    Consequently, it is quite possible that Ṭáhirih here is asking Bahá'u'lláh (Qurratu'l-'Ayn) to revive unconscious ones with His Revelation.
91. In the Persian Bayán the Báb says that 'Him Whom God will make manifest' will rise from the grave and with his rising all people will also rise from their graves (i.e. the Day of Resurrection).
92. Bahá'u'lláh, *Kitáb-i-Aqdas*, para. 4.
93. A dark makeup.
94. The source for this poem is Nuqabá'í, *Huqúq-i-Zan* (61), taken from a handwritten manuscript in the Department of Oriental Manuscripts, British Museum, London.
95. Bahá'u'lláh states the following: 'The knowledge of Him, Who is the Origin of all things, and attainment unto Him, are impossible save through knowledge of, and attainment unto, these luminous Beings who proceed from the Sun of Truth. By attaining, therefore, to the presence of these holy Luminaries, the "Presence of God" Himself is attained. From their knowledge, the knowledge of God is revealed, and from the light of their countenance, the splendour of the Face of God is made manifest.' (Bahá'u'lláh, *Kitáb-i-Íqán*, p. 142)
96. See *Dawn-Breakers*, pp. 601–11.
97. In addition to alluding to the martyrdom of Ḥájí Sulaymán Khán, the word 'calamity' itself becomes part of the common parlance of the mystic tradition. It implies the suffering endured in the path of search for the Friend or the Beloved, as well as those tribulations with which one is tested after having discovered the Beloved, calamities which ultimately strengthen the certitude of the lover/believer.
98. As in 'The Voice of God's Command' (no. 3), *lá* (no) and *illá* (except) are taken from the phrase *'lá iláha illá-(A)lláh'*, meaning 'There is *no* beloved *except* God' in the Islamic call to prayer. In the last couplet, *lá* (no) has been interpreted to refer to the negation of all things and detachment of self from all in the universe; *illá* (except) refers to the existence of God. To get close to God and to feel His nearness, one should first denounce the world of existence and enter the realm of nothingness. Rumi says in this regard: 'You became "*lá*", therefore take your dwelling by the "*illá*"/Isn't that strange that you are both

the captive and the king.' (Gawharín, *Farhang*, vol. 8, p. 124)

99. *Fuqará* is the plural of *Faqír* meaning 'needy and poor'. In the Qur'án (35:15–17) we find the following: 'O men! ye are but paupers in need of God; but God is the Rich, the Praiseworthy! If He please, He could sweep you away, and bring forth a new creation!'

Faqír in mystical terminology is the one who is detached from all else save God. Also, he is the one who is aware of his dependency on God. It is also employed to refer to the one who has achieved the station of *Faná* or nothingness (in God) (Sajjádí 363–8). Compare this concept to the seventh valley in Bahá'u'lláh's *The Seven Valleys* – the valley of 'True Poverty and Absolute Nothingness'.

100. In some poems 'particles' alludes to souls, whereas in some other poems Ṭáhirih alludes to the 'created' universe as manifesting the attributes of God down to the smallest constituent part (the atom or the particle). This distinction, discussed frequently by 'Abdu'l-Bahá, is used to distinguish the physical or created universe (which is composite and therefore subject to decomposition) from the spiritual world (which is non-composite and therefore not subject to decomposition). Here, then, Ṭáhirih is saying (as she states in other poems) that every created thing bears the attributes or the imprint of the Creator.

101. Refer to note 98 for the meaning of *lá* and *illá*. This line means something like this: Whoever becomes aware of the reality of God's station (i.e. that there is no beloved except God – that all reality, whether in this world or the unseen world, is but some expression of God) would gladly acknowledge and submit to the reality of his own being as having meaning only insofar as it participates in the expression of Godliness. Or stated in a more positive way, whoever realizes the nature of God realizes that his individual reality has no meaning apart from its realization of its divine purpose. This concept of nothingness, then, is not by any means the notion of the obliteration of the self, nor is it to be understood as self-denial or self-effacement in any common sense of these terms but rather self-fulfilment by realizing that the fullest expression of individual power and capacity is in willingly participating in the divine plan of God. See Hatcher, *The Arc of Ascent* for a full discussion of this concept.

102. This is ambiguous – is this Ṭáhirih's heart or the heart of the Prophet? The word *Majnún* means insane and is derived from the classical Persian lover 'who searches for his beloved Laylí'. (Momen, *Basic Bahá'í Dictionary*, p. 143)

103. *Qibáb* means 'tents'. This word in gnostic terminology means the human limitations that hide the station of the perfect man from the people.(Nurbakhsh, *Treasury of Sufi Terms*, vol. 2, p. 85) A Ḥadíth Qudsí says: 'My friends are under my tents (*qibáb*). Except for me no one would know them.' Ṭáhirih may be referring to her own lofty spiritual station, implying that she has raised her tents (*qibáb*) under the tabernacle of the Beloved (the figure of Laylí has been used at times in Persian poems to refer to the beloved).

104. 'Those who sit in fire' may be referring to those with a high spiritual station. Some mystics in the Kurdistan province of Iran (the Kurds) were able to sit in large flaming fires without getting burned.

Fire in gnostic terminology signifies the fire of the love of God that purifies the physical body. Also, fire signifies the perfect man who overcomes his material desires. The 'fire of soul' refers to the fire of unity with God and the station of nothingness that burns away the world of opposites and multiplicity. It also refers to the flame of the soul whose warmth is due to the divine favour and blessing (Gawharín, *Farhang*, vol. 1, pp. 22–7). Ṭáhirih therefore may be saying here: 'The fire of my heart burned all the veils. The fire of my soul is so intensive that it set ablaze the tents of the "fire sitters".' Thus we may compare the fire in her soul with the 'fire of Moses' in the next couplet, though she could also be alluding to the fire emanating from the Manifestation.

105. The fire through which God talked to Moses and commanded him to guide the people. Qur'án (28:29– 32):

> And when he had fulfilled his term and was journeying with his folk, Moses descried a fire on the mountain-side. He said to his people: 'Stay here, for I can see a fire. Perhaps I can bring you news, or a lighted torch with which you may warm yourselves.' When he came near, a voice called out to him from a bush in a blessed spot on the right side of the valley, saying: 'Moses, I am Alláh, Lord of the Creation. Throw down your staff.' And when he saw his staff writhing like a serpent, he turned his back and fled, running on and on. 'Moses,' said the voice, 'approach and have no fears. You are safe. Put your hand in your pocket: it will come out white, although unharmed . . .'

In these verses of the Qur'án we see the fear of Moses when faced with God's power and His astonishment at the extraordinary station bestowed to Him by God (put your hand in your pocket: it will come out white). In this couplet Ṭáhirih refers to the astonishment and anxiety that is felt when one encounters the 'fire of Moses' such as Ṭáhirih has found in the Revelation of the Báb. The Báb refers to His Revelation as God speaking at the mountain of Ṭúr in His commentary on the Súrih of Joseph (53), 'I am the Tree in Ṭúr.'

106. A reference to God or to the Prophet, implying inspiration she needs to convey the concept to the believers. While this image is often used and has various possible meanings, it most often implies that the 'wine' from the Cupbearer is wisdom or knowledge or words adequate to convey to others spiritual verities.

107. It could also be read as a secret that has not been previously revealed.

108. This pronoun is indeed thought-provoking. Is Ṭáhirih including herself as part of those involved in the process of revelation (i.e. the Báb, Bahá'u'lláh, Quddús, etc.) or is she referring to those who have

been transformed (the believers and followers)?

109. incantation, spell, charm or magic

110. *Bahám*, as is in Afnán's version. Fáḍil's version, however, has *híyám*, meaning 'ecstasy' and 'madness of love' or 'ẹxtreme thirst'. Fáḍil's version seems correct to us.

111. fortress, safety or fence

112. 'Pavilion', also means 'banquet' and 'festivity'. 'Banquet' in Sufi terminology indicates ecstasy. If we take this word to mean 'banquet', the line would indicate something like this: 'The security of ecstasy of your nearness is the object of this heart.'

113. *Kúy*: Region of (town), place, district, lane. In Persian poetry, to take residence in (or to desire) the beloved's quarter, symbolizes dedication to the beloved. In gnostic terminology it indicates the station of servitude. (Sajjádí, *Farhang*, p. 397; Nurbakhsh, *Treasury of Sufi Terms*, pp. 283–4)

114. We translated the word *qamám* ('cloud') as 'shadow' here to make the meaning clearer. This phrase and this line can be variously translated and interpreted but in the context of the rest of Ṭáhirih's verse, it would seem here that she is referring to the idea expressed through the writings of the Báb, Bahá'u'lláh and 'Abdu'l-Bahá that physical reality is but a shadowy reflection of the world of the spirit: e.g. 'Know thou that the Kingdom is the real world, and this nether place is only its shadow stretching out. A shadow hath no life of its own; its existence is only a fantasy, and nothing more; it is but images reflected in water, and seeming as pictures to the eye.' ('Abdu'l-Bahá, *Selections*, p. 178) Of course, this concept of phenomenal reality as but a reflection of the world of the spirit (which is the 'real' world) is also quite Platonic, as are so many of the images derived from Sufi philosophy, much of which has its roots in Platonism.

Another reading of this line might be the following: 'The clouds which provide me with shade and comfort from the heat of the sun would be destroyed by the heat of tribulation in the path of your love.' In other words, the tribulations or calamities, though outwardly grievous, burn away the veils that conceal the world of the spirit from my understanding.

115. fierce, intrepid; also a high-minded king or a person with courage, magnanimity and high aspirations

116. The concept here literally is that the lover/believer states that only when the Beloved separates us from all that is not of God will the heart be assured of firmness or constancy.

117. Here the concept of the soul as an emanation from God is clearly expressed, once again revealing Ṭáhirih's exquisite understanding of those concepts that will later become discussed and explained by Bahá'u'lláh and 'Abdu'l-Bahá.

118. The ironic ending here is clearly rhetorical. Having discovered the Beloved and having become afire with the blaze of love for God, the 'burning heart' can find no peace so long as it remains attached to earthly forms. Hence, throughout her poetry, Ṭáhirih expresses a

longing to attain the realm of the spirit, to become annihilated (i.e. reunited with the Beloved), much as Socrates states in the *Crito* of Plato that the true Philosopher King (Socrates' equivalent of the Manifestation) longs for death because the spiritual reality is the 'real' world.

119. As noted in other poems, the mole or beauty mark on the face is alluded to a seed that attracts the bird of the heart which then becomes entangled in the snare of the beloved's tresses.
120. This line calls to mind Desdemona's recounting of how she came to fall in love with Othello by hearing him talk about his heroic exploits in battle.
121. Also: 'good people', 'fair ones' or 'beautiful ones'.
122. This tradition of being in love (or 'love sick') is discussed a great deal in early Arabic mystical verse and later (around the 12th century beginning in Provençal, France) as part of the so-called courtly love tradition.
123. Also: 'Permanence', a name of God.
124. A 'cavalier' or brave solider or king who is adept at horsemanship. We have used the French term *chevalier* because of its beauty, though with appropriate acknowledgements to a similar use by Gerard Manley Hopkins in his poem 'The Windhover' (his allusion to Christ).
125. The fifth part always ends with the word 'I' and rhymes with the fifth part of all other sections. Also, in the first section of the poem, this fifth part rhymes with the pair of couplets of that section.

    The poem is thus like a musical composition in which an introductory part sets the tone and introduces a melody and then repeats that particular melody at regular intervals throughout the piece. In terms of meaning, the fourth and fifth parts are generally connected. They form a complete and meaningful continuity by themselves even if they are separated from the first three parts of the section, except for sections 13 and 17 in which the fourth and fifth lines do not make sense if isolated from the section. Lines 1, 2 and 3, however, usually set the tone for lines 4 and 5.
126. We have translated the word *mihr* as 'sun of your being', though the word can simply imply 'love'. Translating *mihr* as sun gives another meaning to the poem. For example, in Ṭáhirih's poem 'Face to Face' (no. 27) we also find the concept of small particles ascending towards the sun, as if being absorbed by the sun.

    The image of the particles of dust that become light, detach themselves from the earthly world and ascend dancing in the air of the Beloved's face seems appropriate here. Rumi uses this same conceit when he alludes to a mountain beginning to dance because of its ecstasy.
127. A reference to the story of creation in the Qur'án (15:29).
128. *Yád*: 'remembrance'. This word probably should be *yár* meaning 'friend' – hence: 'I am eternal because of the Friend and, at the same time, I am a mortal.' This makes sense; however, in the only copy of this poem we have seen, the word is *yád*. Furthermore, there is little

difference between the two except that remembrance implies prayer or an active role on the part of the transformed speaker, something that the Bahá'í writings often allude to as an essential ingredient in personal transformation or spiritual ascent.

129. We have used 'emboldened' here though the original implies 'disgraced' in a sense usually applied in this tradition to a secret love that has now become disclosed or public.
130. See Qur'án 7:143. Moses asks God to show Himself.
131. The literally meaning here is 'quarter' or 'vicinity' or 'neighbourhood' but the sense of the term is any sort of proximity to the Friend; hence we have employed 'nearness'.
132. The actual word is *hayáhú* or 'clamour'. Rumi uses a similar term, *háy-húy*, to describe the condition of ecstasy: 'I am bored with (my heart is saddened because of) these complaining weeping people/ That clamour and loud cry of the drunk is what I wish.' (Gawharín, *Farhang*, vol. 9. p. 274) Even closer to the sense here is found in another verse from Rumi: 'Under the crystalline sphere, no single person would remain sober,/ since from all sides your clamour is heard.' (ibid. p. 237)

    By translating the word more directly as 'ecstasy', we are not trying to impose an interpretation on the reader but simply conveying more clearly the sense of the word as it is intended here.
133. The phrase 'the torch that illuminates the universe' has been used to refer to Muḥammad and to the sun.
134. The word *A'lá* we have translated as 'the Lord Most High' because it is a title for the Báb used in the Bahá'í texts. Its literary meaning is 'the Higher' or 'the Highest'. In the poem 'Behold the Worlds of God' in Chapter Five we have translated this word as 'high' ('the High Lord'), a title for the Báb, a title that Pharaoh in his ignorance and pride used for himself. Shoghi Effendi used 'Supreme' as a translation for *A'lá* in the Arabic Hidden word.
135. This could also be read as the 'valley of His Love'. The term *vádí* has been translated in Bahá'í literature as 'valley', e.g. *The Seven Valleys*.
136. *Bulbulih*: The sound you hear when pouring wine from a container which has a narrow opening (a long neck with a narrow opening) . The bubbling sound is the result of the air gradually letting the wine out, as from a wine flask. The word has two other meanings both appropriate for this poem: 'Sorrows and difficulties' (e.g. for how long should I hide my sorrows of love); and 'Temptations' (for how long should I hide my temptations of love).
137. Possibly here Ṭáhirih is alluding to her desire to teach the Faith overtly rather than conceal what she has discovered.
138. The sense here is that there is no hope that the speaker may become rational or calm – she is too caught up in the ecstasy she is experiencing. Tavern (*maykhánih*) is a gnostic term – the station of *láhút* (divinity) and Unity of Essence that has filled the cup of all determinations of existence (determinations in God's Knowledge). (Nurbakhsh, *Treasury of Sufi Terms*, vol. 1, p. 160) The phrase here would imply that the

speaker has recognized her divine origin and is determined to remain in touch with her spiritual reality forever.

139. *Himmat*: 'High-mindedness, strong will, bravery, generosity, perfect objective, endeavour.' In gnostic terminology, this is the attention and endeavour of heart with all its spiritual forces turned towards God to obtain perfections for self or for others.
140. 'Am I not your Lord' as this phrase relates to the story of creation.
141. 'Lowly' or 'nonexistent' (all nonexistent particles acquired the attributes of existence by taking on divine attributes). Gnostic term: The person who cannot with the wing of high-aspiration (*himmat*) fly to the stages of divine perfection or to any stage of progress. In that sense, this line refers to the previous section where Ṭáhirih tells how she has been elevated by the power of the love of God to a state of having high aspirations and seeking only God. Another meaning is 'reposeful, restful and comfortable': i.e. the restful particles acquired the attribute of becoming light like dust (selfless) and floating in the air towards the sun (this analogy is also used in other poems).
142. At certain times of the day (sunrise, sunset, etc.) assigned government employees (soldiers) used to play drums to inform people of events. It seems that Ṭáhirih is saying that she is an obedient servant like the ones who beat the drums without failure or delay.
143. *Murgh-i-Shabáviz*: a bird that at night hangs with its claws off a branch and howls – possibly a screech owl. This bird is also alluded to as the one that tells the truth. In the western literary tradition, the owl represents wisdom and warning. In this context, Ṭáhirih is alluding to herself as one who forewarns everyone that the Beloved has come, even though it is the nighttime and few are aware.
144. Again, in mystic terms, the state of poverty and nothingness are the highest condition one can attain, a state of being unaware of the ego or the self and intensely aware of one's unity with the divine reality.
145. This closing section is distinct in tone and content from previous sections. The tone is mild, lacking the energy and excitement of previous sections. Instead, it is a melodious description of Ṭáhirih's heart and her dedication in servitude to her Beloved.
146. Browne, *Materials for the Study*, p. 343.
147. See Gawharín, *Farhang*, vol. 5, p. 228.
148. Sajjádí, *Farhang*, p. 282.
149. A gnostic meaning of the cupbearer is the perfect guide and spiritual leader. We notice that Rúḥu'lláh Varqá, an early Bahá'í scholar and poet who was martyred at the age of 12 along with his father, in his amazingly moving and beautiful *Sáqí-Námih* uses the image of the cupbearer to refer to 'Abdu'l-Bahá, the son of Bahá'u'lláh who was appointed by Bahá'u'lláh as His successor and the Centre of His Covenant.
150. Gawharín, *Farhang*, vol. 6.
151. *Futúḥ* (Victory), also can mean: relief; achieving a thing when it was not expected to be achieved. (Gawharín, *Farhang*, vol. 7, p. 68) It is also a gnostic term implying the relief of the wayfarer's heart. Rumi

uses a similar analogy: 'And from the atmosphere in which the Phoenix of the soul/ formerly has seen the flight and victory (*futúḥ*).' Rumi also uses the term to mean salvation. (ibid.)

152. Literally, the 'wine of the spirit', *Ṣahbá*, wine from red grapes. In gnostic terminology it refers to the ancient manifestation of God's attributes at the beginning of creation (the day of 'Am I not?'). (Nurbakhsh, *Treasury of Sufi Terms*, vol. 1, p. 111) Wine in gnostic terminology is the ecstasy of the gnostic as a result of the mention of God, an ecstasy that makes him intoxicated. (ibid. p. 108) The sealed wine (*raḥíq-i-makhtúm*) is the wine the righteous will drink of in the Day of the End according to the Qur'án 83:25–6: 'Choice sealed wine shall be given them to quaff,/ The seal of musk. For this let those pant who pant for bliss.' Since the twin Revelations of the Báb and Bahá'u'lláh are understood by Bahá'ís to be the time of the end or the Day of Resurrection, then her allusion to wine throughout the poem alludes to the Revelation itself (the revealed scripture) as well as the spiritual power unleashed by the appearance of the Prophet of God to transform both the individual and civilization as a whole.

153. According to myth, the salamander could live in fire; hence, the word came to allude to a person or thing that could endure fire. Here Ṭáhirih is clearly alluding to herself as one who delights in the fire (intensity and calamity) of being a follower of the new Revelation. Thus, she is saying that since she is one of those immersed in the fire of this Faith, she would like to be given a draught of the choice wine of the Revelation.

154. As she does so often in her poetry, Ṭáhirih here alludes to the beauty of the face of the Beloved as a symbol of her love for the spiritual station or beauty of the Manifestation of God, by using a traditional image of Persian poetry of the 'moonlike' face.

155. The 'Friend' is common in mystic verse, referring either to the Prophet of God or to some other spiritual luminary – for Rumi, for example, it was Shams of Tabríz. For Ṭáhirih the term always alludes to the Manifestation, though sometimes she speaks of the Báb, sometimes of Bahá'u'lláh and sometimes of both at the same time.

156. See Qur'án 7:139: 'And when God manifested Himself to the mountain he turned it to dust! and Moses fell in a swoon.'

157. Both the physical world and the spiritual world – i.e. I will be in a state of complete ecstasy or love and therefore oblivious.

158. Considering the gnostic meaning of the tresses of the Beloved (which means the multiplicity and confusion of the physical world), this passage could be interpreted as follows: Do not abandon me to the confusion and sufferings of the physical world; grant me spiritual solace to remove my sorrow and affliction.

159. Here we see that once the ecstasy of nearness has been attained, the mystic longs to attain that state again. One experience only increases the desire for more and greater sojourns into the realm of nearness.

160. *Azal*: Ancient Eternity; the Covenant of God with humankind at the

dawn of creation when man responded with 'Yes, yes' to His call of 'Am I not your Lord?'

161. In gnostic thought, the worlds of *malakút* and *jabarút*; in a more general sense, the spiritual realm or the realm of pure forms.
162. This is, no doubt, the same sea alluded to in the previous poem, 'The Realm of Ecstasy'. (no. 17)
163. The analogy of the sea and the pearl used here is similar to onc wc discovered in Rumi's poetry. Ṭáhirih says, 'Take me by His ocean so that I might plunge into that water' (i.e. become annihilated and obtain a pearl that is my soul – meaning that, as a seeker, she would discover the pearl of her own soul in God's ocean).

    In Rumi's poem, the shore represents the physical world and the sea the world of spirits. In one verse a drunken man is asked about his identity. He responds: Half of me is at the shore; the other half is a pearl.
164. Literally, a sheet spread on the ground to set dishes of food for a picnic.
165. One might interpret this and the verse that follows as asking Bahá'u'lláh to manifest His divine mission, to shine His radiance and to summon the angelic believers to serve His Faith.
166. The *ḥúrí* is a handmaiden who dwells in paradise, alluded to in the Qur'án. Bahá'u'lláh explains that these are figuratively the spiritual mysteries that will in the next life become unveiled or clear. The *qilmán* is the male equivalent of the *ḥúrí*, a young lad who serves in paradise.

    This entire setting is meant to convey the idea that when the Manifestation appears, both heaven and earth rejoice and feel the results of this joyous occasion.
167. Now that Ṭáhirih has described how all of creation celebrates the joyous occasion of the new Revelation and she has called on the cup-bearer to bestow the wine on the 'heart-weary' lovers, she returns to the theme of her personal part in this process.
168. From a famous couplet of a poem by Firdawsí quoted here by Ṭáhirih with minor change (see Dihkhudá, *Lughat*, vol. 44, p. 297).
169. A title of the Báb.
170. In the verses that now follow Ṭáhirih goes beyond praising this moment in the history of humankind or even Prophets – she tries, with stated humility, to allude to the exalted station of God. It is a remarkable piece of writing in which she explains clearly that however much one adores the Prophet, it is God that gives them all power and authority, that all religions are products of one divine plan and one light of knowledge and that, consequently, all conflict among religions is ludicrous and ill-founded.
171. Here Ṭáhirih employs the rhetorical device known as *sprezzatura*, a form of self-effacement used by such poets as Petrarch, wherein the poet laments his or her inability to praise adequately the beloved while in the midst of doing it. In effect, she is using eloquent praise of God to exclaim her own inability to praise God.

172. *Qá'im* ('the one who is standing') refers to the Báb. *Qayyúm* means that which has no beginning, which is eternal, independent, self-subsisting; it was a title used in the Báb's and Bahá'u'lláh's writings for Bahá'u'lláh (just as *Qá'im* is used for the Báb). On one occasion it has been used by the Báb to refer to Himself. (Ghadimi, p. 640) Here as elsewhere, Ṭáhirih is clearly aware that the Báb and Bahá'u'lláh are both Manifestations and integral parts of one divine process. In some poems she even alludes to the events that will take place in the history of the Bábí and Bahá'í Faiths after her death.

173. This would seem to allude to the Prophets and probably means, along with the following lines, that even those who to us are perfect reflections of God's attributes (i.e. the Manifestations) profess their utter servitude and subservience to God.

174. See Bahá'u'lláh, *Kitáb-i-Íqán*, p. 178. A reference to the Manifestations. This couplet could also refer to mystics who performed miracles and said: 'I am God.'

175. This axiom would seem to allude to the same truth that 'Abdu'l-Bahá discusses in *Some Answered Questions* that one cannot imagine a creator without a creation. Therefore we cannot imagine a time when humankind (the fruit of creation) did not exist.

In one respect the fruit refers to the Revelation of Bahá'u'lláh, which was the fruit of the Revelation of the Báb and which completed the Bayán. In these couplets Ṭáhirih is addressing the divine reality in Bahá'u'lláh, the eternal reality of the Primal Point (which is manifested in all the atoms of the universe and grants life and existence to them). This is also the reality that manifested itself at every age and its manifestation at this age is the purpose (the culmination and consummation) of all religions of the past:

> A Revelation, hailed as the promise and crowning glory of past ages and centuries, as the consummation of all the Dispensations within the Adamic Cycle, inaugurating an era of at least a thousand years' duration, and a cycle destined to last no less than five thousand centuries, signalizing the end of the Prophetic Era and the beginning of the Era of Fulfilment, unsurpassed alike in the duration of its Author's ministry and the fecundity and splendour of His mission – such a Revelation was, as already noted, born amidst the darkness of a subterranean dungeon in Ṭihrán – an abominable pit that had once served as a reservoir of water for one of the public baths of the city. (Shoghi Effendi, *God Passes By*, p. 100)

176. The word *Khudá* in this and other couplets means 'God'. A related word *Khudávand* means 'God, owner, chief, or master'. In old Persian, it was also used for kings. Therefore, another reading of this couplet is: Because of you, the majesty of the kings and of the majestic ones is manifested.

177. Literally, 'the first of the last', though we presume this is an allusion

to the Quranic passage of the Manifestations being 'the first and the last; the Seen and the Hidden'. (57:3)

178. Though quite elliptical in nature, this is one of Ṭáhirih's profound indications of the sophistication of her understanding of the concepts discussed by 'Abdu'l-Bahá in the *Lawḥ-i-Aflák* of the chain of being and the manner in which all creation reflects divine attributes.

179. Here Ṭáhirih alludes to the concept discussed in the Qur'án and in the writings of the Báb and Bahá'u'lláh of the successive revelations of God throughout history as one continuous process.

180. This is quite subtle (and humorous). In effect, she is stating that if logically she as a human being with limited understanding can only perceive or understand the individual names of God as they become manifest to her (as opposed to the unified Essence itself), then relatively speaking, her belief in the Divine Unity is mere polytheism – a belief in the various expressions of divine virtue. Consequently, her inadequate understanding of and expression of God is (relatively speaking) mere blasphemy. But, she goes on to note, if she is a failure in this regard (an infidel), she is still a product of this same Divine Creator; therefore, how bad can she be? Here Ṭáhirih dares to be coy with God Himself.

181. The humour in this couplet is delightful. In effect, she is setting forth an incontrovertible argument proving that God must love and accept her because it would be against His nature to do otherwise, just as it would be counter to her nature not to falter at times. Therefore, in the last two couplets she asks for the amount of grace (wine) appropriate to one such as she.

182. Literally, this line states that if she becomes nonexistent (the state of nothingness or selflessness for which the mystic strives), then God can grant her existence (of another sort). Here, too, she is being playful, stating that since God is Creator and Omnipotent, were she to become nonexistent, He could create her again in some other form.

183. Quoted in Nabíl, *The Dawn-Breakers*, p. 286.

184. Nabíl, *The Dawn-Breakers*, pp. 285–6.

185. Bahá'u'lláh has stated that it was during that this four-month period of incarceration that He felt 'the first stirrings of God's revelation within His soul'. (Shoghi Effendi, *God Passes By*, p. 101)

186. While various versions of this poem exist, we have composed a version by careful comparison of the Nuqabá'í, the Martha Root and the Afnán versions and by modifying two words that seem to have been copied erroneously in all existing versions.

187.

> Undeterred, unruffled, exultant with joy, Ṭáhirih arose, and, without the least premeditation and in a language strikingly resembling that of the Qur'án, delivered a fervid and eloquent appeal to the remnant of the assembly, ending it with this bold assertion: 'I am the Word which the Qá'im is to utter, the Word which shall put to flight the chiefs and nobles of the earth!' Thereupon, she invited them to embrace each other and celebrate so great an occasion.

On that memorable day the 'Bugle' mentioned in the Qur'án was sounded, the 'stunning trumpet-blast' was loudly raised, and the 'Catastrophe' came to pass. The days immediately following so startling a departure from the time-honoured traditions of Islám witnessed a veritable revolution in the outlook, habits, ceremonials and manner of worship of these hitherto zealous and devout upholders of the Muḥammadan Law. Agitated as had been the Conference from first to last, deplorable as was the secession of the few who refused to countenance the annulment of the fundamental statutes of the Islamic Faith, its purpose had been fully and gloriously accomplished. (Shoghi Effendi, *God Passes By*, pp. 32–3)

188. A reference to a well-known saying: 'We did not know You fully, and we did not worship You properly.' The couplet thus implies that the veil has been lifted from the face of the One about whom it was said, 'We cannot know You properly.'
189. The advent of the Manifestation compared to the arrival of dawn is a commonplace image in Bábí and Bahá'í scripture.
190. In Persian poetry, *Ṣanam* is 'idol' or 'the Beloved'. *Ṣamad* is Arabic for a leader or chieftain. The Báb referred to Himself in the *Qayyúmu'l-Asmá'* with terms such as 'the Arabian Youth' and 'the Persian Youth'. These are references to His descent from Muḥammad and His Persian heritage. He also called Himself 'the Eastern Western Youth', perhaps a reference to His divine aspect which is neither eastern nor western in origin. (Muḥammad-Ḥusayní, *Yúsif-i-Bahá*, pp. 60–1)
191. *Fá* is Fars or Persia, perhaps an allusion to the spread throughout the land of the Bábí religion; *Ṭá* is the city of Ṭihrán, the birthplace of Bahá'u'lláh, thus the source of the new light or knowledge that would illumine the world; and *Há*, the letter *H*, is a variable symbol but it is a reference to the Divine World of the Absolute. It could also be a reference to the Báb since He used the letter *há* to refer to Himself in the *Qayyúmu'l-Asmá'*.
192. 'Moon' and 'moon-face' are allusions to the beauteous face of the Beloved – in this case the manifestation (the Báb or, more likely, Bahá'u'lláh). The idea of this being a 'full' moon would further make it likely that Ṭáhirih is alluding to Bahá'u'lláh as the completion of the process whereby the Promised Day has been fulfilled.
193. In gnostic terminology, the sea alludes to the manifestation of the divine spirit throughout the universe. (Gawharín, *Farhang*, vol. 8, p. 492)
194. Karbilá is the desert where the Imám Ḥusayn was martyred. Water was scarce in the battle in that harsh and dry desert. When 'Abbás, a member of the holy family, went to get water, the enemy cut off his hand. Thirst, search for water and the dryness of the desert are indispensable motifs in the story of Karbilá. S͟hí'í Muslims often remind themselves of the Karbilá episode before drinking water by mentioning Imám Ḥusayn's name.

195. The moon here (as usual) alludes to the beauty of the face of the beloved. The arc and snare have double meanings. The arc refers to the bow which shoots arrows as the glances of the eye pierce the heart of the lover. The snare trembles the multitudes and disperses dynasties.
196. The original reads 'Aḥmad Muṣṭafá', titles of Muḥammad.
197. This alludes to the trembling of Muḥammad when the revelation took place. In Súrih 74:1, the verse states, 'O thou, enwrapped in thy mantle!/ Arise and warn!' According to a ḥadíth, when Muḥammad was leaving the cave of Ḥarra' where He would go to meditate and pray, He heard a voice. He looked all around but saw no one. He then heard the voice for a second time and saw the angel Gabriel in the air. He became frightened and rushed home trembling and asked His wife to cover Him with blankets.
198. The Báb uses similar phrases in *Ṣaḥífiy-i-'Adlíyyih*, pp. 2 and 4.
199. In Platonic philosophy there exists on the spiritual plane a 'form' or 'idea' of beauty from which particular objects assume an individual expression of this quality. But beside the beauty of the Beloved, these forms are trivial.
200. While this could be mere hyperbole, one becomes impressed through Ṭáhirih's poetry of her remarkable knowledge – she often alludes to future events. Consequently, she may well here be alluding to her awareness of her later martyrdom.
201. Here, too, Ṭáhirih could be alluding to the physical presence of the Prophet or, more likely, her ascent to the spiritual realm, something she longs for in many of her poems.
202. *Fá*, should be a reference to the province of Fárs, an allusion to the Báb. Also the word *bihjat* ('joy') is a reference to Bihjat (Karím Khán-i-Máfí), the believer with whom she had corresponded.
203. A reference to the city of Ṭihrán, an allusion to Bahá'u'lláh.
204. 'Mirrors' could convey different meanings. In the Báb's writings, the hierarchy of the spiritual world is symbolized by a chain of mirrors, each reflecting in itself the image of a higher mirror. God or the Primal Will is at the top of this sequence or chain of reality. Then, in descending order, are the mirrors that represent Manifestations who reflect perfectly the attributes of God, the mirrors that are the first believers in each revelation (e.g. the Letters of the Living), the mirrors that are the other believers who reflect the light of the first believers. (See Persian Bayán, pp. 5, 203, 208)

Thus, the 'drop of spring (new) rain' are the latest 'mirrors' of the Primal Will: the Báb (the 'joy of Fars') and Bahá'u'lláh (the 'delight of Ṭihrán'). In the third couplet, the transformation of *Há* to *Abhá* refers to the transformation of the Primal Will as it is reflected in the Báb's Revelation to the reflection of the Primal Will in the Revelation of Bahá'u'lláh.

Because of the immaturity of the people and as an act of kindness to them, the Báb revealed His station to the public gradually and in stages. First He was known as the gate to the Hidden Imám, then as the Imám himself, next as an independent Prophet and finally as the Lord, the Manifestation of God's names and attributes. Though a few believers could see His true station in His earliest writings, to the average or common believer the magnitude and severity of the new Revelation was not originally known. Bahá'u'lláh explains that if the Báb had revealed His station at the beginning of His mission, people would have done to Him immediately what they eventually did (execute Him). Even a gradual disclosure of the mission of the Báb caused severe tests for some believers. To reduce the magnitude of the shock associated with the new Revelation, the Báb hid His true station from the majority of the people. In one epistle to Muḥammad S͟háh He says: 'In brief, I hold within My grasp whatsoever any man might wish of the good of this world and of the next. Were I to remove the veil, all would recognize Me as their Best Beloved, and no one would deny Me.' (The Báb, *Selections*, p. 15) The notion of appearance of the Manifestation of God from behind the veil is seen in Ṭáhirih's poems, as in the sixth couplet in this poem.

The Báb explains in His writings that in the mirror of the station of 'the Gate' the sun of the station of the Imám is reflected and in the mirror of the station of Imám, the sun of Prophethood, and in the mirror of Prophethood, the sun of Lordship is reflected. These various aspects of the Manifestation could also be what Ṭáhirih is alluding to in this couplet.

This may also be an allusion to the prominent early believers since 'mirror' was a title the Báb bestowed on them. For example, in the following passage He addresses His followers as 'Mirrors', warning them that, though having recognized Himself, they may still fail to recognize the Manifestation of the Latter Resurrection (Bahá'u'lláh):

> Beware, O concourse of Mirrors, lest on that Day titles make you vainglorious. Know ye of a certainty that ye, together with all those who stand above you or below you, have been created for that Day. Fear ye God and commit not that which would grieve His heart, nor be of them that have gone astray. Perchance He will appear invested with the power of Truth while ye are fast asleep on your couches, or His messengers will bring glorious and resplendent Tablets from Him while ye turn away disdainfully from Him, pronounce sentence against Him – such sentence as ye would never pass on yourselves – and say, 'This is not from God, the All-Subduing, the Self-Existent'. (The Báb, *Selections*, p. 166)

205. *'Amá* was explained above (the stage of the Essence of God (*aḥadiyya*, as opposed to the stage of Manifestation or *waḥidíyya*). *Há* is the Arabic letter equivalent to number 5 (the word *Báb* also adds up to 5). *Abhá* is the superlative form of *Bahá'* and means 'most glorious'. The line could thus imply the desire to ascend from the stage of being 'glorious' to being 'most glorious', or, more likely, this alludes back to the first

couplet and the transition from the Manifestation of the Báb (represented here by *Há*) to the Manifestation of Bahá'u'lláh (represented here by *Abhá*). In other words, the Faith of the Báb which appeared in the region of Fars (*Fá*) will be followed by the Faith of Bahá'u'lláh in the city of Ṭihrán (*Ṭá*).

If we take the letter *Há* to symbolize the Absolute, the phrase might refer to the process by which the Unknown Absolute (the 'Hidden Treasure') desired to make itself known by manifesting itself gradually until it becomes understood in its greatest glory (*Abhá*).

206. *Húsh*. The Báb explains that in all things the Sun of Will (i.e. the Primal Will) is seen, since it is due to the Primal Will that everything becomes existent (see the Persian Bayán, pp. 85 and 107). The use of the word *húsh* thus means 'soul', 'life' or 'spirit' in this context. (See also Gawharín, *Farhang*, vol. 9, p. 327)

207. The 'hidden treasure' is a most important and weighty tradition explicated in detail by Bahá'u'lláh (see *Kitáb-i-Aqdas*, pp. 174–5), that alludes to the entire process by which creation is brought into being as a manifestation of divine attributes whereby human beings might come to understand spiritual concepts and, ultimately, to know God. In a general sense, the Manifestations represent the principal means by which the hidden or concealed attributes of God are made understandable, both through their person and through their words or utterances.

208. *Lá mithl-u-mirá'*: we assume this is a poetic way of using the Arabic expression *Lá mithl wa lá mirá'*, meaning 'It has no equal without any doubt'. This most probably alludes to the passage in the Kitáb-i-Íqán in which Bahá'u'lláh states the following regarding the Báb: 'He also saith that the Qá'im will reveal all the remaining twenty and five letters. Behold from this utterance how great and lofty is His station! His rank excelleth that of all the Prophets, and His Revelation transcendeth the comprehension and understanding of all their chosen ones.' (p. 244)

209. *Ibqá*: To sustain, to protect, to keep alive, to establish, to strengthen, to protect someone's life, to leave intact and in place, to be kind and benevolent.

210. The source of this piece is Nuqabá'í, *Huqúq-i-Zan*, p.162.

211. *Sh'án* also means 'work' or 'affair'. See Qur'án 55:29: 'Every day doth some new work employ Him.'

212. 'Man and djinn' has been mentioned numerous times in the Qur'án, usually in conjunction with the lack of their recognition of the Messengers of God and their punishment in hell. Ṭáhirih here says that in facing this great Manifestation, both man and djinn are offering their lives. Súrih 55:12–13 defines 'man' and 'djinn': 'He created man of clay like that of the potter. And He created the djinn of pure fire.' This same súrih has other references to the nature of 'man' and 'djinn' and various verities about the fundamental nature of creation, each of which is followed by the refrain: 'Which then of the bounties of your Lord will ye twain [men and djinn] deny?' For

example: 'O company of djinn and men, if ye can overpass the bounds of the Heavens and Earth, then overpass them. But by our leave only shall ye overpass them.'(32); 'A bright flash of fire shall be hurled at you both . . .' (35); 'On that day shall neither man nor djinn be asked of his sin.' (39) One can also refer to, for example, 7:177–8 and 41:25 for references to the lack of recognition of God's Messengers. In 41:29 we see that even man and djinn mislead the infidels.

213. We have changed the word slightly from *nasayyarat* to *tasayyarat*, assuming that this is most probably a reference to the Qur'án (18:45): 'And call to mind the day when we will cause the mountains to pass away, and thou shalt see the earth a levelled plain, and we will gather mankind together, and not leave of them any one.'
214. Nuqabá'í, *Huqúq-i-Zan*, p. 152.
215. Dihkhudá, *Lughat*, vol. 33, p. 111.
216. Since 'tresses' in Persian literature sometimes alludes to the manifestation of God's attributes and the 'beauty spot' to the Hidden Essence that is not manifested, Ṭáhirih might here be alluding to the two Manifestations of God (the Báb and Bahá'u'lláh). See Sajjádí, *Farhang*, p. 184 and Narbakhsh, *Treasury of Sufi Terms*, vol. 7, p. 59.
217. The two tresses are like two traps for the bird of the heart and the beauty mark on the face is compared to a seed that the bird is after.
218. Municipal officer or police officer.
219. The word 'cooked' in Persian can also mean 'wise' or 'mature' or 'experienced', as opposed to 'raw' which can imply the opposite. Rumi says: 'The outcome of my life is but three words:/ I was raw, I cooked, then I burnt.' Ṭáhirih here may be alluding to a poem by Rumi in which he observes: 'No raw person will understand the condition of the cooked (the wise one). Therefore, one should shorten the conversation.' In this case, Ṭáhirih plainly states that these two men of 'authority' don't have the slightest idea what they are talking about, so why should she bother to try to argue with them.
220. One morning is the face and the two nights are the tresses hanging on the two sides of the face. However, symbolically, Ṭáhirih here may well be alluding to the two Prophets (the Báb and Bahá'u'lláh) which together bring about the dawn of the new Revelation after the nighttime darkness of the decline of Christianity and Islam, or more likely, the transition from Islam to the Bábí Faith immediately followed by the transition from the Bábí Faith to the Revelation of Bahá'u'lláh.
221. The cask is alluded to as 'pregnant' because it is full and because its swelling shape resembles the image of a pregnant mother. The enigmatic allusion to the 'maiden' could also be translated as 'daughter' or 'virgin'.
222. Literally, 'illegitimate child'; it might be an allusion to the birth of Christ. Thus Ṭáhirih here would be saying that the divine spirit of Christ has now appeared once more in the twin Manifestations of the Báb and Bahá'u'lláh (i.e. the Second Coming).

223. While this couplet is open to a variety of interpretations, it would seem to allude to the new Revelation (the wine) which has been given its potency through the Holy Spirit (like the maidens of heaven in 'The Tablet of the Holy Mariner' and like the maiden who appears to Bahá'u'lláh in the Síyáh-Chál (or like Ṭáhirih herself). The cask or container in such an analogy might represent the new law or religion that will convey this wine to those followers who are dedicated (who surround the cask in anticipation of the new wine). Thus, there is one child from this marriage of earth and heaven (the new laws and the newly unleashed spirit), that child being the twin Revelation of the Báb and Bahá'u'lláh, one father (God) but two mothers (the Báb and Bahá'u'lláh) who give birth to this miraculous transformation of humankind.

224. This could be translated literally as 'bring one for cash and two on loan' – meaning possibly 'Bring both (one drink now and the two for later) though I can afford only one right now'. Here again Ṭáhirih is possibly alluding to the fact that at the time she is penning this verse, the draught of wine is the newly revealed truth of the Bábí Dispensation but she also is aware that in the near future both Revelations will be combined.

225. Here, too, the allusion to a single vintage (or revealed truth) but two containers (i.e. the two eyes and the two Revelations). The mysterious part of the image is the allusion to a Tartar or Turk. In Persian poetry this refers to the yellow race who lived north of the Caspian Sea and northeast of Iran. These peoples often used to attack the Persian states for plunder and pillage. Since they were plunderers, brave, beautiful, impatient and unkind, in Persian poetry the word has been used to describe the attributes of the Beloved. (See Gawharín, *Farhang*, vol. 3, p. 80)

226. Here Ṭáhirih shifts perspective and speaks directly to the Beloved, the Tartar, and alludes to the more than 20,000 Bábí martyrs who died rather than recant their Faith, just as she knows that she too will do. She also employs here a mixed metaphor. The brow is the symbol of the beauty of the Beloved but also its sword-like shape alludes to the fact that following the path of love of the Prophet will result in martyrdom.

227. This is a complex allusion. First, the beauteous eyes of the Beloved cast a spell on the peoples of the world causing them to lay down their lives in the path of the Beloved. Second, the word 'nation' does not appear. The line in the original reads: 'Bound by the spell cast by your eyes, one *m* and two *l*s' – the word *milal* composed of three letters (one *m* and two *l*s) means 'nations'.

228. The word 'opposing' is implicit and alludes to a Persian proverb which states that a gentleman keeps his word, as opposed to someone who says one thing at one time and the opposite at another. Here, as in so many poems, Ṭáhirih alludes to the cruelty or coyness of the Beloved. In effect, she is saying that if the reunion promised by the Beloved is to be kept, then when will she be reunited with her Beloved (i.e.

when will she be allowed to escape the bondage of earthly existence and ascend to the celestial realm).

229. Here as elsewhere Ṭáhirih finds exaltation in being considered an outcast by society in order to serve the Cause of God. As is usual in the mystic tradition, the state of 'poverty and nothingness' is perceived as the loftiest of conditions. In effect, she is saying to the Beloved: Cause me to suffer whatever abasement or humiliation you wish in the path of your love so long as I can remain your obedient servant.

230. As in 'Face to Face' (no. 27), the soft-blowing wind from the east. In the story of Solomon, the wind which was his obedient servant used to take the news of all that happened across his kingdom to him. (Shamissa, *Talmíḥát*, pp. 333,337) Therefore the wind is the bearer of news.

231. Related to *Há*, the Arabic letter equivalent to number 5. It is a symbol that appears four times in the Bahá'í symbol for 'the Greatest Name' (at both ends of the upper and lower horizontal lines). It symbolizes the Hidden Absolute or God. According to Afnán's footnote, it refers to Bahá.

232. Here *Há* would seem to imply the Divine mysteries – hence, the line implies 'those who have been overwhelmed by having experienced a vision of the divine reality'.

233. This would seem to be Ṭáhirih's allusion to the future when the Bábí Faith is in disarray after the execution of the Báb, the slaughter of most of the Letters of the Living (including Ṭáhirih herself) and Bahá'u'lláh is exiled to Baghdád where over the next years (1853–63) He reorganizes and revives the Bábí community, including the community in Persia by sending teachers and communication to those disheartened believers.

If one accepts this interpretation, one is also faced with the realization that Ṭáhirih has a spiritual station of sufficient magnitude that she has knowledge of these future events, a foreknowledge demonstrated in many of her poems as well as in accounts of her conversations with other believers.

However, the Báb also refers to Himself as the 'Iraqi Youth'. (See Muḥammad-Ḥusayní, *Yúsif-i-Bahá*, p. 62)

234. Those separated from God.

235. The Báb referred to Himself as 'The Eastern Western Youth' or the 'Iraqi Youth' (Muḥammad-Ḥusayní, *Yúsif-i-Bahá*, p. 62), perhaps because His Faith encompassed the Arab world and He addressed the people while in Iraq (west of Iran).

236. Here the Báb is being alluded to not only as Qá'im and founder of a new Revelation but as the 'Primal Point' from which all future progress is begun or generated. In particular, He is alluded to here as the Gate which prepares the way for the Revelation of Bahá'u'lláh. Refer to the Persian Bayán pp. 57–60 on the opening of the gates of the hearts of the believers by the Gate (the Báb Himself).

237. *Ṭá'í*: related to *Ṭá*, the Arabic letter *ṭ*, equivalent to number 9 and

used in the Bahá'í writings to indicate the city of Ṭihrán. Since in the first couplet there are implied references to Bahá'u'lláh (*Há* and the face of Bahá'), this word should also be taken as an allusion to Bahá'u'lláh. Another interpretation is that the victory of *Ṭá* refers to the victory of Moses over Pharaoh as described in the Súrih of Ṭáhá (*Ṭá* refers to Ṭáhá). Therefore: His benevolence is pouring over the people of victory of Ṭáhá (divine victory), in which case the victorious ones here would be the Bábís who succeed in spite of the persecutions and machinations of Náṣiri'd-Dín Sháh (who by analogy would represent the Pharaoh).

238. 'Veil' has different meanings in the Sufi terminology: The 'veil of grandeur' (*ḥijáb-i-'izzit*) means 'wonderment and loss in God' since God's Essence is beyond understanding. (Sajjádí, *Farhang*, p. 166) This couplet appears to refer to this veil: e.g. 'Though in the past you have been veiled by wonderment and remoteness, now you can see God. Unravel the veil.' Another related meaning of 'veil', of course, is the negative sense of that which keeps one from God (selfishness and sins).

239. *Fá'í*: Related to *Fá*, the Arabic letter *F*, indicating Fárs, the province in which Shíráz is located. Probably a reference to the Báb Himself.

240. Another meaning of veil in Sufi terminology is 'the intermediary between God and creation' (Mu'ín, *Intermediate Persian Dictionary*). In this couplet the exact same term of 'veils of grandeur' of the previous couplet is used but here it should mean the 'World of Command': The evident face has suddenly appeared in the station of Manifestation; therefore, do not pay attention to 'you shall not see me'.

An Islamic ḥadíth refers to God as being behind 70,000 veils (or 70 in another version) of darkness and light. Gnostics have associated many meanings with veils. (Refer to Gawharín, *Sharḥ-i-Isṭiláḥá-yi-Taṣawwuf*, vol. 3–4, pp. 164–79.) One meaning of the veils of light is God's attributes since they veil us from God's Essence. In this respect, the veil in the first couplet should refer to veils of darkness and the veil in this couplet to veils of light (come out of the veils of darkness; God is manifested in veils of light).

Bahá'u'lláh states: 'At the time when We were hidden behind countless veils of light thou didst commune with Me and didst witness the luminaries of the heaven of My wisdom and the billows of the ocean of Mine utterance.' (Bahá'u'lláh, *Tablets*, p. 143)

241. A quotation from the Qur'án: when Moses asked God in Sinai to show Himself, God answers: 'You shall not see me.'

242. *Furqán* means: distinction, what distinguishes between truth and falsehood; a title for the Qur'án itself as indicated in the following: 2:185, 3:3 and 25:1. In the Qur'án, however, this title has been mentioned two times regarding the Truth given to Moses: 'And when we gave Moses the Book and Furqán for your guidance' (2:50); 'And we gave Moses and Aaron the Furqán and the Light and the Admonition (*dhikr*) for the God-fearing.' (21:48)

The word *Furqán* can also refer to the special station of the Báb. The Báb makes a distinction in His writings between Muḥammad as a messenger of God, the human aspect of Muḥammad who only repeats what God says, and the reality of *Furqán* as the Word of God. He explains that in this dispensation the reality of *Furqán* has appeared: as opposed to the time of Muḥammad when God's verses were revealed only at specific times, God's revelation at this age takes place continuously and without any interruption (*min dún-i-zavál wa lá iḍmiḥlál*). (See commentary for the Súrih of Kawthar in an article by Nádir Sa'ídí, *Payám-i-Bahá'í*, June 1998, p. 12.)

243. *Rabb-i-A'lá* ('the High or Transcendent or Supreme Lord') is a title used in the Bahá'í writings for the Báb. The Báb used this title for Himself. In the Qur'án, Joseph's brother who brought Joseph's shirt to Jacob is called *Bas͟hír* meaning 'the one who brings good news' or the 'Herald of Glad Tidings'. The Báb considers Himself as the bearer of the good news of the coming of 'Him Whom God shall make manifest'. In this regard He says: 'Take ye firm hold of the garment of the Joseph of Bahá' from the hand of the Exalted Transcendent (*A'lá*) Herald of Glad Tidings. The garment should be placed upon the head in order that one might be endowed with insight.' (*Qámús Íqán*, vol. 4:1875, trans. Stephen Lambden, *The Journal of Bahá'í Studies*, vol. 8, pp. 2, 36–7)

Therefore, the terms *A'lá* (High) and *Furqán* have twofold meanings. They are both mentioned in the Qur'án in relation to the story of Moses and both also refer to the special station of the Manifestation of God at this age. The literal translation of this line is thus: 'The name *A'lá* was established through the named one.' This could mean that the name *A'lá* (Supreme) could not have its real significance until it was assigned to the true representative of God on earth, the Báb. The Qur'án gives an example of this when the name was assigned to the wrong person and therefore completely lost its meaning: in response to Moses' call to God, the Pharaoh said, 'I am your supreme Lord.' (79:24) According to this interpretation, Ṭáhirih is saying here that the Manifestation of God is the one who gives meaning to the phrase 'Supreme Lord' and no one else.

244. The greater, the greatest; the word used for the Greatest Name.
245. The 'Most Great Lord'.
246. The Báb refers to Himself as 'God's Greatest Paradise'. See Muḥammad-Ḥusayní, *Yúsif-i-Bahá*, a book about the Báb's commentary on the Súrih of Joseph.
247. *Sará'irhá*: 'mysteries'. A Persian plural of the Arabic word *sará'ir* which is itself a plural. Persians (e.g. Rumi) have at times made a plural from an Arabic plural word. Rumi uses the word 'mystery' to refer to the reality of the prophets and the hidden nature of the perfect man. (Gawharín, *Farhang*, vol. 5, p. 4) In that sense, this couplet means that the reality of all Manifestations of God is revealed in this new Revelation.
248. The word here is *'ars͟h*, literally meaning 'throne', 'mansion', 'tent'

or 'highest heaven'. In gnostic terminology the 'Universal Soul'. It seems to imply in this context a kingdom, as in the biblical passage where Christ states, 'In my Father's house are many mansions.' (John 14:2) The word *'arsh* has been used by the Báb to mean the Manifestation of God as well as the believers in Him. (Persian Bayán) If we take it to allude to the believers, this couplet would seem to refer to the high spiritual bounty and station bestowed on prominent believers, such as Ṭáhirih herself.

249. This term is variously used in the writings of the Báb to signify an exalted state of existence or even the heavenly realm. The Báb refers to Himself as the 'Throne of Bahá'. In that sense *Bahá* means the Word of God that became manifest through the Revelation of the Báb. In a Bahá'í context, this is the 'Greatest Name', alluding to the personage of Bahá'u'lláh and to the concept of the perfection or completion of a process.

250. See the poem 'The Dry Bones' (no. 10); there are in the Qur'án various passages alluding to the fact that even after people die and turn into dust, God will definitely recreate them: e.g. 13:5, 32:10, 34:7, 17:49, 17:98. Also many verses of the Qur'án emphasize that God is capable of a new creation (*al-khalq al-jadíd*): e.g. 14:19, 35:16, 50:15. See also Ezekiel 37:1–6. In general, this refers to those who are spiritually dead and are in need of the resurrection which occurs whenever a new Manifestation appears (see Bahá'u'lláh, *Kitáb-i-Íqán*, p. 116 and throughout). Here specifically and in previous scriptures, the resurrection that would encompass the entire earth is the appearance of the Báb and Bahá'u'lláh.

251. *Taẓahhur*: literally, 'to go somewhere at midday'; here it means a person who ventures out in the midday sun to disclose what was hidden.

252. Ṭáhirih seems to be asking for God's assistance to be able to reveal the true reality of the Revelation of the Báb which was gradually disclosed to the believers because of their lack of preparedness. Of course, Ṭáhirih did perform such a task at the conference of Badasht.

253. This may be an allusion to the various 'cycles' or dispensations of successive Prophets.

254. This line could be variously interpreted. Is she addressing the Báb who repeatedly expresses His love for Bahá'u'lláh to assist her? Is she addressing Bahá'u'lláh Himself? Our sense is that she is addressing the Báb, asking for assistance to sustain her until Bahá'u'lláh reveals Himself.

255. This poem with some differences and an additional closing verse indicating Fayḍ as the poet is seen in the collection of poems by Fayḍ-i-Káshání, p. 171.

256. Rumi uses the terms 'the cock of the sky' and 'the cock of the soul of revelation' in his poetry in reference to the mythical cock with one wing in the west and another in the east, the head under the empyrean (God's throne) and the feet in the sky. When this mythical cock crows all the cocks on the earth will also crow. In Rumi's poetry this

cock has been interpreted to mean the perfect man or the spiritual guide. (Gawharín, *Farhang*, vol. 4, pp. 260, 261) Regarding His Revelation, the Báb writes in *Ṣaḥífiy-i-'Adlíyyih*: 'The cock crowed on the tree from the branches of paradise.'

257. As in so many other poems, this can be 'friend' or 'the Friend'.

258. This line is intriguing. Perhaps Ṭáhirih envisions herself as a traveller or seeker who, having viewed the dawning of the new Manifestation, no longer needs to wander about in the darkness. The Báb refers to this Revelation as the morning after the ending of the darkness of night: 'O, Qurratu'l-'Ayn, you are the dawn after night.' (Muḥammad-Ḥusayní, *Yúsif-i-Bahá*, p. 16) On another occasion He addresses the unbelievers as those who move in the darkness of the night (the interval between Islam and His Revelation) and do not obtain or see the fruit of the Islamic Revelation which is the Báb Himself. (Persian Bayán, p. 211) He says that the unbelievers, looking at themselves at night, assume that they have a light of themselves. They are ignorant of the fact that upon the arrival of the day, no light remains for them and they dissolve when they face the light of the sun (paraphrase of Persian Bayán 72).

The Arabic *al-qawm as-surá* and the Persian phrase of *s͟habruwán* indicate those who move around at night (thieves, police, etc.) who stop their activity when the morning comes. It also indicates wayfarers, those who pray at night, who are close to God and spiritually refined. A poem of K͟háqání says: 'The night travellers have seen the Ka'ba of soul manifest as the morning/ They have seen the morning unveiled as the Ka'ba pilgrims' (the pilgrims at Mecca take their shirts off and put on a robe). (Gawharín, *Farhang*, vol. 6, p. 26)

259. Quoted in Shoghi Effendi, *God Passes By*, p. 75.

260. Quoted in 'Abdu'l-Bahá, *Memorials of the Faithful*, p. 200.

261. This poem with some variations appears as the ending lines of a *muk͟hammas*, which, according to Muhít Tabátbá'í, belongs to Muḥammad Táhir-i-Qazvíní, though they are not found in all editions of his poems. According to Tabátbá'í, this poem was composed a hundred years prior to Ṭáhirih. This information was provided by Mr Azíz Hakímian from an article published in *Majalliy-i-Hunar va Mardum Viz͟hih Námih Irán va Pakistán*. We also came across poems using some phrases that appear at the end of each couplet of this poem in Fayḍ-i-Kás͟hání's collection (p. 609) and in Rumi's poems *Diván-i-Kámil-i-S͟hams-i-Tabrízí* (p. 327).

262. The group of poems discovered by D͟huká'í Bayḍá'í are complicated in language at times with elaborate philosophical and religious language that is not easily understood by the ordinary reader. They are not melodious outpourings of a lover's heart as we see in this poem. The poems 'The Announcement' (no. 4), 'The Primal Point' (no. 35), 'The Dry Bones' (no. 10) and others belong to the group discovered by Bayḍá'í. Nuqabá'í also believes that this poem is not from Ṭáhirih but is by Ṭá'ir of Isfahan, a Bahá'í who lived at the time of 'Abdu'l-Bahá. Mr Nuqabá'í makes a reference to Fáḍil-Mázan-

daráni's *Ẓuhúru'l-Haq*, vol. 8 that expresses the same belief.

However, what these scholars might have presumed is that Ṭáhirih wrote in a single predictable style. As we will see in this volume, Ṭáhirih was capable of various modes and styles and may well have changed the forms and tones of her verse as her situation changed and her writing developed. In short, there is no hard evidence in support of these theories at this time.

263. *Ṣabá* is a term used often in the Bahá'í writings and a number of times in Ṭáhirih's verses to represent a wind blowing from the east to the west. It is a Sufi term alluding to the divine fragrances blowing from the spiritual realm, wandering the world in search of a pure heart where it can make its home.

264. In the original, Ṭáhirih says 'small' or 'tight mouth', emphasizing the beauty of the face of the beloved but also alluding to the mystical concept of speech as an attribute of God and especially to its transcendency beyond human understanding. (See Nurbakhsh, *Treasury of Sufi Terms*, vol. 1, pp. 48–9)

265. The eyebrow of the beloved in Persian poems is many times what causes the lovers to lose their minds and sacrifice their reputations and status in society for the sake of their beloved.

266. We were not able to locate these two manuscripts in the collections of the British Museum Library even though they are referenced as OR54e and OR27261. We presume these numbers are erroneously entered.

267. *Lát* was the second biggest idol in pre-Islamic Arabia. The idol was placed on a square rock in Ṭá'if and was worshipped by the Thaqíf tribe. After the Thaqíf tribe became Muslims, Muḥammad ordered the destruction of the idol and the building of the Mosque of Ṭá'if in its place. (See Mu'ín, *Intermediate Persian Dictionary*, p. 1770)

Manát was an idol worshipped by some pre-Islamic Arabs. The non-Muslims stole the idol, took it to India and built a place for it called Súmanát. Later on, one of the Muslim kings of Iran conquered India, destroyed Súmanát and took away its jewellery. (ibid. p. 2023)

268. It is not clear whether she is here referring to her own death or to the death of the Báb (which precedes her own martyrdom by two years). Either makes sense, though since she is speaking of separation and the sorrow she feels at that separation, it would seem logical that her longing for nearness to her beloved (the Báb in this case) is coupled with her longing for death that she might once again attain that nearness.

269. There is ambiguity here, too. Is she talking about her decision not to take her own life but to remain behind and teach or is she talking about being revived or recreated by her sense of His love for her?

270. At the time of creation, God blew the breath of life into Adam's body of clay. (See Qur'án 15: 28–9) This concept of the soul as God's breath is also similar to the more literal Bahá'í notion of the soul as an emanation from God:

> Therefore, the proceeding of the human spirits from God is through emanation. When it is said in the Bible that God breathed His spirit into man, this spirit is that which, like the discourse, emanates from the Real Speaker, taking effect in the reality of man. ('Abdu'l-Bahá, *Some Answered Questions*, p. 206)

271. There is a difference among some of the versions of this poem. In particular, Nuqabá'í's version has a couplet after the second couplet and another after the fifth couplet of Aryanpoor's version. We have left these out in favour of Aryanpoor's version of the text.
272. In the original the first half couplet also ends with 'I am'. This is a style of poem in which the two halves of the first couplet end with the same word and all the following couplets also end with that same word.
273. 'Milk and sugar' implies milk mixed with sugar. Also, sugar symbolizes the lips of the beloved or a kiss.
274. Minute particles or dust that become illuminated in sunlight. The word 'dust' here could also imply that the speaker has perished or has become annihilated.
275. The phrase here could be interpreted 'with shame' (restraint as opposed to the shameless adoration of the servant), 'with culture', 'with knowledge', etc.
276. Could also be 'slave' or 'thrall'.
277. The cloister (*dayr*) and shrine (*ḥaram*) are used in Persian literature in contrast with each other. The cloister alludes to the dome under which the infidels used to worship, in contrast with the shrine where the believers would worship. (Gawharín, *Farhang*, vol. 4, p. 20)
278. Both 'heart-breaker' here and 'heart-ravisher' in the following quatrain are synonymous with the notion of 'beloved' in Persian.
279. *S͟háhid*: In Rumi's poetry, this term refers to the spiritual guide and the perfect man.
280. The phrase 'sand beneath the feet' has become synonymous in Persian for one who feels humble and lowly in station.
281. This could also be translated as 'intoxicated with the wine of your countenance'.
282. This could be translated simply as 'mistakes' or unworthiness rather than some explicit sins.
283. See Maneck, 'Ṭáhirih', p. 47.
284. This is clearly an allusion to the more than 20,000 Bábís who had by this time (1852) given up their lives rather than recant their belief in the Báb.
285. Here Ṭáhirih seems to envision her own martyrdom and her reunion with the Báb, who here is alluded to in traditional poetic terms of Persian mystical verse as a lover who tortures his beloved by keeping himself remote. But in this passage, she imagines him approaching her.
286. Khotan was a city in eastern Turkistan famous for its musk deer. The

musk fragrance is frequently used as the scent of attraction between lover and beloved in Persian verse.

287. Khátá is northern China and the Chinese were considered infidels by Muslims. Hence the couplet implies that even the infidels (Mongol invaders who instead of destroying Islam became converts) could not disturb Islam but her beloved (the Báb or Bahá'u'lláh) will cause such a commotion as to cause the religion to re-examine its traditions and especially the concept of the continuity of revelation.

288. From this point on she is addressing the king, Náṣiri'd-Dín Sháh.

289. Browne and Lewis have adopted the common meanings of 'you have denied the Absolute' – e.g. the unseen reality and spiritual verities – and have taken the liberty of inserting the word 'both' (both God and the destitute).

290. Possibly an allusion to the reward of being a martyr to the Bábí Faith.

291. The actual word is *manzil* and refers to a stopping place on a journey – perhaps a caravanserai – in Rumi's poetry it has been interpreted to mean a stage that the wayfarer should tread, a spiritual stage. (Gawharín, *Farhang*, vol. 8, pp. 255, 269) But Ṭáhirih here might also be speaking of this place as a stage in the progress of the true seeker, i.e. this world of multiplicity or materiality, as opposed to the spiritual world where the self is united with the divine reality. Ṭáhirih could also be telling the king to put away any vain notion he might have of some relationship with Ṭáhirih, a *manzil* of 'I' and 'we'.

292. In addition to alluding to the king's suggestion that he and Ṭáhirih might become conjoined in marriage, there is another philosophical meaning here. 'I and we' alludes to selfishness, pride and arrogance. (Dihkhudá, *Lughat*, vol. 43, p. 3) For example, Rumi says: The ladder for most people is 'I and we'./ The end result is a sudden crash!' (Falling off the ladder). 'I and we' also means the world of multiplicity and duality as opposed to the spiritual world of unity. (Gawharín, *Farhang*, vol. 8, p. 483)

293. This couplet could be translated two ways. If her allusion to 'nothingness' is the Sufi sense of annihilation, then her final statement might not be a sarcastic remark that he should go chase after his hollow dreams of power and possessions but rather a reminder to him that the true attainment for a soul is 'true poverty and absolute nothingness'.

294. The same word here is used for both the joints in the human body and the joints in a flute made from a reed or cane. Thus, she creates a pun that causes an analogy between the sad melodies of a flute and the sad verses emanating from her body. A famous poem by Rumi employs the same analogy: 'Listen to the flute, the story that it is telling you. It is complaining about separations . . .' One implication of Rumi's verse is that the reed is lamenting being cut out from the reed bed as a symbol of man's separation from his origin (God). Ṭáhirih's use of the flute also alludes to the flute's complaint of its separation from God, as echoed in the Arabic phrases in the couplet that follows.

295. This couplet is most probably the song her body is intoning.
296. 'Placeless' implies proximity to God or to the divine realm.
297. According to Nuqabá'í, this poem is not from Ṭáhirih but from Ṣuḥbat-i-Lárí, a non-Bahá'í poet from the city of Lár, though Nuqabá'í states that Ṭáhirih was fond of reciting it. The version of the poem we are using is different from Afnán's version (which combines this poem with another), whereas the version which appears in books by Browne, Root and Nuqabá'í is a single piece. Also, Afnán's version has an additional couplet at the end which we have decided not to include here. It would be translated something like: 'If you are greedy for permanence and eager for attaining/ the absolute Existence of the Beloved, listen to the call.' This poem is found with some variations in the collection by Ṣuḥbat-i-Lárí with the last line indicating Ṣuḥbat as the poet.
298. This couplet alludes to Qur'án 7:172: 'And when thy Lord brought forth their descendants from the reins of the sons of Adam and took them to witness against themselves, "Am I not", said He, "your Lord?" They said, "Yes, we witness it." This we did, lest ye should say on the day of Resurrection, "Truly, of this were we heedless . . ."' There is a reference to 'Am I not your Lord?' and the reply of 'Yes' in the Persian Bayán, p. 16.
299. In Iran they used to beat drums to inform people of important events and happenings. Government representatives used to beat drums to gather people to read an announcement or an order. Up to a few decades ago, drums were beaten several times a day to inform people of the sunrise, sunset, etc. The word 'drum' does not exist in this line; however, the word 'beat' does, so that the concept of the drum calling out is implicit.
300. Nuqabá'í has this in the first person: 'I did beat' and 'my heart responded'.
301. The implication here is that the armies pitch their tents as a result of hearing the drums' affirmative response to the call 'Am I not?' One interesting point is that there exists in Ṭáhirih's verse a mixture of allusions to calamity and suffering such that it is often difficult to determine when the suffering is physical and truly painful and when this is an allusion to her great love and longing to attain the presence of the Beloved. If we take some of these passages as literal (she is bemoaning her hardship as a believer), we have trouble with those accounts that describe her as always joyous and radiant, even as she approached her death.
302. This couplet alludes to Ṭúr, Mount Sinai where Moses witnessed the burning bush. This allusion is employed by Ṭáhirih in a number of poems. According to scripture, Moses became unconscious by the shock of the lightning striking the mountain – hence the 'wonderment' of Moses and the destruction of the mountain itself:

> And when Moses came at our set time and his Lord spake with him, he said, 'O Lord, shew thyself to me, that I may look

upon thee.' He said, 'Thou shalt not see Me; but look towards the mount, and if it abide firm in its place, then shalt thou see Me.' And when God manifested Himself to the mountain he turned it to dust! and Moses fell in a swoon. (Qur'án 7:139)

303. The actual word is 'scale' and implies insignificance. Kháqání, for example, uses the word in the same context to connote insignificance.
304. Rumi uses a fish to symbolize the friends of God, gnostics and the prophets. (Gawharín, *Farhang*, vol. 8, pp. 215–17)
305. In effect, how do you presume to have some concept of the totality of creation or existence.
306. In the original there is only the word *lá*, implying, 'No, there is not any.' The word is the beginning of the phrase 'There is no god except God' in the Muslim call to prayer. By implication, then, to become close to God and to feel His existence, one should first renounce the world of existence and aspire to the realm of nothingness. The Báb uses five versions of this phrase, all beginning with the word *lá* to explain the reality of death – i.e. nothingness (Persian Bayán 32).
307. We found this poem in a rare collection of poems and prose which seems to have been put together more than 40 years ago. Most of what is in this collection appears to have been reproduced using an old printing technology and some have been added in hand writing later on. There is no mention in the collection about the calligraphers, the person or entity that produced it or the date or place of original production.

It is obvious that the poems attributed to Ṭáhirih are not copied from E. G. Browne's work or other extant collections published after Browne. In some poems, the order of couplets and some words differ from all published collections we have come across. This collection contains five poems attributed to Ṭáhirih which we had not seen anywhere. Unfortunately, owing to the passage of time various portions of these poems are faded and unreadable. This single poem we are including is entirely readable except for the first two couplets that are mostly faded but which seem to be an invocation to God. The content, phrases used and style of this poem are definitely the same as what we have noted in the majority of poems attributed to Ṭáhirih.
308. 'Or even closer' and *A'lá* in this quatrain are references to a passage in the Qur'án in which the station of Muḥammad is described. The context is as follows:

The Koran is no other than a revelation revealed to him:
One terrible in power taught it him,
Endued with wisdom. With even balance stood he
In the highest [*A'lá*] part of the horizon:
Then came he nearer and approached,
And was at the distance of two bows, or even closer, –
And he revealed to his servant what he revealed.
His heart falsified not what he saw. (53:4–11)

The station of 'or even closer' in gnostic terminology means the station of 'Nothingness'.

309. *Sivá*: 'Except than', meaning anything which is not of God.
310. *Má sivá*: literally, 'that which is separate'.
311. An allusion to Bahá'u'lláh. Siyyid Káẓim foretold the coming of the Qayyúm: 'Verily I say, after the Qá'im [the Báb] the Qayyúm will be made manifest. For when the star of the Former has set, the sun of the beauty of Ḥusayn will rise . . .' (Quoted in Momen, *Basic Bahá'í Dictionary*, p. 190)
312. i.e. the world of existence, as opposed to the realm of the spirit
313. There are several possible meanings for this quatrain. First, this could be an allusion to the martyrs' refusal to recant their beliefs. This could also be referring to those who did not respond to the Revelation of the Báb and who thereby fell from grace to the depths of selfishness and despondency. But since every other couplet is in praise of the Bábís, it would seem more logical that Ṭáhirih here is referring to those Bábís who, though not yet martyrs, daily risk torture and death by having abandoned all concerns other than fidelity to their beliefs and who, consequently, await the assistance of God. These souls thus await in noble silence relief from the calamities they are experiencing. Another possible meaning is that Ṭáhirih is here foreshadowing her own martyrdom when her body will be irreverently tossed into a well. Finally, this quatrain could be alluding more specifically to the female Bábís who are hierarchically at the depth of society and who have no voice in affairs and await the reformation of society that God will bring to give them relief from their plight.
314. This would seem again to refer to Ṭáhirih's own martyrdom and the fact that the usual preparation of the body for burial would be a cleansing of the corpse prior to wrapping the body in a shroud. It also could refer to her detachment from worldly concerns.
315. 'The Greatest Glory'. Here she seems to allude to those martyrs who preceded her and 'became deserving of the signs of 'or even closer'. *A'lá* and *Abhá* could also refer to the Báb and Bahá'u'lláh.
316. 'This, dear Crito, is the voice which I seem to hear murmuring in my ears, like the sound of the flute in the ears of the mystic; that voice, I say, is humming in my ears, and prevents me from hearing any other . . . Leave me, Crito, to fulfil the will of God, and to follow whither he leads me.' (*The Dialogues of Plato*, trans. B. Jowett, vol. 1, p. 438) The execution/martyrdom of Socrates is then depicted in the *Phaedo*.
317. Here yet again is an allusion to the mysterious nature of Ṭáhirih's station. In other words, this seems to be something other than a mere hyperbole affirming her fidelity. It seems, rather, to indicate the sort of pre-existence attributed by Shoghi Effendi as an ontological aspect of the Manifestations. However, such an interpretation is so speculative as to be specious. An equally valid understanding of this line (the main thesis of which Ṭáhirih alludes to in many other poems) is that

after recognizing the Prophet, she realizes that this relationship is the soul of her existence and her true reality from time immemorial: i.e: that all souls are emanations from God. She also might be speaking as a human being on behalf of other human beings who, from the ancient eternity, accepted calamities by responding positively to the call of 'Am I not your Lord?'

318. *'Ayn-i-Riḍá*: 'The eye of satisfaction and contentment.' K͟háqání uses this term in his poem: 'His speech was asking for a covenant and mine was saying yes (*balá*); Mine was the talk of excuses, and from him was the eyes of satisfaction.' (See Dihk͟hudá, *Lughat*, vol. 35, p. 478)

319. Possibly 'for His sake' or 'for God's glory' because the word *Bahá* is used.

320. *D͟harrí*: in Arabic *d͟harra* means a small particle or a bit of something. In a number of passages in the Qur'án, the word has the connotation of alluding to the most insignificant portion of one's actions – i.e. the least good action shall be made apparent as will the *d͟harra* (smallest action) of evil (see 4:40; 10:61; 34:3; 99:7 and 99:8). A literal translation of this couplet could be: 'I don't possess even a speck of pure deeds; by all that is missing from me, you can see how benevolent and giving He is' (i.e. He is even benevolent and kind to one like me who possesses no good deeds).

321. Shoghi Effendi, *God Passes By*, pp. 32–3.

322. Quoted in Martha Root, *Ṭáhirih the Pure*, p. 102.

323. The entire passage by Bahá'u'lláh (though He makes other similar statements) reads:

> Thus it is related in the 'Biháru'l-Anvár', the ''Aválim', and the 'Yanbú' of Ṣádiq, son of Muḥammad, that he spoke these words: 'Knowledge is twenty and seven letters. All that the Prophets have revealed are two letters thereof. No man thus far hath known more than these two letters. But when the Qá'im shall arise, He will cause the remaining twenty and five letters to be made manifest.' Consider; He hath declared Knowledge to consist of twenty and seven letters, and regarded all the Prophets, from Adam even unto the 'Seal', as Expounders of only two letters thereof and of having been sent down with these two letters. He also saith that the Qá'im will reveal all the remaining twenty and five letters. Behold from this utterance how great and lofty is His station! His rank excelleth that of all the Prophets, and His Revelation transcendeth the comprehension and understanding of all their chosen ones. (Bahá'u'lláh, *Kitáb-i-Íqán*, pp. 243–4)

324. Bahá'u'lláh, *Seven Valleys and the Four Valleys*, p. 39.

325. Bahá'u'lláh, *Tablets*, p. 143.

326. 'Eternal Veil' refers here to the 'incomparability' (*tanzíh*) aspect of God – the hidden nature or the station of *aḥadíyyia* in contrast to 'compar-

ability' (*tashbíh*) aspect of God – the station of *wáḥidíyya*, the station of Manifestation (the Manifest).

327. Aḥmad is a title for Muḥammad. Manifestations that belong to or are from Aḥmad (*Aḥmadí*) refers to the reality that was manifested in Muḥammad, what Islamic philosophers called the Muḥammadan Light (*Núr-i-Muḥammadí*) or the Muḥammadan Spirit (*Rúḥ-i-Muḥammadí*), the Word of God or Holy Spirit which in the Islamic Dispensation was manifested in Muḥammad. In this couplet Ṭáhirih is saying that the same process of manifesting the Holy Spirit which took place with the appearance of Muḥammad is taking place once more – that the same reality of the Holy Spirit that was manifested then is now being manifested again.

328. The dot of the letter *bá*, the second letter of the alphabet. This symbolic use of the letter could be understood in at least three ways: 1) the Hidden Essence became manifest as the Primal Point or Word of God; 2) the Hidden Essence was manifested as the Revelation of the Báb; 3) the Hidden Essence was manifested as the Revelation of Bahá'u'lláh.

Support for the first interpretation might go in the following manner. A ḥadíth from 'Alí referred to in the Bahá'í writings observes: All that is in the Qur'án is in [the phrase] *bismi'lláh*. *Bismi'lláh* means 'in the name of God', a phrase that comes at the beginning of every Súrih of the Qur'án (e.g. 'In the name of God, the Compassionate, the Merciful.') The ḥadíth goes on to note: All that is in *bismi'lláh* is in [the letter] *bá* (i.e. the first letter of *bismi' lláh*). All that is in [the letter] *bá* is in [its] dot [the dot in the letter and the dot is also called a point] and I am the Point (that dot, since the dot is also called 'point'). The point of the letter *bá*, therefore, is the 'Primal Point' or the first manifestation of the Hidden Essence. From that Point the letters come into being and from the letters the words and from the words, in turn, the Book of God comes into being.

In his interpretation of *Bismi'lláhi'r-Raḥmáni'r-Raḥím* ('In the Name of God, the Most Kind, the Compassionate', the opening phrase of each section of the Qur'án), the Báb quotes a ḥadíth from 'Alí who said: 'The mystery of Bismi'lláh (meaning 'in the name of God') is in *bá* (the second letter of alphabet), and the mystery of *bá* is in the dot (the dot which is under the letter *bá*) and I am the dot (point) that is under *bá*.' Shaykh Aḥmad Aḥsá'í also attributes the same phrase to 'Alí. Muḥy'id-Dín Ibnu'l-'Arabí (Ibn-i-'Arabí), the renowned Sufi philosopher, refers to this phrase: 'From *bá* existence came into being and from the dot the praising one was distinguished from the praised one.' 'Abdu'l-Bahá in His commentary on *Bismilláhi'r-Raḥmáni'r-Raḥím* refers to this phrase in Ibnu'l-'Arabí's work. (*Maḥbúb-i-'Alam*, pp. 151–2)

Support for the second interpretation derives from the idea that the Hidden Essence was manifested in the Báb. The Báb called Himself 'the point of *bá*' meaning the Manifestation of God in the Revelation of Bayán (the Bábí religion) since the word Bayán begins with the letter *bá*. Similarly, He referred to Muḥammad as the 'point of *fá*' since the word *Furqán*, a title for the Qur'án, begins with the letter *fá*. He used similar titles for Christ and Moses, calling them the point of the first letter of the holy book of their Revelation. (Refer to Asráru'l-Á<u>th</u>ár, Letters *káf* to *yá*, p. 234, under the word *nuqṭah*).

Support for the third interpretation – that the letter alludes to Bahá'u'lláh – proceeds as follows: Siyyid Káẓim Ra<u>sh</u>tí made a connection between the letter *bá* and the word *Bahá*. In *<u>Sh</u>arḥ-i-Qaṣídih-i-Lámi'yyih* (A Commentary on the Ode Rhyming in the Letter L), he prophetically alludes to the word *Bahá* by cryptically indicating that the *point* (the dot of the letter *bá*) is related to the letters *há* ('h') and *alif* ('a'). The three letters – *bá, há* and *alif* – form the word *Bahá*. Therefore he says that the dot in the letter *bá* is related to the word *Bahá*. He also indicates that the letter *bá* in the phrase 'In the Name of God, the Merciful, the Compassionate' is Bahá'u'lláh. (Cf. *Qámús Íqán*, vol. 4:1875, trans. Stephen Lambden, *Journal of Bahá'í Studies*, vol. 8, no. 2, pp. 31–2)

Of course, since the twin Manifestations of the Báb and Bahá'u'lláh are ontologically the same, both being the Word of God and manifestations of the Hidden Essence, all three interpretations basically convey the same meaning. In one place Siyyid Káẓim explains that *Bahá* (glory) in reality is the 'Primordial Light' and the 'Greatest Name' through which God created the heavens and the earth and whatsoever is therein. He also explains in another one of his writings regarding the word *Bahá* that 'it is the light of lights, the very Light which illuminates the lights'. (Cf. ibid. p. 32)

329. *Há* is a letter of the alphabet and is the first letter of the word *Hú* meaning 'He' referring to God or to the Essence of God. *Há* refers to the station of *Aḥadíyya* which is the station of the Hidden Treasure before the manifestation takes place. This Hidden Essence of *há* becomes manifest from the point of *bá*. Reference to *há* as the Essence that is not manifested is also made in couplet three of the poem 'Salutation and Praise' (no. 21): 'When your praise was commanded by *'Amá*,/ You were transformed from *Há* to *Abhá*! All praise!' In that case the couplet refers to the Manifestation of Bahá'u'lláh – *Abhá* means 'the Most Glorious', is a word from the same root as the word *Bahá* and is a title used for Bahá'u'lláh: e.g. Jamál-i-Abhá which is translated as 'the Blessed Beauty'.

330. This alludes to the distinction between the essential reality of God and the manifest attributes of God as discussed by 'Abdu'l-Bahá in *Some Answered Questions*, pp. 202–4.

331. According to Martha Root, some attributed this poem to Nabíl, the Bahá'í historian. We have used the version that appears in Root, <u>Dh</u>uká'í Bayḍá'í and Browne, which are all quite similar. Afnán's version is quite different; it is a mixture of this poem and 'The Announcement' (no. 4) but with the couplets arranged in a different order than they appear in either poem as we present them in this volume.

There are about 20 differences between Browne's version and that which appears in Root's book – some minor and some substantial. Overall, Browne's version makes the best sense. In each case where there is a difference, we have opted for the choice that best complies with what we understand the poem to be doing.

332. The east wind; cf. 'Face to Face'(no. 27) and 'The Impatient Bride' (no. 31)
333. The use of moon or moon-face to allude to the Prophet, besides a cultural connotation of a beautiful face, also has in this instance the obvious implication of a source of light which is a reflection of another source, just as the Manifestation is a reflection of God's power and light. And yet, in relation to the earthly reality, the Manifestation is often alluded to as the source of light, the sun itself.
334. *Mutajammilá*: in some versions the word is *mutjallila* meaning 'victorious in station and glory'.
335. *Jabarút*, the realm of omnipotence (the realm of *jabarút* as opposed to *násút*).
336. Those who suffer in the path of God.
337. I will warn him so that he becomes aware.
338. The word used for 'destruction' here is the Arabic word *lá*. As in 'Meditation on My Death' (no. 32), the word *lá* implies, 'No, there is not any.' It is the beginning of the phrase, 'There is no god except God' in the Muslim call to prayer. By implication, then, to become close to God and to feel His existence, one should first renounce the world of existence and enter the realm of nothingness. Therefore, the use of *lá* in this instance would imply that God will subject one who is faithless or weak to those tests that will demonstrate the emptiness of being attached to the things of this world (i.e. the desire for wealth, fame, etc.).
339. This couplet reminds one of God's answer to Moses when the Prophet asks God what to tell the people is the source of His new knowledge: 'Tell them I am that I am.' (Exodus 3:14). The sense would seem to be that God or God speaking through the Báb is affirming the essential eternality and self-sufficiency of the Deity.
340. A reference to Qur'án 7:171.
341. *Muraqqa'* may mean 'eternal' or 're-planted' or 'transplanted' – the concept of the Divine Lote Tree in the writings of Bahá'u'lláh which alludes to the reappearance of the same spirit in the personage of a new Prophet. In some versions the word *muraffi'* is used, meaning 'the bestower of exaltation and the uplifter': 'Through me was the Bayán exalted.' If read *muraffa*, it would mean 'I am the elevated tree of life'.
342. 'Ye who have glimpsed' is a translation of the word *shuhadá* meaning 'witnesses', a title the Báb used in the Persian Bayán for His believers. (See p. 22)
343. *Nár* ('fire') is used by Browne and others. Dhuká'í Bayḍá'í uses the word *thár* (blood or revenge). 'Fire' might allude to Moses' vision of the Eternal in the form of the burning bush. But if the word is *thár*

('blood'), the bloody face might allude to the martyred Imám Ḥusayn, especially since the last line alludes to Karbilá where the Imám's head was severed and where many devoted believers sacrificed their lives. Furthermore, it was a vision of the martyred Ḥusayn covered with blood that served for the Báb as the onset of His Revelation. (See *Ṣaḥífiy-i-'Adlíyyih*, p.14) This interpretation seems further confirmed by the allusion in the last couplet to believers sacrificing their heads as a token of fidelity.

344. 'The King of Karbilá is a title used for the Imám Ḥusayn who was martyred in Karbilá. The poem thus says that the same Truth has now been manifested in the new Revelation.

345. *Haykal*: 'temple', usually alluding to the human body as in the *Súriy-i-Haykal*.

346. *Hát lak*: 'Come forward. It is yours.'

347. The 'fire of Sinai' alludes to the appearance of God to Moses on Mount Sinai and the 'light of Paran' alludes to Muḥammad. (See letter written on behalf of Shoghi Effendi, 26 December 1941, in *Lights of Guidance*, p. 494) Hence, Ṭáhirih is here saying that this same power has appeared once again.

348. *Ons*: In gnostic terminology, the effect of God's beauty on the heart of man. (Mu'ín, *Qurratu'l-'Ayn*, vol. 1, p. 379)

349. While it is tempting to see this as an allusion to the 'attributes of Bahá'u'lláh' (and it may well be), we have left it to the reader to decide if Ṭáhirih here means all those Prophets who have perfectly personified divine attributes or specifically alludes to Bahá'u'lláh.

350. *Kun fa kán*: 'Be and it was.' A slightly modified version of *Kun fa yakúnu* ('be and it is'). In relation to God's authority and power, this phrase alludes to the process of new creation (Qur'án 2:117, 3:47, 3:59, 6:73). More specifically, this passage alludes to the fact that creation comes into being through the Prophets whose power is primarily demonstrated through speech or utterance. In this case, Ṭáhirih seems to be alluding to the Prophet Himself who has come into being to manifest divine attributes. In the Persian Bayán the Báb symbolizes the Primal Will by the first letter of *kun* (be). The couplet in this regard refers to the station of the Manifestation of God. In Persian poetry *Kun fa kán* has been used to mean the whole creation, the whole universe. (See Dihkhudá, *Lughat*, vol. 40, p. 265) In that sense this verse might mean 'appeared to the letters of all creation'.

351. This would specifically seem to refer to the Christian concept of Christ as God (the Trinitarian doctrine) which Muḥammad denounces in the Qur'án as does Bahá'u'lláh in the Kitáb-i-Íqán. In effect, Ṭáhirih is stating that God is exalted above incarnation or having a literal Son (branch) and since God is eternal, He is likewise exalted above the concept of root (origin or beginning). The same applies to the Word of God symbolized by the 'Tree of Truth' in the Báb's writings.

352. When the Word of God appears through the Manifestation of God, it is like the dawning of the sun. When the Manifestation of God

leaves this world, it is like the setting of the sun. The Báb says in the Persian Bayán (pp. 22, 64) that even in His absence, the Manifestation is still a guide for people in a mysterious way.

353. *Aḥad*
354. *Ṣamad*
355. In this analogy, God is the sun (the source of all light) and the Prophet is the moon (the intermediary between the sun and the world of existence). Accordingly, the moon travels to each constellation where it acquires the attributes of the four elements of material reality whereupon it is then ready to receive the divine mysteries. In other words, Ṭáhirih is here portraying how the Prophets come into being (as does Bahá'u'lláh in the Súratu'l-Haykal).
356. The 12 constellations were assigned virtues into groups of three to represent the four elements (earth, air, fire and water). 'Constellations' could refer to various ages, each like one of the four elements with specific characteristics. Therefore, the Word of God (the moon travelling through constellations) appears in a different manner at each age.
357. Once the Prophet is assigned a corporeal form (see the Súratu'l-Haykal), the soul of the Prophet associates with this 'human temple' and God reveals to this Being all the divine mysteries. This verse can also be understood as: The Temple from which the Prophet uttered the secret of Bahá from various constellations.
358. The twin Revelations of the Báb and Bahá'u'lláh reveal the same divine truth that was revealed to Moses and the Prophets of old: i.e. God is one and His revealed truth is one truth.
359.
> Among the Prophets was Noah. For nine hundred and fifty years He prayerfully exhorted His people and summoned them to the haven of security and peace. None, however, heeded His call. Each day they inflicted on His blessed person such pain and suffering that no one believed He could survive. How frequently they denied Him, how malevolently they hinted their suspicion against Him! Thus it hath been revealed: 'And as often as a company of His people passed by Him, they derided Him. To them He said: "Though ye scoff at us now, we will scoff at you hereafter even as ye scoff at us. In the end ye shall know."' Long afterward, He several times promised victory to His companions and fixed the hour thereof. But when the hour struck, the divine promise was not fulfilled. This caused a few among the small number of His followers to turn away from Him, and to this testify the records of the best-known books. These you must certainly have perused; if not, undoubtedly you will. Finally, as stated in books and traditions, there remained with Him only forty or seventy-two of His followers. (Bahá'u'lláh, *Kitáb-i-Íqán*, pp. 7–8)

360. *Taqarrud*: Beautiful singing of a bird or human.
361. *Badá*: A modified version of *badá'ah* meaning 'new'. Perhaps this

is the word *bidá'* misspelled. *Bidá'* means 'a change in God's Will'. In the story of Noah, God changed His mind several times regarding the flood, changes which tested the people and caused them to doubt the authenticity of Noah's claim to be an intermediary (Prophet) sent from God.

In other words, this entire poem may allude to the testing of people (what Bahá'u'lláh in the Kitáb-i-Íqán calls the 'judgement' of the followers of the previous religion) whenever a new Prophet appears.

362. Bahá'u'lláh, *Gleanings*, p. 14.

363. Ṭáhirih asks, 'What was the wish of Adam?' One would think that the wish of Adam was to remain in paradise but that is not the case according to many Islamic scholars and philosophers including Ibnu'l-'Arabí. They interpret the fall of Adam as the process of the manifestation of God's names and attributes. Paradise has been interpreted to mean the world without differentiation, the realm of the Absolute. The earth is, on the other hand, the world of existence in which God's names and attributes are manifested. Long before the fall of Adam, God told the angels 'I am placing within the earth a vicegerent' (Qur'án 2:30) according to Ibnu'l-'Arabí. Therefore, the fall of Adam was not necessarily a negative thing. Adam wished what God desired which is the manifestation of God's names and attributes (the process of creation). According to Sam'ání's interpretation: 'When Adam ate the forbidden fruit – the "wheat" – he was simply expressing his desire to busy himself with his Beloved.' (See Murata, *Tao of Islam*, p. 65) Neither the Qur'án nor the Old Testament indicates what the forbidden tree or tree of knowledge was. Muslims have interpreted it as wheat and Jews and Christians as apple. (Shamissa, *Talmíḥát*, p. 68) The desire of Adam, therefore, was to do what God had planned for him at the expense of being expelled from paradise.

As Murata, referring to Farghání's interpretation, writes: 'The fall had to occur so that the Hidden Treasure could become completely manifest. The Garden was a domain in which people lived in relative undifferentiation, so the possibility inherent in the existence could not become manifest. The root meaning of the Arabic word for Garden, janna, is concealment . . .' Adam's wish therefore was not paradise but manifesting God's attributes on earth. The famous poem of Háfiẓ relates to this interpretation:

> My father sold the garden of paradise for a grain of wheat
> I will be a disobedient (child) if I do not trade it for a grain of barley.

Perhaps the secret of Adam Ṭáhirih writes about is Adam's wish to descend to the physical world and to manifest God's attributes. The process of creation is, however, an ongoing process. A Manifestation of God in this age is the same phenomenon as the process of the creation of Adam. Therefore, Ṭáhirih calls this 'the mystery of the beginning and the end' in the fifth couplet.

Of course, God gave the power of choice and free will to Adam. Adam selected the hard alternative. Instead of staying in the realm of the divine (pure spirit and undifferentiated), Adam chose to manifest God's names and attributes in the world of existence. This is, according to 'Abdu'l-Bahá, the trust that the mountains could not carry but humans could. (Refer to *Some Answered Questions* regarding 'Abdu'l-Bahá's interpretation of the verse in the Qur'án on this subject.) Adam's free will and Satan's free will, both were what God wanted. Without an alternative, goodness does not mean anything. Therefore, a necessary condition for the manifestation of God's attributes is the free will to choose otherwise (as Satan does in Genesis). Couplet nine of this poem apparently refers to the fact that even Satan who was made of fire (refer to the Qur'án on Satan's reluctance to prostrate in front of Adam, 2:32) was created by God.

This is the situation of every human being and does not refer solely to Adam and to God's Manifestation at the Day of the End. Couplet/quatrain ten refers to this:

> Therefore, though I am one with free will
> living in the dawning of this new age,
> for Him there is no beginning
> and there is no end.

Man's choice of good and bad, however, takes a new meaning with the new Manifestation of God. With the new creation, man's purity of wish is tested again. Therefore, Ṭáhirih at the end of her poem refers to the revelation of the Bayán:

> Lo, make the concealed mysteries of Adam –
> Both the first and second of these –
> manifest in the world
> by your elucidation of the Bayán:
>
> The first truth is to discern in the Bayán
> the revelation of the Divine Beauty;
> The second truth is to manifest your insight
> with an appropriate portion of service.

364. *Áyat*: 'sign', as in *Áyatu'lláh* (the Sign of God), a title used for high clergy.
365. Is Ṭáhirih here referring to the unity of humankind, the unity of humankind with the rest of creation or the unity of herself with the rest of the heavenly concourse who serve as the educators of humankind?
366. The 'beginning' is a reference to the story of Adam and the 'end' is a reference to the Manifestation of God in this age. As in the tenth

couplet/quatrain, Ṭáhirih is alluding to the fact that in each and every age since the beginning of creation until God's new creation in this age, people have been free to accept or reject the call of God. This is an eternal principle.

367. This line combines *Qadar* – measure of things (vs. *qaḍá*) – and *Qadar* – free will. This is an important ontological and theological point. Bahá'u'lláh states:

> And now, concerning thy question regarding the creation of man. Know thou that all men have been created in the nature made by God, the Guardian, the Self-Subsisting. Unto each one hath been prescribed a pre-ordained measure, as decreed in God's mighty and guarded Tablets. All that which ye potentially possess can, however, be manifested only as a result of your own volition. Your own acts testify to this truth. (Bahá'u'lláh, *Gleanings*, p. 149)

This is a reiteration of a point made by Muḥammad in the Qur'án (54:49; 5:21; and 42:27). See also this same point discussed by 'Abdu'l-Bahá in *Some Answered Questions* chapter 35 where *qaḍá* and *qadar* are translated as 'predestination'.

368. This is in the precise context that Bahá'u'lláh discusses free will when He states that without the capacity to recognize the attributes of God through the Prophet and without the capacity of free will to choose whether or not to respond to that recognition, how could humankind be held accountable: 'It follows, therefore, that every man hath been, and will continue to be, able of himself to appreciate the Beauty of God, the Glorified. Had he not been endowed with such a capacity, how could he be called to account for his failure?' (Bahá'u'lláh, *Gleanings*, p. 143) As part of this process of search and discovery is the capacity of human beings to recognize the Prophet even though He may appear among us as an ordinary human being.

369. This concept of free will being a property possessed by all human beings is explained by the Báb in *Ṣaḥífiy-i-'Adlíyyih*, p. 21.

370. Qur'án: 15:26–31:

> We created man of dried clay, of dark loam moulded;
> And the djinn had We before created of subtle fire.
> Remember when thy Lord said to the Angels, 'I create man of dried clay, of dark loam moulded:
> And when I shall have fashioned him and breathed of my spirit into him, then fall ye down and worship him'.
> And the Angels bowed down in worship, all of them, all together,
> save Eblis: he refused to be with those who bowed in worship.

Djinns, who were created of fire prior to the creation of man, are the symbol of free will. That's why the most important of them, Satan

(Eblis), had the choice to tell God that he would not bow down in worship of Adam, since he himself was created out of fire but man was created only from clay. See the chapter on fire in Murata and Chittick, *The Vision of Islam*, p. 96; also 'The Measuring Out', p. 104, for a discussion of free will and predestination.

Also refer to the Súrih of Jinn (72) of the Qur'án. This súrih was revealed when opposition to Muḥammad had reached its climax. In spite of the severe opposition to the Prophet, the djinn followed the Prophet. Here we see that man disobeys God but djinns obey Him. Man's free choice to accept or reject the message is explained in this súrih (verses 11 and 14).

371. See the Persian Bayán, pp. 112–14.

372. This is a fairly loose translation of what is literally *máhiya* – in Arabic it results from the combination of two words, *má* (what) and *hiya* (that). The combination means 'what there is, a thing'. 'What there is' as used in the Qur'án (2:271) sounds more appropriate. (For an example of this grammatical usage of *má* (what) refer to Kamálí Dizfúlí, *Qur'án Thiql-i-Akbar*, p. 132.)

The intent of the line seems clear – that knowledge or recognition of the Prophet is inadequate without subsequent obedience to the laws the Prophet brings, a concept incorporated by Bahá'u'lláh in the opening passages of the Kitáb-i-Aqdas.

373. Rumi also uses this word to mean 'free will': 'In my ode there is both *jabr* (predestination) and *qadar* (free will), but ignore both./ Since there would be no outcome from this subject except tumult and dispute.' In another verse, Rumi alludes to this age-old debate in the following couplet: 'Between the people of "predestination" (*jabr*) and those of the "free will" (*qadar*),/ The dispute will continue till rising of the dead (the Day of Resurrection), O son (O my son).'

374. Perhaps alluding here to a single portion of the spiritual meaning concealed in the delicate design of this leaf – implicitly, all of the created universe may unfold to him its hidden secrets.

375. This could also be read as 'one letter from this Sina writing' (i.e. divine writing).

376. *Qadar*, as in 'The Twin Duties' (no. 39), alludes to the concept of God creating everything as He deems appropriate. More particularly it refers here to the concept articulated in 'The Twin Duties' – that human beings are all created with free will but that the capacity of each individual is meted out according to a pre-ordained measure. In effect, Ṭáhirih here seems to be alluding specifically to what she has revealed poetically to Bihjat in 'The Twin Duties' about the essential nature of creation and the concept of *Qadar* versus the concept of predestination.

377. This poem consists of 27 couplets in Afnán's version and 28 in Nuqabá'í's. There are many differences of words between Afnán's version of this work and Nuqabá'í's, though the order of the couplets is the same in both. We have taken out the last six couplets of this poem, five of which are repeated in 'The Announcement' (no. 4),

'The Kaʻba of Your Face' (no. 28) and 'The Twin Duties' (no. 39).

378. The Báb, *Selections*, p. 7.

379. Nuqabá'í's footnotes, based on Samandar's history, affirm that Bihjat is Karím <u>Kh</u>án, known as Bihjat, who was an intermediary between Ṭáhirih and others. In effect, he would deliver people's requests and letters to her. The word *Bihjat* means happiness, so the line could also be read as 'I pour in the cup of happiness with gladness . . .' Afnán's version is quite different: 'Bestow me wine from the pure sea /Pour it in (my) cup (O) Bihjat with gladness (or pour in my cup of happiness with gladness)'. Afnán's version can also be read as: 'I bestow wine from the pure sea/ I pour (it) in Bihjat's cup with gladness (or I pour in the cup of happiness with gladness).'

 However, the main point that should not be lost here is that the metaphor 'pour into the cup' means to fill someone's mind with information or knowledge or understanding.

380. As in various other poems, this term means 'cloud', 'sky' or, connotatively, 'the divine realm'.

381. *<u>Dh</u>ikr*: a title of the Báb. Hence this could be translated as: 'He will mention naught else except God' or 'He will manifest the same attributes of God as does the Báb'. This is important because in the next line this personage identifies himself as *Quddús*, which could allude to the historical figure Quddús or to *Quddús* ('Pure One') as an attribute of God, such as is used in the Qur'án (59:23 and 62:1).

382. The word *Quddús* or 'pure' is a name of God in the Qur'án (59:23 and 62:1). Therefore this may be a reference to God. Or, as further allusions to early Bábí history in this poem will demonstrate, this could be an allusion to Quddús, the last Letter of the Living, who had a special station, as is demonstrated by the obeisance paid to him at the battle of Fort Ṭabarsí.

383. This could be read as this 'station' or this 'occasion'. We have put this line in italics and quotes because 1) it is in Arabic; 2) it seems to represent the first-person statement of the holy personage being described by Ṭáhirih. It may be an allusion to Qur'án 11:107 regarding the Day of the End in which God will be acting as He deems, separating those deserving paradise from those deserving hell fire. This would also refer to Qur'án 55:29 describing God as acting differently in each age according to the needs and capacities of the people at that stage of human spiritual evolution. See also the Persian Bayán, p. 44.

384. The word *'Ayn* is seen in Islamic ḥadí<u>th</u> and elsewhere as meaning 'The Chosen people of God'. (See Dih<u>kh</u>udá, *Lughat*, vol. 35, p. 480)

385. This may well be an allusion to the Letters of the Living, the first 18 disciples of the Báb, the most prominent of whom were Ṭáhirih, Quddús and Mullá Ḥusayn. This makes sense for several reasons. For example, a few lines later, Ṭáhirih speaks in the first person plural, implying that she is among those on the ark who have cut themselves off from all save God.

386. 'Fire' in Persian literature at times alludes to the grandeur of God's

Essence and the glory of the Absolute Being. The couplet says that from these noble people, the glory of God (Him of whom it can be said 'none is changeless save Him') is glowing.

387. 'self-sufficient', 'eternal'
388. Traditionally, earth, air, fire and water constitute the four substances from which physical creation is composed. Here Ṭáhirih alludes to the fact that every element and every composite creation reflects the attributes of God inherently.
389. *Baytu'l-Qadar*, an Arabic term literally meaning the house of measure but in this context most probably alluding to the divine authority that determines the measure and destiny of the world.
390. *Qahr*: also means 'anger' and 'victory'. An attribute of God mentioned in the Qur'án which has been interpreted as God's power to exhort His will throughout the universe. This can refer to God's ability to bring the universe into existence according to the 'measure' (*qadar*) pre-ordained by Him.
391. This refers to the Báb or to God. God enforces His will through the manifestation of the Primal Point. That is, the universe is created as God wills by the First Mind. The new religion is then established through the manifestation of the Primal Point.
392. This is the concept that all creation begins from a single point (*nuqṭih*), just as words derive from the point at which the pen touches the paper. Also, of course, these lines allude to the Báb as the 'Primal Point': 'I am the Primal Point from which have been generated all created things. I am the Countenance of God Whose splendour can never be obscured, the Light of God Whose radiance can never fade. (The Báb, *Selections*, p. 12) This couplet can also be understood as 'the reason for your anger, Lord of the Bayán, is naught but the hitting (as with bullets) the Point (the Báb) in the open (in public)'.
393. *Bidá'*: 'Beginning'; it is also an allusion to a new Revelation of God.
394. This observation coincides with what Bahá'u'lláh states, that without the appearance of the Báb, the past would not be consummated nor the future begun.
395. Here Ṭáhirih would seem to be alluding to the fact that after the Báb's execution in 1850, His body was put in the open by the civil authorities that it might be devoured by beasts, thereby leaving unfulfilled the prophecy that the body of the Qá'im would not be desecrated. Unknown to the authorities, the Bábís in the night took the remains of the Báb and his young companion and hid them away until they were finally interred on Mount Carmel in 1909. One can thus observe in this poem a very specific allusion to early Bábí history.
396. *Dalíl*: 'reason', 'guide' or 'way'. The Báb Himself foresaw this period after His execution when virtually every Bábí leader would be executed or imprisoned, and thus expressed this request to the forthcoming Prophet (Bahá'u'lláh):

> Shouldst Thou dismiss the entire company of the followers of the Bayán in the Day of the Latter Resurrection by a mere sign

> of Thy finger even while still a suckling babe, Thou wouldst indeed be praised in Thy indication. And though no doubt is there about it, do Thou grant a respite of nineteen years as a token of Thy favour so that those who have embraced this Cause may be graciously rewarded by Thee. Thou art verily the Lord of grace abounding. (The Báb, *Selections*, p. 7)

However, Ṭáhirih might also here be stating that, in truth, there is no true respite between the coming of the Báb and the appearance of Bahá'u'lláh.

397. *Rúḥ-i-Akbar*: We took this to mean the same as *Rúh-i-A'ẓam*, also meaning 'the Most Great Spirit', referring to 'the First Mind' or the 'Word' or 'Command' of God.
398. *Qaṭúr*, 'thick', when combined with *saḥáb* means a cloud that contains much moisture, that is capable of bestowing great bounty. Here Ṭáhirih seems clearly to be alluding to herself as the herald of the new Day as she announces when she appears unveiled at the conference at Badas͟ht.
399. In addition to its obvious use as an image of concealment, the cloud here – as it is explicated by Bahá'u'lláh in the Kitáb-i-Íqán – also alludes to the fulfilment of Christ's prophecy that He would come in the clouds.
400. This seems clearly an allusion to Bahá'u'lláh. We see a reference to the 'Sun of Bahá' in the Arabic Bayán, p. 6.
401. i.e. the invisible Sun becomes manifest or visible.
402. The image of the cycle here would seem to allude to Ṭáhirih's desire to observe the advent of the fulfilment of Bahá'u'lláh's promised world order when humankind will at long last understand the divine process by which God has from time immemorial educated His creation through the Manifestations. Here Ṭáhirih is describing how, after the cloud has released its drops, it still exists as a thin veil or smoke so that the sun appears to emerge through it.
403. It is these qualities, perhaps, that led D͟huká'í Bayḍá'í to believe that the poem is not by Ṭáhirih. However, Martha Root includes this poem in her book and Hádí Ḥasan quotes the first couplet of this poem in his small selection of Ṭáhirih's verse. Nuqabá'í includes this poem in his collection but Afnán does not.
404. Bahá'u'lláh, quoted in Shoghi Effendi, *God Passes By*, p. 115.
405. The cupbearer, a very important figure in one of Ṭáhirih's longest poems ('The Cupbearer', no. 18), is clearly symbolic of one who conveys the revelation (the Prophet) or more generally, one who bestows fortune – a kind of subaltern of God who bestows calamities on the loved ones of God that they might be prepared spiritually by being tested and detached from earthly affections.
406. Here Ṭáhirih seems to note the irony that there seems to be no ostensible logic as to what one receives in this life. Yet she clearly implies that though she receives the 'dregs', it is preparing her for something more, as the remainder of the poem makes clear.

407. Literally this reads 'has remained steadfast'. This commonplace image of love as a battlefield is particularly inventive here. Usually the battlefield image is employed to represent the coy games between the lover and the beloved but here Ṭáhirih portrays the battle as a stark testing of the believers to see if they will remain faithful in their conviction when the inevitable tests come.

408. The word 'parrot' is intriguing here, as is the couplet itself. The parrot has been used symbolically in Rumi's *Mathnaví* and has been interpreted to mean 'the receptive wayfarer, the pious one, etc.' (See Gawharín, *Farhang*, vol. 6, pp. 246–7) The problem here is to determine if this is a positive or negative description. Is she contrasting the piety of the wayfarer with the pretentiousness of the false Shaykh, or is she using 'parrot' to imply a similar sort of mindless worship in which one simply 'parrots' the words of others without thought or reflection?

The verse works either way: 'let the pious one pray and the false Shaykh hurl accusations' or 'let the shallow follower say his prayers and the false Shaykh be pretentious'. In the end the true believer (the 'one out of a hundred thousand') will be the victor.

409. The actual line states, 'let us see who will catch the ball in the field' but the sense is that we will see at the end of the contest who will emerge victorious. The literal translation of this metaphor would not work well in English.

410. 'Powerful'. We have made a correction here to what seems to have been a typographical error in order for this word to make good sense.

411. Literally, 'I have burnt'. Perhaps an alchemical image here of how the gold is purified from the dross by the process of fire, an image that Bahá'u'lláh uses in the Hidden Words. In these images, the fire symbolizes the testing of the servant.

412. *Vujúd*: Existence or Essence (of God).

413. This line is in Arabic. The word 'tablet' (*Lawḥ*) might allude here to the tablet of Moses on which God engraved His will with fire.

414. *Sharr*: Evil, wickedness, injury, as opposed to *khayr* meaning 'goodness'.

415. *Makín*: Seated, established, the one honoured by the king, the one with grandeur. Refer to Qur'án 81:20: 'The possessor of strength, established in the presence of the Lord of Throne' (referring to Muḥammad or to Jibrá'íl according to some).

Also refers to Qur'án 56:12–16, 'In the Garden of bliss. A multitude from among the first and a few among those of latter times, on thrones inwrought, Reclining on them, facing each other.' This súrih describes the station and reward bestowed to the good believers on the Day of Resurrection.

416. 'Am I not', alluding to the passage 'Am I not your Lord?'

417. *Asbaq*: Foremost. A similar word is used in Qur'án 56:10–11.

418. The idea of sanctification as a divine bestowal. Sanctification is a translation for *tanazzuh*, which is similar to *tanzíh* and this word is normally used for 'sanctifying God from any likeness, names and

attributes'. It is the opposite of *tashbíh*, which refers to describing God in human terms and ascribing attributes and perfections to God. Contrasting these two approaches to God is a common notion in Islamic and Sufi philosophy which appears in various forms in Ṭáhirih's poems. Considering this interpretation of the verses, Ṭáhirih is reminding herself of the fact that in her admiration of those special souls she should not ascribe to them any likeness to God.

یـــا الهـــا در تنـــزه بـــایـــدم

ذکـــر تقـــدیســـی ز ایشـــان شـــایـــدم

شـــایـــدم لطفـــت نمـــایـــد دستگیـــر

وا رهـــم از ایـــن شـــؤونـــات حقیـــر

هیـــچ را از مـــن بگیـــری ای حبیـــب

هستـــی محـــض آوری بیـــرون ز جیـــب

یـــا الهـــا حـــق ایـــن شـــاهنشهـــان

وا رهـــانـــم از شـــؤونـــات خَســـان

یـــا الـــه الحـــق رب العـــالمیـــن

یـــا حبیـــب الصـــدق خیـــر الغـــافـریـــن

* * * * *

ز طوطی دعا دعوی از مدعی است
ببینیم تا گوی میدان که برد

«۴۳»

ای ز اشراق جمال المقتدر
سوختی اَحجاب قدسی سر به سر
دیگر ای رب قدیر با بها
بس نمانده قدر ذر ذرّی بجا
از حجابات سرادقهای مجد
از مقامات مُسترهای حد
یا الها سوختم ای کردگار
از شراریات ربانی نضار
یا رَبَم دریاب از احسان و جود
تا مشرف آیم از جذب الوجود
یا جمیل و یا عزیز ْبا بهاء
اشرق اللوح مِن النار البداء
سوختم ای کردگار مقتدر
از شراریات افکیات شر
پاک بنما یا حبیب العارفین
قلب را از آنچه نافی بالیقین
تا مرفع آیم اندر بسط عدل
وا رهم از شأن غیریات هزل
یا الها غیر تو نبود مرا
جز توام نبود نصیر از ماسوا

ریــز در جــام طهــور طــاهــره
از تغنــی هــای نــور طــاهــره
تــا کــه آرد روح اکبــر در ظهــور
هــا انــا البشــار بــالســرّ القطــور
در تــرفــع آیــد و انــدر سمــاء
تــا کــه آیــد وجهــت طلعــت بهــاء
آمــدم کــایــد بــرون از احتجــاب
ریــزم از رشحــات نــوری سحــاب
شمــس را بیــنم مــدور در سمــاء
هــا انــا الحق المُطلع فــی عمــاء

«۴۲»

جــوانــی چــه آورد و پیــری چــه بــرد
بُــت خــوردســال و مــی ســالخُــورد
بت خــورد ســالی کــه یــک جلوه اش
ببــرد از دل اندیشهٔ خــواب و خــورد
مــی ســالخــوردی کــه یــک قطــره اش
نخورد آن که مُرد و نمرد آن که خورد
ز یــک خُــم دهــد ســاقــی روزگــار
تــو را صــاف صــاف و مــرا دُرد دُرد
هــزاران اسیــر وِیَنــد و یکــی
غبــار عــلایــق ز قلبــش ستــرد
نــه بازی است رفتــن بــه میدان عشق
کــه از صــد هــزاران یکــی پــا فشــرد

یا الها حق آن شاهنشهان
متکی بر مسند احسان عیان
جملگی بگذشته از اقیاد هست
مست و سرخوش از منادی الست
دیدن بگذشتنی بگذاشتند
آنچه را بایستشان برداشتند
یا الها همت اعلایشان
آفرین بر همت والایشان
غیر وجه پاکت ای رب وجود
جملهٔ عالی فنای صرف بود
ز ارتفاع همت و قدر بیان
در ترفع تا بساط لا مکان
بس مکین در صدر انماط الرفیع
جملهٔ ذرات از ایشان بدیع
یا الها از تفضلهای تو
یافتند این قدرت ابهای تو
لیک یا رب بایدم عفر خدین
نزد آن ذری کز ایشان شد بعین
زانکه ایشان اسبقند و اشرفند
ذی وجود امنعند و ارفعند
یا الها خود به ایشان داشتی
داشتی و داشتی و داشتی
کردهٔ ایشان مقام لامثال
بردهٔ ایشان الیٰ بیت الجلال
بردی از ایشان شؤون خود داده ای
آنچه را خود بوده او را کرده ای

بس ترنم‌های با فحوای او

اینکه غیرم نیست خلاق الوجود

آورم آن را که خواهم در شهود

هان نگر ای سامع آیات حق

آمدت امر الهی با نَطَق

در نگر در راکبین فُلکیه

عده عین اَحرُف بس نوریه

ریزد از ایشان شرار ناریه

مَن هوَ لیسَ سواهُ باقیه

زانکه آمد امر حق با استتار

چار ارکان را نمود املای نار

ما شنیدیم و اطاعت کرده‌ایم

غیر ما اَنزَل ز خود بُبریده‌ایم

هان ایا سامع نگر در منظره

آمد آن سرّ عظیم مستره

بار الها این چه شور با شرر ؟

اوفتاد از شطرهٔ بیت القدَر ؟

باعث قهرت خداوند بیان

نیست جز تحریق نقطه در عیان

ز آنکه این نقطه بُود سرّ بدا

نیست غیرش را وجود از ما بدا

یا الها هر که او را در ربود

خود ربود اما از او غافل نبود

یا الها بعد نقطه مهلتی

نیست دیگر از دلیل حکمتی

هان بیار اسرار آدم را عیان

اول و ثانی به اشراق بیان

اول او بود اشراق جمال

ثانیش اتیان بماهی از فعال

«۴۰»

یا ربا دریاب بهجت را کنون

تا که یابد سرّ اعیان الفنون

حرفی از این ورقهٔ سینائیه

ناید او را محتجب درخافیه

یا الهآ شاهدی با نصر و فر

میرسانم سرّ آیات قَدر

«۴۱»

عرف فرمایم من از بحر ظهور

ریزم اندر جام بهجت با سرور

در گذارد سالهای ما مضیٰ

آید او با جلوه‌های ما بدا

آید از شطر عمائیه نزیل

آن مطهر از دلیل و قال و قیل

ذکری از غیر خدا نارد عیان

ها انا القدّوس فعال لشان

ها شنو تفرید من جذبای او

هان نگر ای بهجتم در منظره
تا ببینی وجه آیت مظهره
پرسی از ما از سرائرهای سرّ
تا که آئی در مقام مستسر
گوی ای با فر و عزت ظاهره
بهجت ای نور فؤاد طاهره
آرزوی حضرت آدم چه بود؟
سرّ او را ظاهر آور در وجود
هان شنو تفرید جذبانی ما
تا بیابی سرّ بدء و انتها
زان خداوند جلیل مقتدر
خلق فرموده قدر را ذی قدر
تا بیابد او به عالم اختیار
اظهر ظاهر بصعد این دیار
جمله را مختار از روز ازل
کرد محبوب حبیب لم یزل
چونکه غیرش را نباشد پس وجود
اول از مختاریان ز اتش نمود
این منم مختار در بدء و بدا
نیست او را ابتدا و انتها
بهجتا دریاب اسرار حقیق
ریختم در جام تحقیق رشیق

اصل ثابت بود از روز ازل
بس مطهر بود از حد و علل
فیض او ظاهر ز آیات صمد
اسم او پس مستقر اندر احد
پس قمر از او ملمع در عیان
گشت سایر بر بروج آسمان
چون به هر برجی رسید و وارهید
جلوه‌اش را در مقام تازه دید
از عناصر هیکل با استوا
شد منطّق او به اسرار بها
جلوهٔ ربانی انوار شد
جذبهٔ فارانی شرار شد

«۳۸»

بشنو از ما بهجت اسرار اله
تا که آئی در ادای ما گواه
در تغرد آمدم از امر حق
با تو از شأن مضی و ماسبق
بعد اظهار بداع کردگار
نوح کو قائم شد از امر القدار
سر توحید الهی را رساند
اهل وحدت را الیٰ ساحل کشاند
کشف اسرار توهم را نمود
باب انوار تعلم را گشود

طلعت حق است با عز و وقار
گشته از استار عزت آشکار
هیکل با استواء با بها
در تبلج از بروقات ثنا
هان به نطق او آمد از جذب و دود
جملهٔ ابواب مغلق را گشود
ها ! ندای با صفای هات لک
میرباید زنگ ریب ووهم و شک
ها اشارتهای پنهانی عیان
گشت از وی جلوه گر اندر زمان
نار سینائی به دوران آمده
نور فارانیت تابان آمده
اسم اعظم با مسمیٰ شد عیان
کرد واله جملهٔ کرّوبیان
جلوه گر بر کل اسما آمده
سوی بزم اُنس حق رهبر شده
الله الله این چه لطف است و عطا
در تظهر از هویات بها
این چه قدر است وچه عز است وچه شان؟
گشت ظاهر بر حروف کُن فکان
نه غروب او را مصور نه طلوع
نه اصول او را مقدر نه فروع

کسی ار نکرد اطاعتم، نگرفت حبل ولایتم
کُنمش بعید زساحتم، دهمش به قهر به باد "لا"

صمدم، ز عالم سرمدم، احدم، ز کشور لا حَدَم
پی اهل افئده آمدم، هلموا الی لمقبلا

قبسات نار مشیتی انا ذا الست بربکم
بگذر به ساحت قدسیان بشنو صفیر بلیٰ بلیٰ

منم آن ظهور مهیمنی منم آن سفینهٔ ایمنی
منم آن مَنیت بی منی و لقد ظهرتُ مجلجلا

شجر مرفع جان منم، ثمر نهان و عیان منم
ملک الملوک جهان منم، و بی البیان فقد علا

شهدای طلعت ثار من! بدوید سوی دیار من!
سر و جان کنید نثار من، که منم شهنشه کربلا

«۳۵»

جلـوه هــای لاحــدیِ احمــدی
شد ملئلا از حجاب سرمدی
طلعتِ "ها" در هویت مستتر
گشت او از نقطهٔ "با" مشتهر

«۳٦»

طلعات قدس بشارتی، که جمال حق شده برملا
بزن ای صبا تو به ساحتش، به گروه غمزدگان صلا

هله ای طوائف منتظر، ز عنایت شه مقتدر
مــه مستتــر شــده مشتهــر، متبهیاً متجمــلاً

شده طلعت صمدی عیان، که بپا کند عَلم بیان
ز گمـان و وهـم جهـانیـان، جبـروت قـدسه اعتـلا

به سریر عزت و فخر و شان، بنشسته آن شه بی نشان
بزد این صلا به بلاکشان، که گروه مدعی ولا

چو کسی طریق مرا رود، کُنمش ندا که خبر شود
که هر آنکه عاشق من شود نرهد ز محنت و ابتلا

بـر فـراز سـدرهٔ ابهـیٰ شـوم
قـابـل قـربـانـی اعلـیٰ شـوم

«۳۴»

باخته جان به ولایش همه شاهد با شید
ایستاده به وفایش همه شاهد باشید
روز اول کـه رسیـدم بـه مقـام ازلی
محو بنموده سوایش همه شاهد باشید
دورها کو زده این چرخ مدور در حین
ایستادم به وفایش همه شاهد باشید
نیست مقصود مرا غیر رضایش بالله
آمدم عین رضایش همه شاهد باشید
قرة العین نگر با نظر پاک صفی
کیست منظورُ بهایش همه شاهد باشید
خواهم از فضل خداوندی قیوم قدیم
ریزدم خون به بهایش همه شاهد باشید
رنجهایی که کشیدم ز مرور ایام
در ره قرب وَلایش همه شاهد باشید
نبودم ذره از پاک ز کل مفقود
ازمن از فضل و عطایش همه شاهد باشید
خواهم از بدع برون آوردم از ابداع
تا کنم جان به فدایش همه شاهد باشید

بـایـدم دریـابـی ای رب العطـوف
از کمـال لطـف یـا رب الـروف
حـق آنـان کـامـدنـد و آمـدنـد
قـابـل قـربـانـی کـویـت شـدنـد
یـافتنـد آن کنـز غیبـی العیـان
از تلطفهـــای نصـــری نهـــان
پس به صدر شمسهٔ اعلیٰ شدند
قـابـل آیـات "اوادنـیٰ" شـدنـد
وا رهیـدنـد از شـؤونـات سـویٰ
درگـذشتنـد از جمیـع مـا عـدیٰ
قـادر قیـوم یـا رب القـدیـر
نـاصر محبـوب یا حـی النصیـر
این چه عـالم آمد از تو در بروز؟
کشـف گـردیـده همـه سرّ الـرمـوز!
زمـرهٔ احبـابـت ای رب البیـان
جملگی وارستـه از کـون و مکـان
چشم خود بر بسته از کل الشؤون
وارهیـــده از اشـــارات الظنـــون
خُرس صُمت افتاده در قعر القعیر
منتظـر بـر نصـرت حـی النصیـر
یـا الهـا یـک نظـر فـرمـا نظـر
پــاک ایـم از شـؤونـات الغبـر

لمعـات وجهـک اشـرقـت، و شعـاع طلعتـک اعتـلی
ز چـه رو "الست بـربکـم" نـزنـی؟ بـزن کـه بـلی بـلی

بـه جـواب طبـل اَلَست تـو، ز ولا چـو کـوس بـلی زدنـد
همـه خیمـه زد بـه در دلم، سپـه غـم و حشـم بـلا

من وعشق آن مه خوب‌رو، که چو زد صلای بلی بر او
بـه نشـاط و قهقهـه شـد فـرو، کـه انـا الشهیـد بکـربـلا

چو شنید نالۀ مرگ من، پی ساز من شد و برگ من
فمشـــی الی مهـــر ولا، و بکـــی عـــلی مجلجـــلا

چـه شـود کـه آتـش حیـرتـی، زنیـم بـه قلـه طـور دل
فسککتـــه و دککتـــه، متـــدکـــدکـــا متـــزلـــزلا

پـی خـوان دعـوت عشـق او، همـه شـب ز خیـل کـروبیان
رسـد ایـن صفیـر مهیمنـی، کـه "گـروه غمـزده الصـلا!"

تـو کـه فلس مـاهـی حیـرتـی، چـه زنـی ز بحـر وجـود دم؟
بنشیـن چـو طـاهـره دمبـدم، بشنـو خـروش نهنـگ "لا"

به دیار عشق تو مانده‌ام، ز کسی ندیده عنایتی
به غریبیم نظری فکن، تو که پادشاه ولایتی

گنهی بود مگر ای صنم، که ز سرّ عشق تو دم به دم
فهجرتنی و قتلتنی، و اخذتنی بجنایتی

شده راه طاقت و صبر طی، بکشم فراق تو تا به کی؟
همه بند بند مرا چو نی، بود از غم تو حکایتی

عجز العقول لدرکه، هلک النفوس لوهمه،
به کمال تو که برد رهی؟ نبود بجز تو نهایتی

چو صبا برت گذر آورد، ز بلا کشان خبر آورد
رخ زرد و چشم تر آورد، چه شود کنی تو عنایتی؟

قدمی بنه تو به بسترم، سحری به ناگهی از کرم
به هوای قرب تو بر پرم، به دو بال و هم بجناحتی

برهانیم چو از این مکان، بکشانیم سوی لا مکان
گذرم ز جان و جهانیان، که تو جان و جاندهِ خلقتی

جذبات شوقک الجمت، بسلاسل الغم و البلا
همه عاشقان شکسته دل، که دهند جان به ره ولا

اگر آن صنم ز ره ستم، پی کُشتنم بنهد قدم
فقد استقام بسیفه، فَلَقد رضیت بما رضی

سحر آن نگار ستمگرم، قدمی نهاد به بسترم
و اذا رایتُ جماله، طَلَعَ الصباح کَانمَا

نه چو زلف غالیه‌بار او، نه چو چشم فتنه شعار او
شده نافه‌ای به همه خُتن، شده کافری به همه ختا

تو که غافل از می و شاهدی، پی مرد عابد و زاهدی
چه کنم که کافر و جاحدی، ز خلوص نیت اصفیا

به مراد زلف معلقی، پی اسب و زین مغرقی
همه عمر منکر مطلقی، ز فقیر فارغ و بی نوا

تو و مُلک و جاه سکندری، من و رسم و راه قلندری
اگر آن نکوست تو درخوری، وگر این بد است، مرا سزا

بگذر ز منزل ما و من، بگزین به مُلک فنا وطن
فاذا فَعَلت بمثل ذا، و لقد بَلَغت بما تشا

به وقت مرگ گشودی ز پرسشم لب شیرین
چنانکه باز بمانم ز نو دمیده حیاتی

«۲۹»

در ره عشقت ای صنم، شیفتهٔ بلا منم
چند مغایرت کنی؟ با غمت آشنا منم
پرده به روی بسته‌ای، زلف به هم شکسته‌ای
از همه خلق رسته‌ای، از همگان جدا منم
شیر توئی، شکر توئی، شاخه توئی ثمر توئی
شمس توئی، قمر توئی، ذره منم، هبا منم
نخل توئی، رطب توئی، لعبت نوش‌لب توئی
خواجهٔ با ادب توئی، بندهٔ بی حیا منم
کعبه توئی، صنم توئی، دیر توئی، حرم توئی
دلبر محترم توئی، عاشق بی نوا منم
شاهد شوخ دلبرا گفت به سوی من بیا
رسته ز کبر و از ریا، مظهر کبریا منم
طاهره خاک پای تو، مست می لقای تو
منتظر عطای تو، معترف خطا منم

دور دهان تنگ تو عارض عنبرین خطت
غنچه به غنچه گل به گل لاله به لاله بو به بو

ابرو و چشم و خال تو صید نموده مرغ دل
طبع به طبع و دل به دل مهر به مهر و خو به خو

مهر تو را دل حزین بافته بر قماش جان
رشته به رشته نخ به نخ تار به تار پو به پو

در دل خویش طاهره گشت و ندید جز تو را
صفحه به صفحه لا به لا پرده به پرده تو به تو

«۲۸»

سجود وجهک فرضا علی فی الصلواتی
تو را پرستم اگرْ فی المثل چو لات ومناتی
به چشم خویش نظر کن مرا مگو ز چه مستی
در آئینهٔ رخ خود بین مرا مپرس ز چه ماتی
نرفته در عتباتت ز مهر کعبهٔ رویت
روان ز چشمهٔ چشم من است شط فُراتی
خدای عالم وآدم مربی همه اشیاء
تو را وفا بدهد یا مرا ز غصه نجاتی
حیات من نه زجان و ممات من نه زمرگ است
مِن الوصال حیات من الفراق مماتی

بــذل روحــی فــی هــواه هیــن
تجمد القوم السری عند الصباح
رام قتلی لحظه مِن غیر سیف
اَسکـرتنـی عینــه مــن دون راح
قــد کفتنــی نظــرة منــی الیــه
مــن بهائــی فــی غــداة فــی رواح
هـام قلبی فی هـواه کیف هـام!
راح روحــی فــی قفــاه ایــن راح
لم یفــارقنــی خیــال منــه قــط
لم یـزل هـو فی فـوادی لا یـراح
ان یشاء یحرق فـوادی فی النوی
او یشــاء یقتـل لـه قتـلی مبـاح

«۲۷»

گر به تو افتدم نظر چهره به چهره رو به رو
شرح دهم غم تو را نکته به نکته مو به مو

از پــی دیــدن رُخــت همچــو صبــا فتــاده ام
خانه به خانه در به در کوچه به کوچه کو به کو

میـرود از فـراق تـو خـون دل از دو دیـده ام
دجله به دجله یم به یم چشمه به چشمه جو به جو

رب اعظم رب اعلیٰ شأن او
رب اکبر روضهٔ رضوان او
عرش‌ها با رفعت شأن بها
بس سرائرها مرفع از سما
الله الله ای قدیم لم یزل
قادر حی عطوفِ لا مثل
یک نظر فرما به انظار رحیم
زنده گردان هذه العظم الرّمیم
تا نمایم نطق از اسرار تو
در تظهر آورم اضمار تو
جز توام مقصود نبوَد در بنا
جز توام معبود ناید در ثنا
سرّ وحدت را تو فرما آشکار
چند گردم در سما خورشیدوار
ای حبیب حب محبوب بها
جذب فرما این عبید مبتلا
بر بساط عز وحدت مستقر
ساز از الطاف خود بی‌حد و مر

«۲۶»

یا ندیمی قم فَان الدیک صاح
غن لی بیتا و ناوِل کأس راح
لَست اصبر عن حبیبی لحظة
هل الیه نظرة مِنی تباح

گاه بخوان سگ درت، گاه کمینه چاکرت
فرق نمیکند مرا، بنده یکی و نام دو

«۲۴»

ای صبا بگو از من آن عزیزهائی را
این چنین روا باشد طلعت بهائی را
ابر لطف آن محبوب، رشحه رشحه میبارد
بر هیاکل مطروح، محو سرّهائی را
نسمهٔ عراقیش، میوزد بسی روحا
زنده مینماید او، هیکل سوائی را
باب رکن غربیش، شد مفتح ابواب
لطف او شده سائل، اهل فتح طائی را
بابیان نوریه، جملگی برون آئید
از حجاب های عز، بنگرید فائی را
طلعت مبین ناگه، طالع از حجاب عز
مشنو ای عزیز من، نطق "لَن ترانی" را

«۲۵»

غیر او مشهود نبوَد در عیان
محو موهومات شد اندر بیان
اسم اعلیٰ از مسمیٰ شد متین
شد برون فرقان حق از آستین

خال به کنج لب یکی، طرهٔ مشک فام دو
وای به حال مرغ دل، دانه یکی و دام دو

محتسب است و شیخ و من، صحبت عشق درمیان
از چه کنم مجابشان؟ پخته یکی و خام دو

صورت ماه طلعتان، زیر کمند گیسوان
کس به جهان ندیده است، صبح یکی و شام دو

حامله خُم ز دُخت رَز، باده‌کشان به گِرد او
طفل حرام‌زاده بین، باب یکی و مام دو

ساقی ماهروی من، از چه نشسته غافلی
باده بیار می بده، نقد یکی و وام دو

مست دو چشم دلربا همچو قرابه پر ز می
در کف تُرک مست بین، باده یکی و جام دو

کشتهٔ تیغ ابرویت، گشته هزار همچو من
بستهٔ چشم جادویت، میم یکی و لام دو

وعدهٔ وصل میدهی لیک وفا نمیکنی
من به جهان ندیده‌ام، مرد یکی کلام دو

چه ظهور آن شهِ ما عَرَف، عظمت شئون جلاله
به جهانِ جان شده از شرف، حسنت و عز مقاله

همه جانِ جملهٔ اِنس و جان، شده در قدوم وی ارمغان
بهِ تعشق آمده عاشقان، قتل سبیل وصاله

طلع البهاء و اشرقت، ظهر البهاء و المعت
قلل الوجود تسیرَت(۱)، فلکا لوجه جماله

همه آیه های مسلسله، ز لسان او شده نازله
همه انبیاء مهروله، متبرجا بجماله

---

(۱)ـ در نسخه موجود «نسیرَت» آمده.

«۲۰»

این صدای پا که می آید ز دور
افکند بر هستیم یکباره شور
میشناسم این صدای پای اوست
طرز ره پیمودن زیبای اوست

«۲۱»

حبذا ای بهجت "فا" حبذا
حبذا ای نزهت "طا" حبذا
مرحبا ای رشحهٔ قطر بدیع
در تلألؤ از مرایا مرحبا
چون بیامد مرحبایت از عما
خواستی از ها به ابهی مرحبا
جمله ذرات هوش او معیّن
یافتی آن کنز اخفیٰ مرحبا
نازل آمد از خداوند جلیل
جوهری لا مثل مرا مرحبا
هان بگیر این منظر با استتار
زان درخشان وَجهَت "فا" مرحبا
باش با ما در تغرد ای حبیب
تا بیابی سرّ ابقا مرحبا

ز کمان آن رخ پر وَلَه، ز کمند آن مَه ده دله
دو هزار فرقه و سلسله متفرقا متسلسلا

همه موسیان عمائیش همه عیسیان سمائیش
همه دلبران بقائیش متولها متذللا

دو هزار احمد مصطفی ز بروق آن شه باصفا
شده مضطرب، شده در خفا مُتدثرا مُتزملا

بحر الوجود تموجت لعل الشهود تولجت
شفق الخمود تلجلجت، بلقائه متجملا

ز غم تو ای مَه مهربان ز فراقت ای شه دلبران
شده روح هیکل جسمیان متخففا متخلخلا

هکل جمال ز طلعتش، قلل جبال ز رفعتش
دول جلال ز سطوتش، متخشعا متزلزلا

دلم از دو زلف سیاه او، ز فراق روی چو ماه او
به تراب مَقدم راه او، شده خون من متبلبلا

تو وآن تشعشع روی خود، تو و آن تَلَمَع موی خود
که رسانیم تو به کوی خود، متسرعا متعجلا

هله ای گروه عمائیان بکشید هلهلهٔ ولا
که ظهور طلعت ما عیان شده فاش و ظاهر و برملا

بزنید نغمه ز هر طرف که ز وجه طلعت ما عَرَف
رَفَع الغطاء و قد کَشَف ظلم اللیال قد انجلا

برسید با سپه طرب، صنمی عجم، صمدی عرب
بدمید شمس ز ما غرب، بدوید الیه مُهر ولا

فوران نار ز ارض فا، نَوَران نور ز شهر طا
طیران روح ز شهرها، و لقد علا و قد اعتلا

طیر العماء تکفکفت، ورق البهاء صَفصَفت(۱)
دیک الضیاء تذرقت(۲)، متجمَلا متجلـلا

ز ظهور آن شه اله، ز اَلَست آن مَه ما لهه
شده آلهه همه والهه، بتغنیات بلیٰ بلیٰ

به تموج آمده آن یمی، که به کربلاش به خرمی
متظهر است به هر دمی، دو هزار وادی کربلا

---

(۱)ـ در نسخ موجود «تصفصفت» و یا «و تصف صفت» آمده.

(۲)ـ در نسخ موجود «تدورقت» و یا «تذورقت» آمده.

در عالم، خود آن اول آخری
به ذرات عالم تو جلوه‌گری
به هر قوم گردیده‌ای رهنما
پرستش نمایند ایشان تو را
به اسمی ز اسماء تو ساجدند
برت جملگی خاضع(و) خاشعند
منور ز نورت کلیس و حرم
توئی مظهر ذات وجه قِدم
کجا من کجا وصفت ای محترم
عدم چون کند وصف ذات قِدم؟
همه شرک محض است توحید من
منزه تو هستی ز تحمید من
اگر مشرک کافرم از تو ام
اگر خاطی قاصرم از تو ام
خطا آمده شیوهٔ بندگان
شده لطف عفو از خداوندگان
یکی جام از لطف سازم کرم
که سوزد همه کفرم ای محترم
ز جام محبت کرم کن مِیَم
فنایم اگر بخش خود هستیم

ز دور ازل منتم ایــن فتــاد

مــرا دایــه از حــب او شیــر داد

شها من به وصفت چه سازم بیان

ثنا خوان تو خلق کون (و) مکان

تـوئی آنکـه خـلاق ایـن عـالمی

خـدایـا تـو قیـوم و هـم قـائمی

شدم منفعل، خوانمت من خدا

خـداهـا شـد از بنـدگـانـت بپـا

انـا الله زنـان بنـدگـان تـو انـد

خـداهـا کنـان چـاکـران تـو انـد

به امر تو شد جمله ذرات خلق

تــوئـی نقطـهٔ اول مــا سبــق

چـو نـور جمـال تـو آمـد عیـان

ثمر خوانـدت از لطف رب بیـان

مراد از شجر نیست غیر از ثمر

شجـر از ثمـر میشـود جلوه گر

بیـان از تـو تکمیـل گـردیـده شد

همـه سرّ پنهـان حق دیـده شد

نبـود ار وجـودت نبـودی بیـان

نمـانـدی در عـالـم ز ایمـان نشان

ز تـو مـرتفـع امـر حـق آمـده

جـلال خـداهـا هـویـدا شـده

تو مقصود دین هر زمان بوده ای

تجـلی بــه هـر دور فـرمـوده ای

نه ختمی، که آخر بدانم تو را

نه بدوی، که اول بخوانم تو را

عبیر از سر گیسوی حوریان
بسوزان تو در مجمر زرفشان
به اهل جنان باب عشرت گشا
به رضوانیان خود تجلی نما
تو از بهر خدمت ز خلد برین
بگو حور(و) غِلمان شود در زمین
به رقص طرب گلرخان سر به سر
در این بزم تابان شود چون قمر
شود زهرهٔ چرخ در مَه بری
عنان بنگرد ماه با مشتری
بساطی بیفکن تو اندر زمین
که گوید ملک در فلک آفرین
به خلق جهان ساقیا ده نوید
که شد شام غم، صبح عشرت رسید
به غمدیدگان ده تو جام صفا
به عشاق دلخسته بر زن صلا
که عین ظهور ازل آمده
جمال خدائی هویدا شده
به این مژده گر جان فشانم رواست
از این مژده خوشوقت رب علاست
ز حق جلوه گر آمده نور او
سراسر جهانی شده طور او
یکی جام می در دهم این زمان
که در مدح این شه گشایم زبان
قبولش اگر نیست این مدحتم
چه سازم که گردیده است عادتم

ز صهبای دوشین خُمارم اگر

ز جام دگر بر تو هوشم ز سر

به زلف تو ساقی چو دل بسته‌ام

ز قید دو عالم همه رسته‌ام

مرا از ازل مذهب(و) دین نبود

بجز مهر تو هیچ آئین نبود

به عهد ازل من نمایم قرار

ز ایمان کنم حُب تو اختیار

چو حُب تو را کرده باشم قبول

بده جامی از مِی ندارم ملول

کرم ساز جام مِیَم دم به دم

که مستغرقم من به دریای غم

نسازد کفایت مرا جام می

مرا بر تو ساقی بَرِ بحر وی

که تا اندر آن بحر غوص آورم

فنا گشته از خویشتن بگذرم

ز عمان دل بشکنم این صدف

من آن گوهر جان بیارم به کف

بیا ساقیا شد جهان، نوبهار

زمین چون زمرد شد از سبزه‌زار

بهار است بشکفته شد گلستان

بساطی بیفکن تو در بوستان

مغنی نوازد نی و چنگ و رود

به عشاق دلخسته آرد سرود

برون شو تو ساقی از این پیرهن

قمیص بهشتی درآور به تن

هو المحبوب

بیا ساقی ای شاهباز فتوح
ایاغی کرم کن ز صهبای روح
یکی جام می باز سازم کرم
که سوزد سرا پای من تا قدم
بیا ساقیا ده یکی جام می
که از دل رود جمله غمهای دی
حیاتی ز نو بخش بر مردگان
ایاغی کرم کن به افسردگان
سمندر صفت چون درین آتشم
کرم ساز ساقی می بی غشم
ز روی مَه افکن در این دم نقاب
درآ از در(و) ده تو جام شراب
ز جام طَهورم تو سرشار کن
به جانم تجلی از آن یار کن
چوموسی کنم منصعق خود زنور
نما مُندَک این کوهِ تن همچو طور
بسوزان وجودم همه سر به سر
که از دو جهانم نباشد خبر
به این غم نشین ساقیا مِی بیار
پریشان مدارم چو زلف نگار

خرقه و سجاده به دور افکنم

باده به مینای بلور افکنم

شعشعه در وادی طور افکنم

بام و در از عشق به شور افکنم

بر در میخانه بود جای من

عشق عَلَم کوفت به ویرانه‌ام

داد صلا بر در جانانه‌ام

بادهٔ حق ریخت به پیمانه‌ام

از خود و عالم همه بیگانه‌ام

حق طلبد همت والای من

ساقی میخانهٔ بزم "الست"

ریخت به هر جام چو صهبا ز دست

ذرهٔ صفت شد همه ذرات پست

باده ز ما مست شد و گشت هست

از اثر نشئهٔ صهبای من

عشق به هر لحظه ندا میکند

بر همه موجود صدا میکند

هر که هوای ره ما میکند

کِی حذر از موج بلا میکند؟

پای نهد بر لب دریای من

هندوی نوبت زن بام توام

طایر سرگشته به دام توام

مرغ شباویز به شام توام

محو ز خود، زنده به نام توام

گشته ز من درد من و مای من

باقیم از یاد خود و فانیم
جُرعه‌کش بادهٔ ربانیم
سوختهٔ وادی حیرانیم
سالک صحرای پریشانیم
تا چه رسد بر دل رسوای من
بر در دل تا "ارنی" گو شدم
جلوه‌کنان بر سر آن کو شدم
هر طرفی گرم هیاهو شدم
او همگی من شد و من او شدم
من دل و او گشت دلارای من
کعبهٔ من خاک سر کوی تو
مشعله افروز جهان، روی تو
سلسلهٔ جان، خَم گیسوی تو
قبلهٔ دل، طاق دو ابروی تو
زلف تو در دیر، چلیپای من
شیفتهٔ حضرت اعلاستم
عاشق دیدار دلاراستم
راهروی وادی سوداستم
از همه بگذشته تو را خواستم
پر شده از عشق تو اعضای من
تا کِی و کِی پند نیوشی کنم؟
چند نهان بلبله پوشی کنم؟
چند ز هجر تو خموشی کنم؟
پیش کسان زهد فروشی کنم؟
تا که شود راغب کالای من

من شدم از مهر تو چون ذره پست
و ز قدح بادهٔ عشق تو مست
تا به سر زلف تو داریم دست
تا تو منی، من شده ام خودپرست
سجده گه من شده اعضای من
دل اگر از تست چرا خون کنی؟
ور ز تو نبود ز چه مجنون کنی؟
دم به دم این سوز دل افزون کنی
تا خودیَم را همه بیرون کنی
جای کنی در دل شیدای من
آتش عشقت چو بر افروخت دود
سوخت مرا مایهٔ هر هست و بود
کفر و مسلمانیم از من زدود
تا به خَم ابرویت آرم سجود
فرق نه از کعبه کلیسای من
کِلکِ ازل تا به ورق زد رقم
گشت هم آغوش چو لوح و قلم
نامده خلقی به وجود از عدم
بر تن آدم چو دمیدند دَم
مهر تو بُد در دل شیدای من
دست قضا چون گِلِ آدم سرشت
مهر تو در مزرعهٔ سینه کِشت
عشق تو گردید مرا سرنوشت
فارغم اکنون ز جحیم و بهشت
نیست به غیر از تو تمنای من

چنان ز ابر بقا بارید گوهر
که افتاد از نظرها سنبل تَر
ندارد قدر آنجا مشک عنبر
که باشد سنبل ریحانهٔ تو
چون پادشاهی، گاهی نگاهی
بر این اسیرت، ای شهسوارم

«۱۷»

ای به سر زلف تو سودای من
و ز غم هجران تو غوغای من
لعل لبت شهد مصفای من
عشق تو بگرفت سرا پای من
من شده تو آمده بر جای من
گر چه بسی رنج غمت برده‌ام
جام پیاپی ز بلا خورده‌ام
سوخته جانم اگر افسرده‌ام
زنده دلم گر چه ز غم مرده‌ام
چون لب تو هست مسیحای من
گنج منم بانی مخزن توئی
سیم منم صاحب معدن توئی
دانه منم صاحب خرمن توئی
هیکل من چیست اگر من توئی؟
گر تو منی، چیست هیولای من؟

ای دلستانم جز تو ندارم
جانم نثارت ای تاجدارم
منم ای سرو قد دیوانهٔ تو
از آن دو نرگس مستانه تو
شدم از عارض جذبانهٔ تو
اسیر عشق جاویدانهٔ تو
مُردم به کویت در آرزویت
جز وصل رویت قصدی ندارم
ز عشقت گر بسوزد استخوانم
به جز نام ترا بر لب نرانم
به پای آن کسی صد جان فشانم
که یک بارم بَرَد بَر خانهٔ تو
گاه از وصالت شادم نمائی
گاه از فراغت سازی نزارم
چنان گرم از مِی ات ای دل ستانم
که دلسرد از بهشت جاودانم
من آن مرغ رمیده ز آشیانم
که نشناسم به جز کاشانهٔ تو
باز آ به پیشم، بین قلب ریشم
تا کی گِذاری، در انتظارم؟
شده هر موی زلفت یک کمندم
که بر عشق تو کرده پای بندم
شدم ای دلبر بالا بلندم
هلاک از غمزهٔ فتانهٔ تو
قد بلندت، سرو روانم
زلف کمندت، مشک تتارم

بُـوَد سـوی ی تـوام راز نهـانـی
که زآنم هست عیش و کامرانی
شـدم چـون آشنـا ای یـار جـانـی
بـه بـزم خـالی از بیگـانـه تـو
ای مـاهـرویـم ای مشـک مـویـم
یـارم تـوئـی تـو ای شهـریـارم
به عرش جان چوتوجانانه ای بود
که قهر از عارضت افسانه ای بود
بـه زیـر دام زلفـت دانـه ای بـود
بـه دامـم درفکنـد آن دانـه تـو
در محفـل خـود بـارم ده ای یـار
پیـش رقیبـان منمـا تـو خـارم
فـراق رویـت ای سلطـان خـوبـان
چو زلفت کرده عالم را پریشان
به هر بزمی درآیم همچو طفلان
کـه شـایـد بشنـوم افسـانهٔ تـو
گر بـر لـب آری یـک بـار نـامـم
در خاک پایت صد جان فشانم
ز درد عشقـت ای مـاه حبیبـان
رمیـدنـد از مـداوایـم طبیبـان
خوش آن دم که علی رغم رقیبان
شـرابـی نـوشـم از پیمـانهٔ تـو

به خیالت ای نکو رو به مدام باشد این دل
به جمالت ای نکو خو به کلام باشد این دل

چو نموده‌ای به افسون به دل حزین پر خون
که مسلسل از نظاره به هیام باشد این دل

به جمال حسن رویت به تتار مشک مویت
به حصار بزم کویت به مرام باشد این دل

چو بخوانیش به محضر بَریَش به عز منظر
به جلال و شوکت و فر به نظام باشد این دل

چه به جذب روی مهوش شده‌ام غریق آتش
نشود دگر که سرخوش به غمام باشد این دل

به تلطف و تکرم به تعطف و ترحم
بِرُبا ز ما توهم که همام باشد این دل

چو ز ماسوی برانی ز خودش به خود رسانی
ز بلاء خود چشانی به دوام باشد این دل

ز دلم شراره بارد که نسب ز نار دارد
ز چه رو ثمر نیارد که به کام باشد این دل

دیــدن رویــش فقــرا را تمــام

غــرقـهٔ دریــای فنــا مــی کنــد

ایــن نــه منــم مــادح رویــش ورا

جملــهٔ ذرات ثنــا مــی کنــد

هــر کــه ز "الّا"ی وی آگــه شــود

خویش در این مرحله "لا" می کند

«۱۴»

چشم مستش کرد عالم را خراب

هرکه دید افتاده اندر پیچ و تاب

گــردش چشــم وی انــدر هــر نظــر

میــربــایــد جملــه اهــل لبــاب

گو چه آید زین دل مجنون محض؟

کــو زده در خیمــهٔ لیــلی قِبــاب

خیمــهٔ آتــش نشینــان پــر شــرر

آتش با شعله زد در هر حجاب

گر نباشد نار موسی در ظهور

از چه کل محوند و اندر اضطراب؟

خواهم از ساقی به جامم طفحه ای

تــا بگــویم بــا تــو سرّ مــا اجــاب

هــان نگر بر مـا به عیـن باصره

تــا ببینــی وجه حق را بی نقاب

آمــد از شطــر عمــائــی در نــزول

بــا تجــلی رخــی چــون آفتــاب

«۱۲»

اگر به باد دهم زلف عنبرآسا را
اسیر خویش کنم آهوان صحرا را
وگربه نرگس شهلای خویش سرمه کشم
به روز تیره نشانم تمام دنیا را
برای دیدن رویم سپهر هر دمِ صبح
برون برآورد آئینه مطلا را
گذار من به کلیسا اگر فُتد روزی
به دین خویش برم دختران ترسا را

«۱۳»

پادشه عشق ندا میکند
در ره معشوق صدا میکند
در صفت طلعت انوار او
خامهٔ توصیف حیا میکند
هر که ز اسرار وی آگه شود
لاجرمش جان به فدا میکند
شمس که در روز ضیاء رُخش
دهر پر از نور جلا میکند
سوی غمش رقص کنان می رود
هر که تمنای لقا میکند
آئینه دان که تجلی در او
طلعت انوار الا می کند

«۱۰»

بحر اعظم هان به فوران آمده
نقطهٔ غیبی به دوران آمده
سر "لا تعطیل" میپرس از قلم
کَت بود محبوب ومقصود از رِمَم

«۱۱»

یا حی یا قیوم!

قُرة العینم بیا اندر نوا
با نواهای نوای نینوا
تا رُبائی جملهٔ ذرات نور
ریزی از اشراق وَجهی نارِ طور
جان من! برخیز با شور و شرر
در نگر با چشم ساقی، در نگر!
کو فتاده جملهٔ ذراتیان
در صعید وعده ، اما صَعقیان
خیز از جا! نور چشم اُنظُرم
یاب ایشان را به جذب اَقدَرَم
تا به کی در قعر یأسی طرحیه ؟
تا به کی مانی تو سرّ خافیه ؟

مهمانِ سرِ خوانت، جمعی ز دل و جانت
جبریل مگس رانت، ها نحن هنیئا لک

برگو به طرب هر دم، با نغمهٔ زیر و بم
درمان ز تو شد دردم، ها نحن هنیئا لک

ای قُرّه بگو هر دم، با قلب تهی از غم
کز طلعت شه خرم، ها نحن هنیئا لک

«۹»

محو موهومات از افهام شد
صحو معلومات از الهام شد
جذب کردی هر صفت را در بیان
حدیت برداشتی هان از میان
سر وحدت را نمودی آشکار
کسرها بیرون نمودی از دیار
کشف استار جلالیات شد
هان اظهار جمالیات شد

این عید سعید آمد، از خُلد پدید آمد
ایام وحید آمد، این عید مبارک باد

هان! طرز دگر سازم، این عید سعید آمد
انوار خداوندی، از پرده پدید آمد

این عید مبارک پی، ها نَحنُ هَنیئا لَک
خلقی به وجودت حیّ، ها نَحنُ هَنیئا لَک

وه وه طربست امروز، سرّ عجبست امروز
دل در طلب است امروز، ها نَحنُ هَنیئا لَک

خلقی به نوا از تو، جمعی به بها از تو
وین فر و ضیا از تو، ها نَحنُ هَنیئا لَک

ای ذات تو لامِن شیئی، یکسان به تو موت و حیّ
ظلمت به ظهورت طی، ها نَحنُ هَنیئا لَک

مستم ز می جامت، دارم طرب از نامت
آسوده در ایامت، ها نَحنُ هَنیئا لَک

طوبی لک طوبی لک، جان از تو برون از شک
برشو بنوا اینک، ها نحن هنیئا لک

برخیز و طرب زا شو، سرسلسلهٔ "با" شو
بیرون ز من و ما شو، ها نحن هنیئا لک

یعنی ز خلاق زمان، شد این جهان خرم جنان
روز قیام است ای مهان، معدوم شد لیل غَسَق

آمد زمان راستی، کژی شد، اندر کاستی
آن شد که آن میخواستی، از عدل و قانون و نَسَق

شد از میان جور و ستم، هنگام لطف است و کَرم
ایدون به جای هر سَقم، شد جانشین قوت و رمق

علم حقیقی شد عیان، شد جهل معدوم از میان
برگو به شیخ اندر زمان، برخیز و بر هم‌زن ورق

بود ار چه عمری واژگون، وضع جهان از چند و چون
هان! شیر آمد جای خون، باید بگردانی طَبَق

گر چه به انظار ملل، ظاهر شده شاه دُوَل
لکن به لطف لَم یَزَل، برهاند از ایشان غَلَق

«۸»

عید آمد، عید آمد، این عید مبارک باد
مبعوث جدید آمد این عید مبارک باد

شد عید خداوندی، باشید به خرسندی
کز چرخ نوید آمد: این عید مبارک باد

«۶»

هان صبح هدی فرمود، آغاز تنفس
روشن همه عالم شد، زآفاق و ز اَنفُس
دیگر ننشیند شیخ، بر مسند تزویر
دیگر نشود مسجد، دکان تقدس
ببریده شود رشتهٔ تحت الحَنَک از دم
نه شیخ به جا ماند، نه زرق و تَدَلُس
آزاد شود دنیا ز اوهام و خرافات
آسوده شود خلق، ز تخییل و تَوَسُوس
محکوم شود ظلم، به بازوی مساوات
معدوم شود جهل، ز نیروی تفرُس
گسترده شود در همه جا فرش عدالت
افشانده شود در همه جا تخم تَوَنُس
مَرفوع شود حکم خلاف از همه آفاق
تبدیل شود اصل تبایُن به تَجانُس

«۷»

ای عاشقان، ای عاشُقان، شد آشکارا وجه حق
رفع حُجُب گردید هان، از قدرت رب الفلق

خیزید کایندم با بهاء، ظاهر شده وجه خدا
بنگر به صد لطف و صفا، آن روی روشن چون شفق

عالمی را از شرر پر شور کرد

آدمی را او سراسر نور کرد

طاهره بردار پرده از میان

تا بیاید سرّ غیبی در عیان

گوی الحمدُ هوَ رّب جمیل

قد تشعشع مِن طرازات الجلیل

«۵»

ای خفته رسید یار برخیز

از خود بنشان غبار برخیز

هین بر سر مهر و لطف آمد

ای عاشق زارِ یار برخیز

آمد بر تو طبیب غمخوار

ای خسته دلِ نِزار برخیز

ای آنکه خُمار یار داری!

آمد می غمگسار برخیز

ای آنکه به هجر مبتلائی!

شد موسم وصل یار برخیز

ای آنکه خزان فسُرده کردت!

اینک آمد بهار برخیز

هان سال نو و حیات تازه است

ای مردهٔ لاش پار برخیز

بـا خـود آینـد بیخـودان هـوا
هـوشیـاران شونـد مست و خراب
بنـده و خـواجـه درهـم آویـزنـد
لا عبیــد یــری و لا اربــاب

«۳»

هـان که امـر مبـرمـم ظاهـر شده
حکـم محکـم آیـهٔ قـاهـر شـده
بـرکَـن اَلباس حدود و پس قیـود
خـویـش را انـداز در دریـای جـود
تا به کی در عـالم پرشر و شور
دور هستی تو ز مقصد دور دور
امر ما ظاهر شده از کاف و نون
گــو مِــنَ الله اِلَیــه راجعــون

«۴»

آمـد او بـا جلـوه هـای سـرمـدی
ظـاهـر او بنمـود وجـه احمـدی
لیـک غـافـل جملـهٔ اربـاب هـوش
از تغـرّدهـای جـذبـای سـروش
احمد است اینکه نزیـل آمد نزیـل
از سمـاء عـزّ بـآیـات جلیـل

«۱»

شمس ابهی جلوه گر گردید و جان عاشقان

در هوای طلعتش چون ذره رقصان آمده

«۲»

در وصل تو میزنند احباب

افتتح یا مفتح الابواب

چه شود گر بر تو ره یابند

کم بقوا ناظرین خلف الباب

تا کی از حضرت تو صبر و شکیب

طال تطواً فهم وراء حجاب

در پس پرده تا به کِی حسرت

ارهم نظرة بلا جلباب

از تو غیر از تو مدعائی نیست

ما لدیهم سوا لقاک ثواب

سکروا فی هواک ثم صحوا

مالهم من لدی سواک مثاب

از سبب ها گذشته اند و حجب

خرقوا الحجب و ارتقوا الاسباب

بنما آفتاب را بی ابر

بگشا از جمال خویش نقاب

تا بمانند عاقلان حیران

خشک مغزان شوند اولوالالباب

اشعار فارسی و عربی

حضرت طاهره